SCIENTISM AND HUMANISM

Scientism and Humanism

TWO CULTURES
IN POST-MAO CHINA
(1978–1989)

by
Shiping Hua

STATE UNIVERSITY OF NEW YORK PRESS

Published by
State University of New York Press, Albany

© 1995 State University of New York

For information, address State University of New York Press,
State University Plaza, Albany, N.Y., 12246

Production by Cathleen Collins
Marketing by Theresa Abad Swierzowski

Library of Congress Cataloging in Publication Data

Hua, Shiping, 1956–
    Scientism and humanism : two cultures in post-Mao China
(1978–1989) / by Shiping Hua.
        p.   cm.
    Includes bibliographical references and index.
    ISBN 0-7914-2421-9. — ISBN 0-7914-2422-7 (pbk.)
    1. Communism—China.   2. Ideology—China.   3. Humanism—China.
4. Scientism.   5. Intellectuals—China.   6. China—Politics and
government—1976–   I. Title.
HX418.5.H88   1995
320.5'323—dc20   94-21098
                                                                            CIP

10 9 8 7 6 5 4 3 2 1

Contents

Preface

This book is a study about the transformation of Chinese political consciousness during the post-Mao era. In a departure from the wisdom of many people that Deng Xiaoping's pragmatic policies during the reform era have made ideological discussions irrelevant, this book holds that any version of pragmatism, especially a version that can command the adherence of both the ruling elites and the people, must inevitably reflect a set of basic predispositions. Though it seems that no single, fixed ideology has existed during the period, ideological dimensions have been persistent, and can be analyzed systematically.

This study consists of an analysis of the ideas of a group of Chinese establishment intellectuals: Hu Qiaomu; Su Shaozhi; Jin Guantao; Wang Ruoshui; Li Zehou; and, Gan Yang. Studying a few intellectuals as spokesmen for the transformation of Chinese political consciousness may seem odd to Westerners, but it is not so odd in the Chinese context because of the special social status that Chinese intellectuals have enjoyed.

I have analyzed the ideas of Hu, Su and Jin from the scientific perspective and that of Wang, Li and Gan from the humanistic perspective. I did so not only because of my conviction that ideas, especially those of the intellectuals, can be analyzed from these two philosophical perspectives, but also because of the different philosophical emphasis of their ideas. This, of course, does not mean that the first three are scientific only, while the last three have only humanistic concerns. Most of the materials that are used in this book had been published between 1978 and 1989, marking the years when Deng Xiaoping came back to power, and the year of the tragic event at Tiananmen.

Although the ideas of these intellectuals were put forward in various scientific and humanistic theories, it seems clear that what most of them, if not all of them, really cared most about was real world politics, that

vii

is, how to save China. These intellectuals did not want to do scholarship for its own sake. Therefore, in the comparison between the ideas of these intellectuals and both those in the West and in the Chinese tradition, from which these intellectuals have drawn strength, similarities and differences are mainly interpreted in terms of differing social realities, and not treated as the whims of some idiosyncratic individuals. Furthermore, the personal experiences of these intellectuals were examined to the extent that they were directly related to understanding their ideas.

Why don't we study some more pure intellectuals? The answer is pure Chinese scholars have rarely been found during this period. For instance, out of the "Four Great Thinkers of Contemporary China" claimed by the Hong Kong media, Fang Lizhi, Li Zehou, Jin Guantao and Wen Yuankai, the first three have made it explicit that they did not want to pursue scholarship for its own sake. This is so in spite of the fact that Fang, Li and Jin have never directly served the ruler as others did, such as Hu Qiaomu, Su Shaozhi, and Wang Ruoshui. In addition, to focus on the few pure scholars won't suit our need, because pure scholars in the Chinese context have never been as influential as those scholars who did not pursue scholarship for its own sake, regarding the transformation of Chinese political consciousness. Therefore, this book is partly an attempt to uncover the political implications embodied in their ideas.

Although most of these intellectuals put forward their theories in the name of Marxism, their theories were ambiguously connected with Marx, and quite often, no necessary connections have existed in between. This is significant because with the exception of perhaps Gan Yang all the other five intellectuals, at least at some point in their careers, claimed that their theories were created in line with Marxism. Even Gan cannot free himself completely from linkage to Marx, because in the eyes of some people he is quite close to Jürgen Habermas (1929–), the leader of the second generation of the Frankfurt School, which is regarded by many Western scholars as a school of Marxism.

It has also been found that although three of these scholars have created their theories in the name of science, an ambiguity has existed between their theories and science. Quite often, what they have really advocated were really various versions of scientism, a situation that had its counterpart in the first half of the twentieth century. Although generally the three versions of humanism are less politicized, their ideas have drifted far from the intellectual roots where they have drawn strength. This drift can be explained in terms of China's socioeconomic and political situation during this period.

This may be connected with what I call a "fill-in" mentality, a situation that has occurred time and again in China's modern and contemporary history. These intellectuals should be viewed as trying to fill in the intellectual vacuum created by the Cultural Revolution by providing political platforms of some kinds of state socialism, the depoliticized middle of the road policies and pluralism or liberalism.

I have purposely restrained myself from consulting the six intellectuals under study, either through correspondence or interviews, with the understanding that although doing so would probably make the study more interesting, it might also jeopardize objective investigation. I had tried to contact some of these figures previously when I was writing some articles about them. The result was that some of them not only responded, but also made detailed comments, while others either responded briefly or did not do so at all.

Growing out of my dissertation at the Department of Political Science, University of Hawaii, this project has benefited first of all from my consultations with my committee, especially with my academic adviser Peter Manicas. The comments of my committee members, Manfred Henningsen, Daniel Kwok, Deane Neubauer, Bob Stauffer, and Steven Uhalley, were taken seriously when I was revising the book.

Major funding for my graduate study comes from a four-year scholarship by the East West Center. The revision of the manuscript was completed when I was a Visiting Fellow with the Program for Cultural Studies, East West Center. My colleagues at the program, Godwin Chu, Paul Clark and Helen Palmer, were indispensable for the accomplishment of this project in the sense that they not only offered intellectual support, but also practical help. China experts Hong Yung Lee, Oliver Lee, Andrew Nathan, Michel Oksenberg, Mark Selden, Alvin So, Steve Thomas, and Tu Wei-ming also shared with me their ideas on the project. I alone am responsible for the views expressed in this book.

With the permissions from *Modern China, Bulletin of Concerned Asian Scholars* and *Asian Thought and Society*, I have reproduced here parts of the articles that I published.

PART I

Origins of the New Thinking

Introduction: Scientism Versus Humanism

The new transformation of Chinese political consciousness started in the late 1970s. Shortly before Deng assumed full power at the Third Plenum of the Eleventh Party Congress in December 1978, the National Conference of Science and Technology was held. Deng said at the conference that the modernization of science and technology had to take priority over the three other modernizations of industry, agriculture and national defense. In the same year, Hu Yaobang who later became Secretary General of the party wrote an article entitled "Smash Superstition, Master Science" for the first issue of *Zhongguo qingnian* magazine after the Cultural Revolution.[1] The superstition refers to Mao's personality cult, while the science refers to the principles guiding the newly started reform. To justify this stand, science was moved from superstructure to economic base, an acknowledgement that would not only free science from ideological restraints, but also enable it to receive the foremost support in development. It was said that "science, as the most active component of productive force, naturally becomes a revolutionary force that pushes human society forward."[2]

Corresponding to this change of ideas, Chinese leaders with backgrounds in natural and applied sciences, such as engineering, have

1

gradually replaced professional revolutionaries. For instance, during the period of 1982–87, those ministers who had backgrounds in political fields decreased from 60 percent to 21 percent of the total number of ministers, while those who are former engineers had increased from 2 percent to 45 percent.[3] Like these ministers, government functionaries are headed now by two former engineers, Secretary General Jiang Zemin and Premier Li Peng. From 1978 to 1985, China sent 38,000 students and scholars abroad to study. Among them, 90 percent studied some aspects of science and technology. Only 3 percent studied humanities and the other 7 percent studied something related to social sciences.[4]

The picture on the unofficial side is similar. In 1987, Hong Kong media listed Fang Lizhi, Wen Yuankai, Jin Guantao and Li Zehou as The Four Great Thinkers of Contemporary China.[5] With the exception of Li, the rest are either currently natural scientists or had training in hard science. Fang is an astrophysicist, Wen is a chemistry professor, and Jin is a former Beijing University chemistry student.

The sudden enthusiasm about science was also reflected in a phenomenon that various intellectual-political trends emphasizing some kind of science seemed to overwhelm a counter trend, the various versions of humanism. People seemed to have been more receptive to the emphasis of science than to the humanistic trends. This emphasis of science was quite often mixed with various versions of "scientism," a term to be defined later. Among the three intellectual trends which by and large originated from official circles, the "scientific" trends of historical materialism and technological determinism were more enduring than the humanistic trend of Marxist humanism.

Historical materialism as exemplified by Hu Qiaomu's theory played an important role in the late 1970s by stressing observing objective laws. Although this version of Marxist scientism has largely lost influence in recent years, it has been inherited by another version of scientism, technological determinism. Born out of some key concepts first put forward by Su Shaozhi in 1978, it argues that to focus on developing productive forces not only can ensure socialism, but also can prevent capitalism.[6] This theory has been serving as the main philosophical basis for the regime's pragmatic approach in policy making after the Thirteenth National Party Congress in 1987. In spite of the 1989 Tiananmen incident, the reform faction, which has been the mainstream of the Chinese ruling elite, has largely remained with this theory.

With this emphasis on productive forces to the neglect of the relations of production, the denationalization of the means of production in China has been fast. According official statistics, the total value produced by state owned enterprises has decreased from 78.3 percent in 1981 to 55 percent in 1992, that produced by collectives has been raised from 21 percent to 35 percent, and that produced by the private sector has increased from 0 7 percent to 10 percent.[7]

The fate of Marxist humanism, the third intellectual-political trend that largely originated from official circles, is not that good. The first nationally noted article about Marxist humanism during the post-Mao era was published in late 1979 by the aesthetic philosopher Zhu Guangqian. Drawing upon Marx's *The Economic and Philosophical Manuscripts of 1844*, Zhu points out that Marxism starts from human nature. Then Wang Ruoshui published his "On Alienation" and Ru Xin, former Vice President of the Chinese Academy of Social Sciences (CASS), published his "Is Humanism Revisionism?"[8]

During the period from late 1979 to 1983, more than 500 articles on the subject were published. These articles involved the following themes: human nature cannot be explained only in class terms; the essence of humanism is to treat humans as humans; the concept of alienation was consistently used by Marx throughout his career; alienation exists not only in capitalist society, but also in socialist society; the disasters in the Maoist era were largely due to Mao's contempt for humanistic principles; humanistic values should be used not only in understanding China's past, but also in understanding its present and the future.[9] Among those who participated in this discussion, Wang Ruoshui apparently was the most influential.

After the Anti-Spiritual Pollution Campaign in 1983 when Wang was purged, Marxist humanism has gradually been losing influence. Press coverage of the issue of humanism gradually faded away in the late 1980s. This is not entirely due to government censorship since, after punishing some banners of Marxist humanism such as Wang and Zhou, the regime finally acknowledged the constructiveness of the concept of humanism.[10] It seems that the gradual loss of appeal of Marxist humanism is not only in accordance with the gradual loss of influence of Marxism in general, but also because it lacks certain qualities that are conducive to the building of a new political culture.

A similar situation has also been identified in unofficial trends in that people seem to be readier to accept a more scientific approach than a humanistic one. Three major editorial boards emerged in the 1980s and they may be viewed as reflecting the general unofficial intellectual trends in China: Zouxiang weilai (March Towards the Future) headed by Jin Guantao and Bao Zunxin; Wenhua: Zhongguo yu Shijie (Culture: China and the World) headed by Gan Yang; Zhongguo wenhua shuyuan (Chinese Academy of Culture) headed by Liang Shuming, Li Zehou and Tang Yijie.

March Towards the Future is noted for its drastic anti-tradition attitudes towards Chinese culture and for its enthusiasm for science. Many of its board members are young and middle-aged scholars who were natural scientists. The board stresses the spirit of science. This spirit refers to the analytical and positivistic tradition of the West. Many of the roughly 100 books, published under the leadership of Jin Guantao, were each printed with more than 100,000 copies.[11] The majority of these books stress the role played by science in shaping society. Some of these books are written by Chinese writers, some are translations.

This group targets the general public rather than small circles of intellectual elites. The books were designed in the less scholarly looking form of pocket books. The books in this series rarely exceed 300,000 Chinese characters in length, or approximately 150,000 English words. Of the two editions of Jin Guantao's most widely circulated book *Xingshen yu weiji (Cycle of Growth and Decline)*, the one within the March Towards the Future series with the title *Zailishi de biaoxiang houmian (Behind the Surface of History)*, is much more readable. It was believed that Jin's theory was the basis for the manuscript of the popular TV series *Heshang (Yellow River Elegy)*. The program was so popular that it was said that one million people attended a meeting to discuss *Heshang* in Guangzhou.[12]

The series of Culture: China and the World is mainly dedicated to publishing translations of foreign books. Its intellectual orientation is the opposite of that of March Towards the Future in the sense that while the later carries a strong tone of science, the former stresses humanism, ethics, aesthetics and religion. This situation is parallel with that of the West in that scientism and humanism have developed side by side, often in polemical opposition. As in the case with March Towards the Future, most of its board members are young and middle-aged scholars. This series published works by Martin Heidegger (1889–1976), Jacques Lacan (1901–), Michel Foucault (1926–1984), Jean-Paul Sartre (1905–1980), Albert Camus (1913–1960), Samuel Huntington (1927–) and Simone De Beauvoir (1908–), a total of 470 books. Apparently, works by these authors were not targeted at the general public, especially the less educated, a situation that is the opposite of the March Towards the Future group. Consequently, some of the works published by this group may or may not have immediate social implications. Among the three sub-series of *Xiandai xueshu wenku (Modern Scholarship), Xinzhi wenku (New Knowledge)* and *Xueshu yanjiu congshu (Scholarship Series)* under Culture: China and the World, the first sub-series is targeted mainly at those professionals who work in research institutes. Gan Yang, who is the leader of this group, is known for his studies on Hans-Georg Gadamar (1900–) and Paul Ricoeur (1913–). His point of departure, however, is closer to Jürgen Habermas

(1929–) in the sense that Gan is critical of not only scientism but also the Chinese cultural tradition. He believes that the best means to build a new culture is to take an iconoclastic stand.

Politically, this group emphasizes professionalism and independence of scholarship. Given the often politicized nature of Chinese scholarship, this approach is both rare and new. Nevertheless, this group advocates depoliticized politics. This attitude is similar to that taken by Vaclav Havel (1936–) who named one of his articles "Anti-Political Politics."[13] This situation is also different from the March Toward the Future group in that some members of Jin's group were later incorporated into the reformist faction of the party despite originating from unofficial circles. These members include Yan Jiaqi and Zhu Jiaming.

The major basis for advocating Confucianism is the Chinese Academy of Culture, the third unofficially originated intellectual group, founded in January 1985, with its honorary president being Liang Shuming, the last Confucianist. Compared with the other two groups, there is less of a consensus in terms of intellectual persuasion within this group. Therefore, it is hard to single out a representative thinker for this group. It seems that Liang who is perhaps a little more obsessed by Confucianism than most other members of this group may not represent the intellectual orientation of this group. The chief spokesmen of this group may include Li Zehou, Tang Yijie and Pang Pu who are joined by some overseas Chinese scholars such as Tu Wei-ming and Yu-sheng Lin. Li, Tang, and Pang are well established scholars who are well versed not only in Chinese cultural tradition but also in Western scholarship. For instance, one of Li Zehou's major books is on Immanuel Kant (1724–1804). This situation has largely excluded the possibility that this group simply wants a restoration of Chinese Confucian tradition, although it stresses the continuity of culture.

There is also a difference between these Chinese scholars who function at home and those who are based overseas. It seems that those who are overseas have taken a more pro-tradition approach, while the mainlanders, with the exception, perhaps, of Liang Shuming, are more cautious in advocating the Chinese cultural tradition. In addition, the overseas scholars seem to be more thorough with the Confucian literature. Three factors may have contributed to this situation. First, they perhaps have less been influenced by the iconoclastic tradition of the Chinese scholarship since 1919. Second, being overseas, thus feeling a bit lonely and helpless, they have perhaps developed a more enthusiastic attitude towards Chinese tradition. Third, this group of scholars started their endeavor in the early 1960s, thus becoming more established than their mainland counterparts who are subject to political oppression.

The Chinese Academy of Culture has been a success. It was said to have an enrollment of several thousand students each semester, many of them college teachers and government officials. Some even use the idiom "luoyang zhigui" (the literature is so popular that paper has become too expensive to buy) to describe the success of this academy. In spite of its popularity, this school can in no way compete with other schools, especially the iconoclastic March Towards the Future group. For instance, while many March Towards the Future books printed about 100,000 copies,[14] Tang Yijie's *Zhongguo chuantong wenhuazhong de ru dao shi (Confucianism, Taoism and Buddhism in Chinese Cultural Tradition)*, a chief book of this group, printed only 14,400 copies.[15] This situation has made Tu Weiming lament that the revitalization of Confucianism perhaps has to begin abroad or from Taiwan, Hong Kong, not from mainland China.[16]

To sum up, this study identifies three versions of scientism during the post-Mao era: the Marxist scientism of historical materialism; a Chinese-style scientism of technological determinism, the empirical scientism of systems theory. Three corresponding versions of humanism have also been identified: Marxist humanism; Confucian humanism; critical humanism. From the perspective of philosophical starting points, the dichotomy of scientism and humanism is drawn not only in line with the Chinese tradition that views intellectual-political trends as more or less in compensation, but also the tension of Max Weber (1864–1920) of formal rationality versus substance rationality. From the perspective of intellectual origins, the three versions of scientism and humanism can be traced back to Western materialistic scientism and Marxist humanism, the Chinese science tradition with its emphasis on technology and Confucianism, and Western empirical scientism and post-modernism. From the perspective of political connotations, the three versions of scientism are viewed as the expressions of state socialism, the current regime's contingent policies and pluralism/liberalism. The political connotations of the three versions of humanism are not as clear as that of scientism.

This study supports the following conclusions:

1. The ideas as embodied in the minds of the Chinese establishment intellectuals, especially those who endorse scientific approaches, are largely responses to China's socioeconomic and political conditions during this period. Consequently, there is an ambiguous relationship between their understandings of science and science as it is actually practiced. The relationship between their ideas and Marx is also unclear. Their ideas have drifted from the origins.

2. In the competition between scientism and humanism, the former is more popular. As two intellectual-political trends that are not only in opposition to, but also complementary with, each other, scientism seems to be dominant, while humanism is marginalized. There are a number of reasons for this: 1) Claiming to be the only way to know the truth, scientism is continuous with the holistic-monistic intellectual-political modes of thought in the Chinese tradition. 2) Since it appears objective, scientism can be understood as a response to voluntarism and ethic-purism that characterized the Cultural Revolution. 3) Pretending to be a panacea, scientism claims to be able to solve all the socioeconomic and political problems created by the Cultural Revolution and reform. 4) The objectiveness of scientism suits the Chinese political culture during a period which is characterized by fragmentation and low level of tolerance. 5) The three versions of scientism are also conveniently in a position to remold Chinese consciousness in correspondence with the three aspects of Chinese political culture, that is, the idealistic, the operational and the tolerated.

3. The momentum of the various versions of scientism and humanism witnessed drastic changes during the post-Mao period. Marxist scientism and Marxist humanism seemed to be more influential in the late 1970s and early 1980s. Then came Chinese style scientism of technological determinism and Confucian humanism. Empirical scientism of systems theory and critical humanism of various species of postmodernism and Western Marxism began to gain much momentum from the mid 1980s. That is to say, intellectually, the momentum is in the direction of empirical scientism and critical humanism; politically, the momentum is correspondingly in the direction of pluralism.

4. In connection with the fourth conclusion above, Chinese establishment intellectuals have been in the process of reforming themselves too. This is a process during which the intellectuals stop seeing themselves as merely the tools of the ruler, but as relatively independent intellectuals who speak for society, or finally, as post-modern intellectuals who speak only for themselves. The philosophical move towards Western mainstream thinking, the political move towards pluralism and the intellectuals' move towards autonomy are apparently the result of the world wide setbacks of Marxism and the failure of China's past practice in socialist policies.

CHAPTER 1

Science, Scientism and Humanism

In the Introduction, we noted that in official circles, there have emerged three intellectual-political trends: 1) historical materialism as represented by Hu Qiaomu; 2) technological determinism as first put forward by Su Shaozhi; 3) Marxist humanism as advocated by Wang Ruoshui. From unofficial circles, there have emerged three intellectual-political trends also: 1) the March Towards the Future group as represented by Jin Guantao; 2) the Culture: China and the World group of Gan Yang; 3) the Chinese Academy of Culture group as represented by Li Zehou.

If we rearrange the order of these six groups, not from the perspective of official versus unofficial, but from the point of view of science, we will find that three of them have by and large adopted a scientific approach: historical materialism; technological determinism; and March Towards the Future group. The other three groups have, however, adopted a humanistic approach: Marxist humanism, the Culture: China and the World group, and the Chinese Academy of Culture group. Interestingly, these six groups could be put in pairs: 1) Marxist scientism (historical materialism) versus Marxist humanism; 2) a Chinese style scientism (technological determinism) versus a Chinese style humanism (modified Confucianism); 3) mainstream Western scientism (empiricism/positivism) versus mainstream Western humanism (critical humanism).

9

In this chapter, the following questions will be discussed: What is science? What is scientism? Why are there three versions of Chinese scientism in the post-Mao era? What is humanism? Why are there three versions of humanism during the period? What is the relationship between the three versions of scientism and the three versions of humanism? Finally, we discuss briefly the role played by Chinese establishment intellectuals in China's political-intellectual arena to answer the question: To what extent do these intellectuals under study represent the Chinese political consciousness during the period?

This chapter is relatively dense and Western oriented. This is because, unless the deeper philosophical issues were clarified, the current issues could not be understood. Since all of the intellectuals under study have drawn strength from the Western philosophical tradition, we need to trace the roots of their ideas. Only when the Western origins are fully comprehended, can the distinct Chinese characteristics be demonstrated.

What Is Science?

It is widely agreed that modern science was born in the Scientific Revolution in Europe during the sixteenth and seventeenth centuries. Modern science is usually characterized by the following four principles and, until very recently, there was the agreement in what this revolution represented: 1) the empirical principle, which stresses the need for observation, hypothesis, experimentation and the return to observation; 2) the quantitative principle, which stresses the necessity to achieve exactitude in measurement, 3) the mechanical principle which stresses the need for formulating general laws or equations which describe and explain behavior; 4) the principle of progress through science.[1] At the turn of this century, these "scientific methods" were introduced into social sciences. As a result, metaphysics that was concerned with the relationship between matter and ideas and ethics were disqualified as part of human knowledge, because they could not be proved right or wrong by the above mentioned scientific principles.

This conventional understanding of science has been under attack in the last half century. Since the 1960s, these attacks have become more systematic. In fact, there has been a consensus among intellectual communities in the last two decades that there is no consensus concerning the meaning of science.[2] In the words of Chinese scholar Liu Qingfeng, "If people in the times of Newton and Galileo were able to tell with confidence what science was, nowadays, no real scientist can say this."[3]

In order to show why we have long misunderstood science, Thomas Kuhn (1922–) says that people who talk about science are not empirical and historical. There have been two tendencies in the history of science. First, Eurocentric Whig popularizers and ideologists saw science as the overcoming of superstition, magic, metaphysics and bad philosophy. Secondly, there were practicing scientists who did not look at how science actually was practiced or developed. They depended upon writing recipe books for students. Kuhn criticizes tendencies in the history of science which equate science with "rationality," or with the idea that scientific progress is a smooth road marked by attention to method.[4]

To the methodological transformations of the classical sciences, the contributions of Baconism as presented in the above-mentioned four scientific principles were very small, because it did not produce new theories in previously established sciences. Aristotle, for instance, stressed both deduction and the need for close observation.[5] Kuhn points out the insufficiency of methodological directives, by themselves, to dictate a unique substantive conclusion to many sorts of scientific questions. For instance, instructed to examine electrical or chemical phenomena, the man who is ignorant of these fields, but who knows what it is to be scientific, may legitimately reach any one of a number of incompatible conclusions. The more they study, say Aristotelian dynamics, phlogistic chemistry, or caloric thermodynamics, the more certain they feel that those once current views of nature were, as a whole, neither less scientific nor more the product of human idiosyncrasy than those current today.[6]

This skepticism towards the conventional understanding of science has been reinforced by scientific advances in recent centuries. For instance, the second law of thermodynamics does not conform to the "four scientific principles" in the sense that it cannot be falsified.[7] Yet, nobody doubts the scientific character of the second law of thermodynamics. Photons cannot be observed by positivistic means, yet nobody doubts their existence and the certain peculiar characteristics that their movements possess.[8]

Therefore, the allegation that pre-modern pseudo science was dominated by deduction of Aristotle and real science was born during the Scientific Revolution that stresses experiments is a myth. However, Baconism has exerted immense impact upon people's understanding of the world, regardless of the different interpretations about it. It made new fields, often those with roots in the prior crafts, available for scientific scrutiny (for example, magnetism, chemistry, electricity and the study of heat).[9] Although it is a mistake to believe that Bacon invented modern science which is characterized by experiments, especially the method of induction, he did contribute substantially to popular misunderstanding.

With the overwhelming doubt towards science in the Baconian sense and the awareness that the development of modern science was a long historical process involving complex social, political and economic factors, there have recently emerged three sorts of attitudes towards science. The first attitude is taken by those who, although aware of recent criticism and usually unwilling to endorse Baconian science on an abstract level, may still largely rely on positivistic methods in concrete studies. There is, accordingly, continuous appeal to operational definitions, to the search for quantitative relations, testing, hypothesis, reliability, validity, falsification and claims that real science is not metaphysical, and not influenced by extra-scientific concerns and interests.

A second adopts what I should call a historicist or a critical realist position. Much in line with Kuhn's critique of the conventional understanding of modern science, this group of people refuse to totally rely on empirical evidence or to endorse any grand generalizations and abstractions in the study of science. A historicist holds that "[K]nowledge, mind and meaning are part of the same world that they have to do with, and they are to be studied in the same empirical spirit that animates natural sciences."[10] But a historicist is not scientistic in the sense that he or she thinks that science can solve all problems. In addition, there will always be politics exactly because even given all the possible knowledge (an unlikely outcome) people would still need to resolve differences.

Historicists reject the four principles—at least as they are usually understood—and define positivism as holding that a scientific explanation must thoroughly eschew appeal to what is in principle beyond experience. Thus, although for historicists, science is empirical, this cannot be understood narrowly. Historicists, unlike positivists, insist that the conceptual (theoretical) and the empirical are intertwined. Moreover, for the historicist, "theoretical terms may have a non-observable reference" and a "valid scientific explanation can appeal to the in-principle non-observable."[11] Experimentation is, of course, desirable, but for the historicists, one can have genuine science where experimentation is impossible. Second, historicists reject the quantitative principle arguing that quantification and the use of mathematics is neither a sufficient nor, sometimes, a necessary condition for science. Third, in contrast to positivists, historicists hold that explanation does not proceed by assumption under general principles or equations which describe and explain behavior. For historicists, since outcomes are products of causal complexity, explanation more generally takes the form of a narrative, as in historical explanation. Finally, historicists are not committed to the idea there is scientific progress or that science can guarantee progress.

The third attitude towards science disagrees with both historicists and those who endorse positivism in specific studies without admitting it in a general sense. Various versions of post-modernism have adopted this attitude. It agrees with Kuhn in renouncing positivism as a legitimate means to approach truth. As a main methodological approach, post-modernists stress the need to identify the ideological implications through analyzing texts. Among the three groups, post-modernism is the least optimistic about human understanding of the world, or even about humans themselves.[12]

As a matter of the pursuit of knowledge, all the three approaches are useful. In a sense, they complement each other. Although positivism does not equal science, its methods, such as surveys and experiments are useful if adopted properly. Without these methods, there would be no modern science. The historicist approach is the most encompassing in terms of methodology. Its weak point is that it does not guide human research as a method. Therefore, researchers who adopt this approach may look only for the things they want to look at, because of human limitations. For one thing cited in the study, ten thousand may have been left out. Post-modernism is useful to warn us about any too optimistic assumptions of human knowledge and human power.

Therefore, this study does not define science. It is fine to accept the four principles as science, as most positivists may want to do, as long as we acknowledge the fact: 1) this science cannot solve all the problems in nature; 2) this science cannot solve most of the problems in human society. It is also fine to call these four principles positivistic principles which do not equal science, as most historicists and post-modernists may want to do, as long as we share the assumption that the science in the minds of these historicists and post-modernists is different from that in the minds of positivists in the sense that this science is the only way that leads us to truth.

As a methodological approach, this study has adopted an eclectic approach. It has drawn strength from historicism. In Chapter Two when discussing the economic origins of the new thinking, survey data is used and interpreted critically. In Chapter Nine when discussing the relations between the new thinking, which can also be called elite political culture, and the mass political culture, the results of surveys done recently by such political scientists as Andrew Nathan and Tianjian Shi have been used. The approach adopted by some of these people is by and large within the mainstream positivistic tradition.

Nevertheless, it is not possible to rely totally on positivistic methods. For instance, James R. Townsend divides Chinese political culture during the Maoist era into the elite political culture and the mass political culture.

Elite political culture is further divided it into a Maoist political culture oriented toward continuing the revolutionary struggle and a bureaucratic political culture oriented more toward political stability and economic construction.[13] Apparently, the current study, if using Townsend's language, deals with China's political socialization from a special perspective: how scientism and humanism as parts of the Chinese elite political culture interact with the mass political culture during the post-Mao period.[14]

In fact, between the two methodological approaches of the configurative and the positivistic in the China field, as defined by Andrew Nathan and Ying-shih Yu, the majority of researchers have adopted the former. Perhaps aware of the possibility that this situation may have been caused by the closure of the Chinese society in the past, thus vigorous testing and scientific survey were not possible, Nathan advocated recently a more positivistic approach because it is now easier to do this kind of research.[15] However, vigorous testing may not be able to solve our problems in the study of China's elite political culture.

The post-modernist methodology may not be able to solve all our problems either. If the pessimistic implication of post-modernism were accepted, no intellectual pursuit would be meaningful. Nevertheless, its method of unmasking ideological implications through analyzing texts as Jacques Derrida (1930–) did is precisely the main method that this study has adopted. This is so in spite of the fact that the current study is more conscious in relating the texts to current social reality. In addition, by having the warning of post-modernism, this study realizes its limitations and accepts the real possibility that it may not offer the only, or even the best, answer to the questions raised.

This study assumes that although the thinkers' ideas come from reality, once these ideas are formed, they have lives of their own. That is to say, although these thinkers live in the same society and share the same civilization, they have responded in quite different ways, because as individuals they have different socioeconomic, political and psychological backgrounds. Therefore, some have adopted "scientific" approaches, others have found humanistic approaches more attractive. However, that does not mean that there are no patterns for the formation of their ideas. Above all, the people have responded to their theories also with certain tendencies, which can also be analyzed systematically and empirically.

The issues involved have also been dealt with from the perspectives of social structure and functions that the New Thinking has played. On the level of structural analysis, the New Thinking has been discussed in the light of the interactions between different aspects of society, mainly the historical, political, economic and social. On the level of functional analysis, New Thinking has been dealt with according to the role that the

Chinese establishment intellectuals have played in general and how the New Thinking which implies different ideologies has helped remold Chinese political culture. I return to the patterns and formation of their ideas when discussing the theoretical assumptions of this study.

What Is Scientism?

Scientism is often viewed as a matter of putting too high a value on science in comparison with other branches of learning or culture. It implies 1) science is unified; 2) there are no limits to science; 3) science has been enormously successful at prediction, explanation, and control; 4) the methods of science confer objectivity on scientific results; and 5) science has been beneficial for human beings.[16]

It is also identified as a form of idolatry, which could also be termed scientolatry. Science is worshipped as omniscient, omnipotent, and the bearer of man's salvation. This scientolatry claims that it can solve all problems scientifically and even examine questions of spirit, values and freedom.[17] Indeed, nowadays, scientism is always pejorative. It is always taken to mean an exaggeration, or over-optimism regarding science. That is, most people, at least in the West, approve of science, but there is considerable skepticism that science can cure everything.

However, people's interpretations about scientism are quite different, a situation that has significant intellectual and political connotations. In brief, Western scholars tend to regard scientism as an exaggeration of Baconian science, or empirical scientism, while the interpretations about scientism offered by some Chinese scholars such as D. W. Y. Kwok are broader. It not only includes empirical scientism but also a materialistic scientism.[18] A generic scientism, technological determinism, has also been found in contemporary Chinese thought by this study.

We have been unable to find "materialistic scientism" in Tom Sorell's classification of scientism. According to Sorell two kinds of scientism have existed: one intends to replace humanities; the other intends to replace philosophy. The first form of scientism is conveyed by Bacon's classification of learning: poetry and history are second-class subjects with limited scope; natural science is both incomparably more inclusive and, in principle, incomparably more valuable. This scientism is called scientific empiricism. It is a negation of metaphysics and an attempt to assimilate humanities into natural science.[19] The other version of scientism in Western philosophy, in addition to scientific empiricism, is a kind of naturalism that tries to assimilate philosophy into natural science.[20]

Similarly, no materialistic scientism has been identified in Hohn Wellmuth's classification. Wellmuth identifies three characteristics of scientism which also replace humanities and philosophy with natural science. 1) The fields of the various sciences, including such borderline or overlapping sciences as mathematical physics, biochemistry, physiochemistry and mathematical logic, are taken to be coextensive, at least in principle, with the entire field of available knowledge. 2) The scientific method, as exemplified in the above mentioned science, is the only reliable method of widening and deepening our knowledge and of making that knowledge more accurate. 3) The third characteristic of scientism is either that philosophy should be made scientific by conforming to the methods and ideals of some particular science, or that the function of philosophy is to correlate and if possible unify the findings of the other sciences by means of generalizing on a basis of these findings, after having rid itself of outworn metaphysical notions. This third characteristic is actually what Sorell describes as "naturalism," which intends to replace philosophy with science.[20]

How do we comprehend both Sorell's and Wellmuth's exclusion of materialistic scientism that includes the Marxist scientism of historical/dialectical materialisms under study in this book? We certainly realize the complexity in which Chinese intellectuals responded to Western science. Therefore, it is unrealistic to find exact Chinese parallels of categories concerning science and scientism in the West. However, it is worthwhile to inquire why Kwok has identified materialistic scientism but Sorell and Wellmuth have not. The fact that materialistic scientism occurred in China during the first half of the century does not seem to be accidental, or aberrational. Similar intellectual trends seem to have emerged during the post-Mao era, both in the name of science.

It seems the main reason is that in the West twentieth century scientism has been by and large various versions of positivism. Materialistic scientism is still in the discourse of metaphysics in the sense that it one-sidedly emphasizes matter to the neglect of ideas.[22] Metaphysics answers the question: What is reality? The central problem involved is the relationship between matter and ideas. Therefore, one-sided emphasis on matter is not only materialistic, but also metaphysical. Although orthodox Marxism which includes historical/dialectical materialisms claims that it departs from metaphysic in the sense that it is "dialectical,"[23] they are similar in the sense that both have the issue of matter and ideas at the center of discussions. Since metaphysics was excluded from Western social sciences at the turn of this century, this materialism stopped being regarded as having anything to do with science. Therefore, there has been no materialistic scientism in the Western academic discussions.

Such is not the case for China. First of all, although China has its own science tradition, modern science is by and large an imported matter. Consequently, China has consistently been one step behind the West in absorbing modern science. Baconian science has never occupied the center of China's intellectual arena as in the West. In addition, the relative strong voice of orthodox Marxism throughout China's modern history is decisive in keeping materialistic scientism alive. Therefore, materialistic scientism was not only one of the main versions of scientism during the first half of the twentieth century, it is still part of Chinese enlightenment today.

Given our better understanding about science in the last few decades, the legitimacy of materialistic scientism as a category in discussions of scientism may have to be considered in this new light. Ontological concerns have a legitimacy in discussions of science and scientism, although we may not go as far as to advocate the restoration of metaphysics as the main paradigm in academic discussions as some scholars have done recently.[24]

The linkage between materialistic scientism and metaphysics has to be noted, because conceptual confusions may arise without the clarification. For instance, although Kwok regards the 1923 debate on science as between "science" and "metaphysics" (*ke xuan zhizheng*),[25] as most people do, he also regards "materialistic scientism" as based on a "materialistic metaphysic."[26] Therefore, the *xuan xue gui*, or metaphysicians as he calls them, may include not only those who were against science, but also some of those who were for science, the materialistic scientists such as Chen Duxiu and Wu Zhihui. Another difficulty with Kwok's classification is that while his empirical scientism is an exaggeration of his four scientific principles, his materialistic scientism has no necessary relations with these principles.

It is also important to clarify the relations between empirical scientism and materialistic scientism, because they carry not only different intellectual connotations but also different political implications. Empirical scientism or, scientific empiricism, is largely modelled on the experimental tradition in Western physical science. By stressing method, Baconian science, which sometimes becomes empirical scientism, does not concern itself very much with ontological questions. It does not care whether the ultimate reality is material or spiritual, or something else. Therefore, scholars functioning in this category may be naturalists such as John Dewey (1859–1952) and Hu Shi (1891–1962), or agnostics such as Herbert Spencer (1820–1903) and Thomas H. Huxley (1825–1895). In fact, most of twentieth century empirical scientisms are all positivisms. They bifurcate facts and values. They hold that value judgments, like claims about God, the soul, etc. are not cognitive. They are neither true nor false. They are merely expressions of emotion or feeling, etc.

The political connection between empirical scientism and liberalism can be identified. Two reasons may account for this situation: 1) The point of departure of empirical scientism is not monistic as is materialistic scientism. It does not care whether the ultimate reality is material or spiritual. Consequently, it is more flexible. This view, accordingly, seems democratic and pluralistic. 2) While Marxist scientism is assumptively deductive, empirical scientism is more cautious by relying on rigorous testing. Induction is more important for empirical scientism. Historically, those Chinese intellectuals who believed in empirical scientism have proved to be more likely to be liberals.[27] Not surprisingly, the majority of Western mainstream social scientists are also liberals, partly because the research methods they adopt are more often than not in the Baconian science tradition.

Marxist philosophy, or historical materialism and dialectical materialism, is not in the Baconian experimental tradition. By saying Marxist philosophy, I am not referring to the various unreductionist interpretations of Marx by Western Marxist scholars,[28] but orthodox Marxism as interpreted by Friedrich Engels (1820–1895) and the Russian Marxists. Specifically, it has two origins in Western philosophy: 1) dialectics in methodology which emphasizes the changing nature of the world and the concept of contradiction; 2) the materialistic tradition in ontology which claims that the ultimate origin of the world lies in the objective world rather than the spiritual world of human beings. This species of Marxism believes that all events were manifestations of the fundamental nature of matter, and that there was one fundamental science which could explain all of these manifestations by means of its grasp of the nature of the material world. This science, however, was not physics, but was the dialectical interpretations of nature and man.[29]

In terms of political implications, all Marxists are socialists. Is there an intellectual link between Marxist science tradition and socialism? There is. First of all, materialism is monistic. That fits state socialism. Materialistic scientism lacks the pluralism and fallibility which is embodied in empirical scientism.[30] Second, some theories in materialistic scientism such as historical materialism and dialectical materialism do not have to be proved. The demise of capitalism and the success of communism are largely deduced from the monistic materialistic assumptions. Third, dialectics stresses contradiction, which can provide intellectual support for the political concept of class struggle.

The fact that discussions about scientism may have to be considered in the light of socioeconomic and political situation is supported by the fact that those intellectual figures from whom scientism is said to have originated may have explicitly disproved scientism. Sorell points out that "the idea that science might save us—might be a panacea—is not easy to find in seventeenth-century writers and it is not in Bacon"; nor is it found in Thomas Hobbes (1588–1679) or Rene Descartes (1596–1650). Neither Bacon, Hobbes or Descartes believed that science is the only source of learning.[31] Clearly, the emergence of scientism cannot simply be viewed as a distortion of intellectual pursuit, but has to be considered in the light of socioeconomic and political conditions.

The Chinese-style scientism of technological determinism is largely generic. Compared with empirical scientism and Marxist scientism, it is more political than intellectual. It is actually a distortion of orthodox Marxism plus some modifications of the indigenous Chinese science tradition. It borrows from Marxist scientism crucial notions such as objective law and the idea that productive forces are the most important in the development of human society. It differs from Marxism in that it downplays the role of relations of production. Su Shaozhi's concept of primary-stage socialism, which was later developed into a kind of technological determinism, or a Chinese style scientism, was accepted by Zhao Ziyang as one of the theoretical basis for the current regime's reform policies.[32]

Chinese science tradition is closely connected with the development of Chinese society, which was highly centralized with one man at the top. China's scientific development was characterized by: 1) politicization (*zhengzhihua*), 2) technologization (*jishuhua*);[33] 3) downplay of comprehensive theories. Politicization refers to the fact that science was influenced very much by politics. This is most clearly demonstrated in astrology, because the movement and formation of stars explain the mandate of the Emperor. Throughout China's feudal history, the development of astrology was not a process during which humans' understanding of this particular science progressed gradually. Rather, its development was a zigzag path; two steps forward, one step backward. New discoveries in astrology were subject to the ruler's political interests.

Technologization of ancient development of Chinese science refers to the fact that those aspects of technology that were useful for the maintenance of the political system were very advanced. China's four big scientific discoveries—paper, the compass, typographic printing, and gunpowder—are examples in point. All these discoveries were closely connected with the central government's desire to control the vast land. None of these discoveries was closely linked with the people's daily life.

A third characteristic of China's scientific tradition is that it does not view the pursuit of knowledge for its own sake, but for solving problems "of this life, in this world."[34]

It is not the intention of this study to set a strict definition for scientism. The main difference I have regarding defining scientism as compared with other scholars concerned is that all the three dimensions of philosophy, ontological, methodological and epistemological, have to be considered. Even Kwok's "four principles" are not a pure method, as some scholars insisted.[35] They are at least as much epistemological as methodological. For practical purpose, an operational definition for scientism that is scientism in its widest possible sense is offered. It could be viewed as the belief that: 1) the objective world has to be understood by way of science, defined in whatever way; 2) science, in whatever sense, can enable us to know fully the world and solve all the problems.

Based on this definition, three species of scientism have emerged during the post-Mao China: 1) Marxist scientism as exemplified by Hu Qiaomu's historical/dialectical materialism. This is actually a continuation of Chen Duxiu's Marxist philosophy in the early part of this century. 2) Empirical scientism exemplified by the systems theory of Jin Guantao. This version of scientism can be viewed as a continuation of Hu Shi's empirical scientism during the Republic period. 3) A Chinese style scientism of technological determinism as represented by Su Shaozhi.

What Is Humanism?

Like the emergence of modern science, humanism originally was also part of the Enlightenment tradition, when all the thinking of the time was designed to make man free. Although all thought of the Enlightenment was concerned with the problem of liberty, different people looked at the problem from different perspectives. Some were more scientific, as were discussed previously, others were more humanistic.

For François-Marie Abouet De Voltaire (1694–1778), liberty meant freedom from the church and from intolerance, freedom of the mind, freedom from misconception and ignorance, the most insidious of all forms of enslavement.[36] For Jean Jacques Rousseau (1712–1778), the precursor of many nineteenth-century romantics who swam against the tide of the rationalism of the French eighteenth-century philosophers (the Encyclopedists), the role of sentiments and emotions were important.

Above all, humanism is closely connected with Kant. It was Kant who explicitly introduced the anthropological question, "what is man?", into philosophy. As a result, the post-Kantian tradition was condemned to what may have thought to be an unfortunate anthropologism. The critique of humanism was thus often directed against Kant, and against the ideals of the Enlightenment that he built into our understanding of what philosophy is.[37]

As general intellectual trends, it has been found that, going side by side with empirical scientism, there has been a what I call critical humanism. This critical humanism covers all of those who have adopted a humanistic approach in philosophy but who are largely not part of the Marxist enterprise, for analytical convenience. One important figure of this group is Michel Foucault (1926–1984), who is known for his post-structuralism. Although Foucault once believed that modern philosophy should be based on the ideas of Marx, Freud and Nietzsche, it is now generally believed that his theory is more profoundly influenced by Nietzsche. This has ensured him an anti-rationalist position. Habermas may be considered another important figure of this group. Habermas is the most important figure of the second generation of the Frankfurt School. Although the Frankfurt School, known for its social critique theory, was profoundly influenced by Marx, Habermas openly renounced Marxism. He believed that criticism of science should replace criticism of society.[38]

Similarly, Marxist scientism has its counterpart too: Marxist humanism. Although Marxism surely encompasses both the scientific and humanistic aspects, people read Marx differently. Orthodox Marxist philosophy, that is, historical materialism and dialectical materialism, developed through the interpretations of the Second International and Russian Marxists, is Marxist scientism. As many malpractices in the former Soviet Union were discovered in the first half of this century, various Marxist groups in Europe began to develop their own theories which sometimes have a humanistic flavor. This is what was later called Neo-Marxism.

Largely developed since the late 1940s, Neo-Marxism encompasses a broad spectrum of theories and departs from orthodox Marxism, which was rooted in the Second International. The main departure of Neo-Marxism on a philosophical level from orthodox Marxism is a more flexible stand regarding base/superstructure relations and recognition of many ideas in the writings of the young Marx. The political implications of this flexible approach primarily lay with the different answers to the notion of whether the worldwide collapse of capitalism and the realization of communism were inevitable. Key figures here include George Lukacs (1885–1971), Antonio Gramsci (1891–1937), the Frankfurt School,[39] Louis Althusser (1918–1990), the Praxis Group in Yugoslavia and a wide range of so-called Western Marxists. Among the various schools of thought of Neo-Marxism, humanism has consistently been a hot topic of discussion. But sometimes

Neo-Marxism is defined in a broader sense. It includes not only Western Marxism, but also the "dissent" theories that emerged from the Soviet Union and Eastern European countries after the Twentieth National Party Congress of the Soviet Union, in which Nikita Khrushchev (1894–1971) criticized Joseph Stalin (1879–1953).[40]

Marxist humanism, however, has much to do with *The Economic and Philosophic Manuscripts of 1844*. The complete texts were not published until 1932. The publication of this book was viewed by Western Marxists as an extremely important text, because they not only became disillusioned with the Russian experience but also were frustrated by the failure of Second International Marxism to explain the European situation. *The Manuscripts*, together with the *German Ideology*, published in 1888, and *Grundrisse (Foundation of the Critique of Political Economy)*, which was written as early as 1857, but was not published until 1939, made a different understanding of Marx possible. These texts soon became tools for the Western Marxists to fight not only Second International Marxism, which later became orthodoxy under Stalin, but also to interpret capitalism in a different way. It was with these texts that humanism and alienation became the new paradigms of the Western Marxists, to replace the old slogans of revolution, class struggle, and the dictatorship of the proletariat.

Confucianism, with its many modern modifications, is the indigenous Chinese humanism. It may be viewed as the counterpart of the Chinese style scientism, the technological determinism that focuses on developing productive forces. In line with the current regime's endorsement of technological determinism, Li Ruihuan, the ideology tsar of the party after the 1989 Tiananmen incident promoted Chinese traditional culture. Confucianism is noted for its ethic-purism and for relying on sense perception for an understanding of the world. By way of demonstration, Liang Shuming's rationality asserts that not only humans, but nature, including mountains and rivers, has a life of its own too. Just like the case with Su Shaozhi whose technological determinism has provided one of the theoretical basis for the reform policies of the current regime, Li Zehou's modified version of Confucianist humanism has been regarded as forming another part of the philosophical basis for the current regime's reform policies.[41]

Theoretical Assumptions

The six intellectual-political trends introduced in this study form a model: Latitudinally, there is the dichotomy of scientism and humanism; longitudinally, there is collectivism (Marxist scientism versus Marxist humanism), the middle of the road (a Chinese-style scientism versus a Chinese-style humanism) and liberalism (the mainstream Western scientism versus the mainstream Western humanism). This model raises the following three questions; 1) Why do the various versions of scientism necessarily have corresponding versions of humanism? 2) How are the political implications embodied in these intellectual trends? 3) How do we locate the Chinese New Thinking vis-a-vis the transformation of Chinese society? These questions can be answered based on three theoretical assumptions.

The first theoretical assumption is that philosophical starting points usually fall into a dichotomy: the scientific (often, scientistic) and the humanistic. The scientific refers to the principles embodied in science in general, not exclusively to natural science. Consequently, the so-called "two cultures" of this book are different from that defined by C. P. Snow who mainly comments on the "cultures" of natural scientists and philosophers.[42] This dichotomy, or sometimes tension, has been consistently perceived by people throughout human history.

In times of ancient Greece, there was Plato (427?–347 B.C.) who advocated a "non-scientific" approach by relying on the cultivation of the proper behavior of philosopher-kings.[43] Correspondingly, there was also Aristotle (384–322 B.C.) who was said to be the Father of Political Science, because he advocated law instead of calling for the goodness of human nature.[44] In modern times, there was John Locke (1632–1704) who tried to introduce the principles of hard science into social science.[45] Correspondingly, there was Jean-Jacques Rousseau who gave inspiration to the romantics by emphasizing sentiments and emotions.[46]

The tension between being scientific and humanistic has been found within individuals too. For Max Weber, he perceives a fundamental tension between the "instrumental rationality" which is "scientific," and "value rationality" which is "humanistic."[47] Of course, we are all familiar with a scientific Marx and a humanistic Marx. Both those who see Marx in these different perspectives have succeeded in finding textual support from Marx's works. Similarly, Kant has not only been regarded as one of the most influential figures in the Western humanistic tradition as was mentioned previously, his ideas have also been regarded as one of the main sources of modern positivism.[48]

The case of Chinese intellectual Wang Guowei at the beginning of this century is even more dramatic. Recent studies on Wang have gone as far as to suggest that this intellectual tension may have been at least partly responsible for Wang's committing suicide. Wang suffered because he felt that those kinds of things that can be loved cannot be believed (humanistic), while those kinds of things that can be believed cannot be loved (scientific) (*keai buke xin; kexin buke ai*).[49]

It seems that a humanistic approach always emerges because the so called scientific approach is unable to answer questions of the universe. But this may be true in the other way around, when one takes a humanistic stand, he or she is likely to be one-sidedly humanistic, just like the case that when one takes a scientific stand, he or she is likely to run into the trap of scientism. Those who endorse both approaches are likely to feel the tension.

The second theoretical assumption of this study is simple; politics is always embodied in theories and different theories carry different politics. From the political perspective, analysis of the elite political cultures in a transitional society could always be conducted in terms of some kind of collectivism (often socialism), middle of the road, and liberalism. Following the advice of Weber, theories are always value-laden.

The third theoretical assumption is that societies can be divided into three forms: traditional; charismatic; rational. This is largely based on Weber's notions of society.[50] Apparently, the Chinese dynasties belong to the category of the traditional, where authority is based on rules handed down from the past and personal status and authority rest with an individual or chief who has been chosen on a traditional basis. The Maoist period may be identified as charismatic bacause authority depended mainly upon success by the leader in coping with the crisis that toppled the traditional order. Chinese elite political culture during the post-Mao period can be viewed as moving towards a rational society where authority rests with rationality. This rationality, or the instrumental aspect of rationality, is characterized by a secularization or separation of religious and governmental practices, which involves a proliferation of administrative regulatory functions, the introduction of impersonal discipline and rules of procedure, and an expansion of economic activity and taxation to finance the emerging bureaucracy. The intellectual trends discussed in this study can be viewed as part of this process.

Nevertheless, if the current study has offered a model, it is a heuristic one, to say the most. First of all, none of the six intellectual trends is the sufficient condition for the existence of the others. Any sophisticated thinker—all of the six intellectuals under study are sophisticated—is always aware of the one-sidedness of taking just a scientific or a humanistic position. Therefore, all of them endorse both a scientific and a humanistic approach. Second, politics, as reflected in the theories, be it state socialism, middle of the road, or liberalism, is not clear cut. For instance, although Wang Ruoshui is put in the category of socialism because he still claims to be a communist, his platform for reform is closer to the Western liberals. Third, the three forms of society, be it traditional, charismatic, or rational, cannot be divided in any rigid way.

Carriers of New Thinking:
The Establishment Intellectuals

This part of the study analyzes the political-intellectual roles played by
contemporary Chinese establishment intellectuals during the post-Mao era,
because they are the carriers of the New Thinking. This may help us to
evaluate to what extent they represent the political mentality of the average
Chinese. We will find that regardless of the intellectual orientations of their
scholarship, these intellectuals are indeed the voice of society on various
levels. The selection of the six intellectuals as a sample will be justified
in the separate chapters which deal specifically with them.

We first explain the phrase "establishment intellectuals." If it were
a century ago, the word "establishment" would have been redundant. In
China at that time and for roughly the previous 2,000 years since the Han
dynasty when the civil service exam was gradually institutionalized, intellectuals by and large belonged to the establishment, the imperial family.
Most of the scholars who had passed exams were recruited into the government bureaucracy. By contrast, it would be unusual to link establishment
and intellectuals in this general sense in the Western tradition. Ideally
Western intellectuals who dwell largely in civil society may not directly
serve the establishment and in actuality they seldom do. With the collapse
of China's last dynasty in 1911 and the subsequent creation of two authoritarian states, the Republic of China (ROC) and the People's Republic of
China (PRC), Chinese intellectuals were to be divided into establishment,
those who directly served rulers of one kind or another, and non-establishment scholars who did not, or only indirectly did so.

A dual role played by these intellectual leaders in serving both the
ruler and the society is the best starting point for analyzing the role played
by establishment intellectuals and consequently we can draw some insights
as to what extent the new awareness represents the mentality of both
intellectuals in general and the people. The tension of satisfying both the
ruler and the people is the distinguishing characteristic of the behavior
of these intellectuals.

This discussion may be useful in that these intellectual leaders have
played crucial roles in China's intellectual and political arenas during the
reform period, yet Western scholarship which has sought to evaluate their
roles has been conflicted. Peter Moody did not explicitly make the
distinction between establishment and non-establishment intellectuals,
although he talked about the relationship between intellectuals when
analyzing the relationship between the ruler and intellectuals.[51] Although
she does not adopt the term "establishment intellectuals" consistently,
Merle Goldman draws this distinction and says that these intellectual
leaders probably numbered only "in the hundreds."[52]

For those who employed this distinction, there has been no consensus as to the basis on which the distinction should be made. According to Goldman, "what distinguished this tiny minority from the majority of China's intellectuals was a sense of responsibility to address issues of political policy in a public forum."[53] This evaluation was connected with the intellectuals' attitudes, which have historical origins not only in ancient China but also in the May Fourth Movement tradition. It has not been clearly demonstrated whether Goldman's sense of responsibility was the only distinction between the establishment and non-establishment intellectuals, or one of many.

The situation may be more complex. During the Hundred Flowers Movement in 1957 many intellectuals, not exclusively the hundreds or so intellectual leaders, rose up to criticize the imperfections of the party in response to the official call. Whether or not because of this same realization, Edward Shils believes that historical traditions may not be as important as the social functions these intellectual leaders perform and that these social functions should serve as the basis on which such a distinction should be made. In contrast to non-establishment intellectuals, the intellectual leaders would then be defined as those who serve and operate within the governing institutions and "are primarily engaged in intellectual activities that define the 'ultimate' or the ideal". . ."and have 'affirmed, accepted and served the ruling authorities.' "[54]

On the relationship between intellectuals and the rulers, Goldman, Hamrin and Cheek hold that it has been more of a "vertical patron-client" pattern. Hamrin and Cheek offer a chart which shows there is a gradation of political involvement for intellectuals from the center to the periphery.[55] They have done so to negate the viewpoint held by Moody who has claimed that the relationship was more of a dichotomy of interests, a result of the fact that the Chinese society was divided into the ruled and the ruler.[56] However, although the patron-client analysis may be more plausible in describing the party-intellectuals relationship than the dichotomy analogy, especially considering the changes brought about by Deng's reform, it may not be able to explain the situation in which establishment intellectuals seem to always go beyond the boundaries set by their party patrons.

Although the analyses offered by these authors bring some light to the question of modern Chinese intellectuals, they are inconsistent, not only with each other, but at times internally so. For instance, David Kelly endorses the patron-client analysis when analyzing the roles played by Wang Ruoshui, but at the same time maintains that Wang's writings "exceeded any 'contractual obligations' to a faction."[57] This break of contractual obligations which seems to be habitual for Chinese establishment intellectuals is not characteristic of patron-client relationships. In addition, those who insist that the relationship between the ruler and the intellectuals was basically a patron-client one have not based this distinction on exactly the same ground. Some have based it on tradition, others on social function.[58]

The intriguing nature of the roles these intellectuals have played has led other Sinologists to leave the question open as to why intellectuals have behaved the way they have. For instance, after a brilliant analysis of Fang Lizhi's intellectual-political career, James H. Williams admits at the end of his article that what was "most important" and "least easily explained" was why Fang had dissented at all, given the high social status and reasonably good living standard Fang had enjoyed within the system.[59] Commenting on Yan Jiaqi, David Bachman and Dali L. Yang say that "the role and activities of insiders as reformers (establishment intellectuals) are doubly difficult to determine."[60] We will make a more rigorous exploration of these issues.

As will be demonstrated when we analyze the careers of the six intellectuals, they seem to have demonstrated the following characteristics: 1) They have all performed very different social-political functions when compared with regular intellectuals. Therefore, a distinction based on social-political functions is necessary. 2) They have all shared common interests with the ruler at one time or another, thus refuting the dichotomy analogy. 3) No evidence has shown that any of them has been in a typical patron-client relationship with the ruler, although all may have been close to a member of the ruling body at one time or another. All have dissented in one way or another, at one time or another. Thus the patron-client analogy is at least not sufficient. 4) All seem to have dissented for reasons of personal interest and intellectual conviction. The aspect of Chinese tradition that has had a more profound impact on them seems to be the general tendency for intellectuals to get more involved in politics than some less central concerns. Why is this?

China's centralized dynastic society was sustained by an organic tripartite whole of common ideology and state theory, that is, Confucianism, the system of prefectures and counties established in Qin (221–107 BC) (*junxianzhi*), and a landlord economy. Confucian scholars, by filling the major posts in the bureaucracy, played the crucial role of gluing these three parts together. Because of this situation, even education served mainly the purpose of training these scholars. For instance, the great majority of academies that flourished in the nineteenth century only taught the texts necessary for success in the civil exams. Because of this lack of any institutionalized mechanism for sustaining intellectual autonomy, those who sought it usually faced political estrangement.[61] Remonstrance was the only way for efficient dissent. Qu Yuan, the scholar-official of Chu during the Spring and Autumn Period (770–476 BC) who killed himself in order to protest against the corruption of the king and the wickedness of his colleagues, and Zhuge Liang, the devoted Prime Minister of Shu during the Three Kingdoms Period (220–280 AD) who served the monarch, no matter whether the monarch was wise or stupid, had been models for Chinese intellectuals for over two thousand years. In fact, some Western scholars have pointed out that "classical Chinese has no word for 'intellectual.'" The Chinese "literati," "scholar" and "gentry" have very different connotations compared with that carried by "intellectual" in the Western context.[62]

The several decades of domestic chaos following the collapse of the Qing Dynasty in 1911 had a two-fold impact on Chinese intellectuals. On the one hand, it destroyed the structural basis for the Confucian style service to the state by scholars. In the early twentieth century, relative intellectual autonomy replaced remonstrance and new scholarship (*xinxue*) which was largely modelled after the Western educational system, replaced old style academies. On the other hand, however, the Confucian scholars' tradition of getting involved with real world politics was reinforced, instead of declining. This was because national salvation called for the political involvement of Chinese intellectuals.

For example, Lu Xun, China's most prominent literary figure at that time, originally planned to become a medical doctor, because of his father's early death and because many Chinese people were suffering from poor health. He then began writing political stories because he realized that no matter how healthy the Chinese were, they could not save themselves without political and national emancipation. Both Chen Duxiu, the first communist theorist, and Hu Shi, the most important liberal theoretician in China prior to the founding of the PRC, were determined originally not to get involved with real world politics, but to devote themselves to raising the political consciousness of the Chinese people. This is because they believed that an emancipation of consciousness should take priority over political action. However, Chen soon found himself the first Secretary General of the Chinese Communist Party (CCP) and Hu the Kuomintang Ambassador to the United States, and were thus unable to resist the temptation to become politically involved.

Chinese intellectuals' active participation in politics during the period in which the CCP and the Kuomintang competed for national power produced unintended results. In other words, the majority of leading intellectuals functioned structurally in two military organizations. This process was called by Yingshi Yu part of the marginalization of Chinese intellectuals. Drawing upon historical experience, Yu argues that during periods of social turmoil, only marginal people such as bankrupt peasants and hooligans function well and unmarginal people such as successful entrepreneurs and intellectuals have to become marginalized in terms of behavior in order to survive in politics. Yu points out that most cadres of the CCP and the Kuomintang, especially those of the middle and lower level, were either marginal people in the first place or those such as intellectuals who became marginalized. Therefore, intellectuals in a sense voluntarily moved to the margin from the center of political arena, the place they used to occupy.[63]

Immense structural changes took place after the founding of the PRC in 1949, which in turn had an enormous impact on Chinese intellectuals. The new system resembled Chinese dynasties in some aspects such as promoting a common ideology and employing a centralized political system with one person at the top. However, crucial differences did exist. Firstly, the political structure in Mao's time, with the exceptions of the 1957 Hundred Flowers Movement and the Cultural Revolution, was more centralized than historical dynasties. Different views were then more tolerated than in the PRC regime. The totalitarian social structure made it easy for people to come up with a "dichotomy" model if the analysis is made largely from the perspective of viewing intellectuals as a whole as Peter Moody did, and with a patron-client model if the analysis is made largely from that of the hundreds or so leading intellectuals as Merle Goldman did. In fact, both Moody's and Goldman's analysis largely drew upon experiences from the Mao era.

Secondly, although Confucianism in dynasties and Marxism in contemporary China both claimed to be all-encompassing, the latter is deficient in many aspects in sustaining the social system. While Confucianism was basically able to explain the universe for most scholars in the largely isolated ancient China where natural scientists did not constitute nearly as large a proportion in the ranks of scholars as today, Marxism cannot do so for most contemporary intellectuals, given the complexity of affairs in the modern world that calls for a division of labor among the intellectuals. Not every modern intellectual, even in Mao's time, devoted himself only to the study of Marxism as most Confucian scholars did with Confucianism.

Thirdly, most contemporary intellectuals do not have nearly as much power as their Confucian scholar predecessors did because of the division of labor among them. In ancient China, the county magistrate, the lowest in the dynastic hierarchy, was dubbed *qipin zhimaguan* (the seventh grade official who is as tiny as a sesame seed). A county magistrate in contemporary China commands enormous power compared with other intellectuals such as the hundreds of thousands of high school teachers and technicians. Only about one tenth of contemporary intellectuals serve in the party and government organizations where political power lies.[64] Among them only a small fraction together with some high ranking intellectual leaders can be called establishment intellectuals. However, about a third of contemporary intellectuals work in the field of education where political power is minimum.[65]

Within this historical and structural context, a group of intellectual leaders has emerged. In terms of number, they only constitute a tiny fraction of the intellectuals as a whole, probably in the hundreds. Within the official hierarchy, they probably have to hold positions above the level of bureau, (*jiu*) which is equivalent to directors of important research institutes and presidents of major universities. Some very famous journalists, novelists and playwrights such as Bai Hua and Liu Binyan, though without administrative posts, may also qualify for this title. In terms of the functions they play, they are closer to dynastic official scholars than to their fellow intellectuals at large in the sense that they not only possess knowledge but also command power.

These intellectual leaders have found themselves playing a dual role of both serving the ruler by joining the establishment and educating the people by practicing their intellectual profession. There are several determinants that have had an impact on their behavior. Firstly, with the common ideology and centralized political system, they are supposed to serve in ways similar to that of Confucian literati. The regime also pretends that they are still officials by giving many of them the title *ganbu* (cadre). Secondly, with the deficiency of Marxism as the all encompassing ideology in sustaining the social system as compared with Confucianism, establishment intellectuals have never felt completely comfortable devoting themselves to serving the ruler, because they are not as convinced by Marxism as their Confucian counterparts were by Confucianism. Consensus was partly ensured by political power. Thirdly, this tension was intensified with the fundamental change in the formation of intellectuals: while almost all Confucian scholars belonged to the establishment, only a tiny proportion of contemporary intellectuals belong to the ruling body. Intellectuals-at-large are competitors as well as alternatives for the establishment intellectuals.

This uneasy marriage between the ruler and establishment intellectuals got worse after Deng's reforms. This situation has made both the dichotomy and patron-client models even more difficult to sustain as effective analytical frameworks. With the self-claimed all-encompassing Marxist ideology in danger of losing all relevance, and the ensuing decentralization of the political system, intellectuals have gained more autonomy. In fact, some Western scholars have even employed the concepts of "civil society" to characterize these social-political changes and "class" to describe the new awareness of the intelligentsia brought about by the reforms.[66]

If these establishment intellectuals were merely part of the ruled as the dichotomy model defines, they could speak on behalf of neither society nor the ruler; if these establishment intellectuals were only clients, as the patron-client model speculates, they could only speak on behalf of the ruler. If, however, as we have found, they have played a dual role, they could represent the voices of a broad base.

They have taken this social responsibility, sometimes at the expense of sophisticated scholarship. Fang Lizhi once writes, "My airing of [dissident] thoughts has much less to do with any unique insights of mine than with the need to express publicly what many people are thinking privately." Once repression ends in China, Fang says, "these overscrutinized words of [his] will return to their rightful state of obscurity."[67] As we will see in the following respective chapters, another two of the so-called Four Great Contemporary Chinese Thinkers, Jin Guantao and Li Zehou, have also made it explicit that they would not do scholarship for its own sake.

Referring to some of my writings about him, Yan Jiaqi said, "If you merely reproduced what I wrote in China without proper explanation, Western scholars would surely say: 'What is the value of these ideas? Nothing new!' "[68] Su Shaozhi wrote to me: "You would be disappointed if you want to write about my ideas, because I have no systematic theory."[69] Even Liang Shuming, who was believed to be "the first one to systematically defend Confucianism and China's tradition"[71] and who was never close to the ruler, refused to be a pure scholar. He regarded himself as an activist.[71] The remarks by Fang, Yan and Su certainly cannot be taken at face value, because their exaggeration about the superficiality of their own works may partly be a sign of modesty. But the circumstantial nature of the modern Chinese scholarship is true. The ideas of these intellectuals have played the important social function of remolding Chinese political culture on various levels and during different periods of time.

CHAPTER 2

Historical Origins of the New Thinking

It may be natural for scientism to emerge during the post-Mao period, and to an extent triumph over the various versions of non-scientism, be it Marxist humanism, Confucianism, or critical humanism, mainly for three reasons: 1) Scientism inherits the Confucian cultural and intellectual tradition which has a holistic approach. All aspects of social consciousness are regarded as an inseparable whole. This intellectual holistic notion is also linked to the monistic political orientation in the Chinese culture where only one legitimate source of truth is recognized. Scientism is also in line with the utopianism embodied in the Chinese tradition. 2) It is a psychological response to what is termed voluntarism and ethic-purism as demonstrated during the Cultural Revolution. 3) It is a practical response to the socioeconomic problems encountered by the Chinese people after the Cultural Revolution.

Cultural Origins:
Holistic-Monistic Chinese Tradition

As with any great intellectual tradition, one can trace many current Chinese intellectual trends to their ancient past. In fact, the Chinese traditional culture is noted for its richness and, quite often, inconsistency. Westerners who study China are often shocked by the looseness in structure and inconsistency in ideas in the Confucian classic *Lunyu* (*The Analects*). In addition, Confucianism is only one of the three major schools of ancient Chinese thought, the other two being Taoism and Legalism. There is also an imported Buddhism. To make the situation worse, other minor schools of thought besides these four can also serve as parts of Chinese tradition in justifying current intellectual and ethical concerns. For instance, Confucianism is noted for its emphasis on family love and its lack of concern about general human love, which is a distinct notion of the Western Enlightenment. This situation has made many people, both Chinese and Westerners, complain that China lacks a democratic tradition. However, the *Mojia*, which flourished more or less simultaneously as Confucianism but gradually lost its influence later, is noted for its *Jian ai*, which literally means "general human love."

Even if one cannot find the origins of some modern notions from ancient texts, one may find them from other expressions of Chinese mentality in the Chinese tradition. For instance, romantic love between men and women is not stressed at all in classical texts and Chinese men were very unlikely to devote themselves too much to women. Courtship as a complicated technique was foreign to most Chinese men. An ideal ancient marriage is *caizi jiaren* (an excellent scholar who has passed the top level civil service exam marries a beautiful woman whom he hardly knows). This is because, as the idiom goes, *"shuzhong ziyou yanruyu"* (a beauty will run into your embrace herself if you have passed the exam by mastering the Confucian classics). These Chinese scholars would be stunned if they discovered that so many men in medieval Europe died in duels because of women. However, the theme of *Hong lou meng* (*The Dream of the Red Mansion*) and *Jin ping mei* (*The Golden Lotus*), two of the so-called *sida qishu*, or four most famous novels in traditional Chinese literature, is precisely about the love and/or lust between men and women, at least on the surface. The theme of romantic love between men and women can also be found in *shi jing* (*The Book of Songs*), which came before the Confucian times. Because of this complexity, my attempt here in trying to trace the roots of the current intellectual trends from Chinese tradition is strict. That is to say I will regard the least disputable aspects of Chinese intellectual thought as a legitimate source for the current intellectual trend. The holistic-monistic notion is one of them.

Chinese philosophy, like philosophies of other great civilizations, has deep roots in pre-civilized times, which generally refer to the times before the period of 800–200 BC. Karl Jaspers calls it the axial period in human history because this is the time when several great civilizations flourished independently in different parts of the world: the civilizations of Greece;

Egypt; India; Babylon; China.[1] It is said that before this axial period, different civilizations shared a common characteristic: they were dominated by religion. After this period, civilizations went their own ways. However, even during the pre-civilized times, the religion of different civilizations had different contents, a situation that had an enormous impact on the development of these civilizations later.

The nature of Chinese philosophy can be better presented by tracing its roots in pre-civilized times and in comparison with the philosophies of other great civilizations, especially that of the Eastern Mediterranean from which Western civilization originated. A brief analysis of religious beliefs and myths during these early times may help us to gain an insight about the development of Chinese philosophy later, because, as Bertrand Russell (1872–1970) has argued, philosophy is a marriage between religion and science.

Let us unfold the two points of Chinese mythology that are of immediate relevance to our discussion both on ontological and epistemological levels. Firstly, compared with its Western counterpart, Chinese mythology is weak in ontology, especially cosmogony. Whatever exists is taken for granted. There is no beginning point of universe, no law giver, no original sin. The Chinese philosophy is not interested in finding *the* truth as Western philosophy is. It is more interested in the concrete this world rather than in engaging itself in abstract discussions about an other world.

Secondly, there is a plural nature in Western mythology, but lacking in the Chinese counterpart, a situation that has enormous implications on epistemology. The gods of Greece are often depicted as quarrelsome and have less respect for the supreme god than their Chinese counterparts. Except perhaps for the two qualities of eternity and powerfulness, there is little difference between these Western gods and humans. Many Western gods are depicted as lustful, drunken and aggressive. Such is not the case with Chinese gods who are often depicted as gentlemen, reminiscent of the ideal Confucian scholars. Chinese gods are much nicer than Western gods. The structure of the Chinese Heaven, that is, the society of gods, is like the society on earth, hierarchical and orderly.

The this-worldly approach in Chinese ontology has impact on epistemology in that while the Western orientation is more precise or objective, the Chinese one is vague. This is why Hu Shi claimed that no epistemology had developed in China.[2] At the root of all Chinese thought is the conception that the cosmic universe is one entity, indivisible into natural and supernatural realms.[3] This situation has also contributed to the fact that there has been a lack of methodology in modern Chinese philosophy. In the West, however, scientific methods have been developed from at least the time of Aristotle to this day.

Marx saw this situation from a different perspective. Marx saw the world transformation from pre-civilized to civilized societies as forming three types: 1) Oriental despotism; 2) Germanic; 3) Greek-Roman. He argued that while the Greek-Roman transformation succeeded in separating natural relations from social relations, the oriental transformation did not. "Natural Relations" refer to blood related relations such as clan and family, while "social relations" are largely based on property ownership.[4]

How to explain the different orientations in Greek and Chinese myths and, indeed, why did the transformation separate natural relations from social relations in Greek tradition, but not in the East? In spite of many problems, the explanation offered by Karl Wittfogel may be the closest. In other words, while many factors may have played roles, the geographic one is perhaps the most important. The place where the Greek civilization originated can be characterized as open, while the Chinese civilization originated from a place which can be called closed. The Greeks who made critical steps in developing Western civilization lived in the tiny city-states that were located near the sea, but were only very loosely connected with each other. In addition, inter-city commerce was important.

The Chinese case is different. China proper is surrounded by high mountains on the West, plateau on the north and sea on the south and the east. The East China Sea and South China Sea are different from the Mediterranean in that the latter is largely an inland lake that connects Europe, Africa and West Asia while the former is connected only with the impassable Pacific. Consequently, commerce has never been as important as agriculture, which in turn called for organized efforts to control water supply. This geographical position gives rise to a united hierarchically structured kingdom, as maintained by Wittfogel. Consequently, the Chinese cities were not designed to be trading places, but political and cultural centers.[5]

The Greeks viewed themselves and the universe as separate from each other. From this point of view, in order to benefit themselves, it was necessary to understand the world objectively, so the world can be better exploited. Various kinds of methods were invented for this purpose. In due course, they succeeded in separating social relations from natural relations, convention from nature. The Chinese, however, saw this differently. For them, human society is an extension of nature. The Chinese tradition is often perceived as "a totally integrated social-cultural-political order presided over by a class which managed to embody within itself both the spiritual and political authority of the society."[6] This is because collective efforts that were required by maintaining the hydraulic system minimized the difference between natural relations and social relations.

The *yin yang* theory in Taoism, which is the one that stresses cosmological concerns, has provided a good basis for the absence of differentiation between natural and social relations. In cosmological use, Tao is the way, the process by which the cosmos operates. It functions through the interaction of two opposed but complementary and inseparable forces, *yang* and *yin*, which are perhaps most usefully compared to the positive and negative poles of an electrical system. Everything acts by an alternation of *yang* and *yin* forces; *yang* is naturally ascendant in certain circumstances and times, *yin* in others. When the natural alternation of *yang* and *yin* is aborted, the result is inappropriate or perhaps harmful or otherwise disadvantageous; but no question of good or bad arises in any absolute, abstract sense.[7]

Therefore, the Chinese view themselves as part of nature. The universe is taken to be one in which humans are just a part of the dynamic mechanism. Based on this understanding, the Chinese traditional society was a triple unity of the social, political and ideological. Harmony is stressed over antagonism. The Chinese rely on intuitive knowledge and direct reflection of the world. Whatever people see is taken for granted. Paradoxes are tolerated.

Monistic Political Tradition

Although there is little argument regarding the holistic nature of Chinese philosophy, it is open to debate whether the Chinese intellectual tradition is monistic in character. But the Chinese political tradition is monistically authoritarian in the sense that there has to be only one legitimate source of power. In traditional Chinese philosophy, Taoism and Legalism served as complements of Confucianism. Confucianism is mainly concerned with social and political relations and has a monistic orientation. Taoism is concerned with cosmological concerns and on the high value of life. Its orientation is holistic. Legalism is mainly concerned with state administration.

Since Confucianism is mainly concerned with the political and social relations of people, the authoritarian traditional Chinese political structure perhaps drew more strength from Confucianism rather than from other sources of intellectual schools such as Taoism. In general, three themes usefully characterize the political structure of the traditional Chinese society, which are: 1) Humanistic and paternalistic; 2) structured in order to suit the needs of water control (hydraulic); 3) despotic and nepotistic. These three features are closely interrelated. They share the common idea that the Chinese society is a hierarchy, with one person who has the sole legitimate power at the top. A monistic power structure can easily adopt a monistic ideology to justify its legitimacy. Actually, China's centralized dynastic society was sustained by an organic tripartite whole of a common ideology and state theory: Confucianism; the system of prefectures and counties first established in Qin (221–107 BC) (*junxianzhi*); a landlord economy.

One may argue that quite often there had to be one legitimate source of power in the West too. However, the power structure there may not be as tight as that in the traditional Chinese society. For instance, although the Emperor of Roman Empire was supposed to be the sole legitimate source of power, local lords had considerable amount of autonomy. The fact that individualistic orientation is never stressed much in the traditional Chinese society is quite unique. Tu Wei-ming, a philosopher and historian of East Asian studies, remarks:

> In the Jewish tradition, it is believed that the personality of an individual can be realized by worship of God; in the Indian tradition, it is believed that one's own real personality can be realized by way of interaction between oneself and Heaven, not through social transformation; even in the Taoist tradition, self fulfillment has to be realized by cutting off one's relations with other people. Only in the Confucian tradition, it is believed that one's self fulfillment cannot be realized without interaction with other people in society.[8]

The Chinese cultural tradition is also noted for its utopianism. In fact, precisely because Chinese philosophy is weak in ontology and epistemology, it is strong in moral teachings. Confucianism is a kind of humanism. Man is believed to be equal in sharing certain traits, the most outstanding one being that man is good in nature. The father and the Emperor have to be examples of good men. Rule by man is generally considered better than rule by law. For the Chinese, family is both a natural relationship and a social relationship. Society is a larger family; family is a smaller society. Hierarchy (in terms of a power relationship) is assumed: the father is at the top within each family, while the Emperor is the father figure of society. In the *Book of Rites* (*Li yun*), which was attributed to Confucius, it was said that in this ideal society, the Grand Course was pursued, and common spirit ruled all under the sky. Thus men did not love their parents only, nor treat as children only their own sons. A competent provision was secured for the aged until their death, employment for the able bodied, and means of growing up to the young. They showed kindness and compassion to widows, orphans and childless men, and those who were disabled by disease, so that they were all sufficiently maintained. Males had their proper worth and females had their homes. In this way selfish scheming was repressed and found no development. Robbers and filchers, and rebellious traitors did not show themselves, and hence the outer doors remained open and were not shut. This was the period of what we call *Datong*, or the Grand Union.[9]

Based on this philosophical understanding, the Chinese people have always cherished the political vision of a Grand Union. As early as the times of Qin, the following beliefs were established: the mandate of Heaven; that rulers need and should heed capable, wise ministerial advisers; that government is to provide peace and order; that government should be humane and paternalistic, giving a high priority to fostering the welfare of the people; that the scope of government was all-encompassing.[10]

The Chinese people's endorsement of the utopian Grand Union is the opposite to the Western tradition. Plato (427–347 BC) desires philosopher-kings. However, the Greek state system was not run in line with what Plato said. Greek city-states were, generally aristocratic democracies. Thomas Moore (1478–1535) talks about utopia where everyone is equal and everyone loves everybody else. But this kind of society was not practiced in the West. Most best known traditional Chinese operas have the theme of happy reunion, or *da tuan yuan*, while the majority of the best known classical Western dramas are tragedies. The Chinese have little difficulty with the idea of Grand Union. Because of this, even Sun Yatsen, the founder of Kuomingtang, endorsed the idea of *datong*. He also added that *datong* is socialism and communism.[11]

Political Origins:
Voluntarism and Ethic-Purism of the Cultural Revolution

Two underlying implications of scientism are objectiveness in terms of intellectual pursuit and neutrality in terms of value judgement. These two qualities are the opposites of voluntarism, which is supposed to disregard conditions, and ethic-purism, which is supposed to put ideology-laden ethics above everything else. Voluntarism and ethic-purism ran rampant during the Cultural Revolution which was prior to the emergence of scientism in the 1980s. There may be connections between the Cultural Revolution and the current surge of scientism which followed immediately.

Before going into details about the voluntarism and ethic-purism that ran rampant during the Cultural Revolution period, we discuss very briefly the question: to what extent did the mentality as demonstrated during the Cultural Revolution represent Mao's ideas? This may help us to have a better understanding of the New Thinking, because most theories in this New Thinking were created in attempts to correct Mao's ideas.

Three factors have to be mentioned in understanding Mao's relationship with Marxism. First, Mao certainly read some texts by Marx; *Capital*, for instance. But he read these through the eyes of a combination of Second International Marxism, which was powerfully influenced by positivism and Darwinian naturalism. Consequently, it is very easy to find reductionist remarks in Mao's works.[12] According to Feng Xianzhi, who for a long time was in charge of Mao's books, Mao said, "I started my Marxism training with Lenin. Marx and Engels came later."[13] Mao's claim has been supported by quantitative studies in the West. For instance, it has been found that in the first four volumes of the *Selected Works of Mao Zedong*, Mao quotes more than ten times as much from the works of Lenin and Stalin than he does from the works of Marx and Engels.[14] Further evidence of this is the fact that Mao used an orthodox Marxist Hu Qiaomu as his personal secretary to draft many documents in the name of Mao. Feng also believed that Mao was better versed in Confucian classics than the works of Marx and Engels.[15]

Secondly, some key texts by Marx from which various branches of nonreductionist Marxism draw strength were not available to Mao at the time when he was writing his main philosophy books *Mao Dun Lun* (*On Contradiction*) (1937) and *Shi Jian Lun* (*On Practice*) (1937). *Grundrisse* was not published until 1939 and the Chinese version of *The Economic and Philosophic Manuscripts of 1844* did not come out until 1957.[16]

However, Mao's ideas were not straight forwardly reductionist, even without the exposure to these unreductionist Marx's works. Bill Brugger and David Kelly pointed out Mao made the following remark before 1949 when the PRC was founded: "Each of man's actions (practice) is guided by his thought, so naturally without thought there can be no action whatsoever." The irony is that, according to them, this remark was deleted from the official text to be published in the *Selected Works* after 1949.[17] This act may have been an attempt taken by Mao to put himself more in line with orthodox Marxism in the early years of the People's Republic.

On some other occasions, Mao seemed to be purposely embracing nonreductionist Marxist writings. For instance, when Mao revised *On Practice* in 1952, he was also revising *On Contradiction*. In the latter work he added a reference to the "Introduction" to the *Grundrisse*. Indeed, that work was the only work of Marx included in the footnotes. Later, Mao singled out the "Introduction" as one of nine works of Marx recommended for high-ranking cadres.[18]

Not only is there ambiguity in Mao's ideas, but also the movements that were supposed to be led by Mao were of ambiguous nature. An anecdote may demonstrate the contingent nature of the nation-wide establishment of the People's Communes. In 1958, one of the first People's Communes was formed in Qiliying, Henan Province. Mao visited the commune. When the leaders were briefing him on how advanced this commune was, Mao murmured to himself, "Good, Good." Mao's murmuring was overheard by a Xinhua reporter. The next day, when Mao was reading newspapers, he found that on the first page of *Renmin ribao* there was a big story with the title "The People's Commune Is Good." The remark was attributed to Mao. Mao's compliment to a specific event, that is, the performance of one commune, was changed into an approval of a very important general policy. Mao was very upset when seeing this. He said, "No, no. The Politburo has not discussed about it."[19] However, once the masses were mobilized, Mao was reluctant, or found himself unable, to calm them down. The People's Commune later joined The General Line and The Great Leap Forward to become one of the Three Red Flags (*San mian hongqi*) of the party. The Three Red Flags serve as the main witness of Mao's voluntarism for many Western Sinologists.

Similarly, the Cultural Revolution was not run according to Mao's blueprint. In January 1967, several months after the start of the revolution, Tan Zhenlin, a vice Premier who was in charge of agriculture, reported to Mao about the political situation in the countryside. He said that attacks on the leaders were enough. In addition, some bad people had tried to fish in troubled water. Mao wrote a 100-character comment, agreeing that the Cultural Revolution should stop.[20] However, the Cultural Revolution Group headed by Jiang Qing and Kang Sheng could not possibly let the revolution stop, because that would deprive them of the power they had seized from the old power holders. In addition, the old power holders wanted to restore the pre-Cultural Revolution order. In February 1967, the famous February Counter Trend (*eryue niliu*) occurred. Some old generals defied the new order set by the Cultural Revolution Group by attacking Jiang Qing, an indirect attack on Mao. The Chairman counter-attacked. Thus, the revolution continued and lasted for ten years.

To say that the People's Commune and the Cultural Revolution were not entirely designed by Mao is not to exempt him from the responsibility in causing so much suffering of the Chinese people. Nor am I suggesting that Mao disproved these two movements. My concern is to try to be as true as possible to history. This may help us to have a better understanding of the New Thinking that emerged after the Cultural Revolution and that was created largely in the name of correcting Mao's ideas.

Spirit of the Cultural Revolution 1): Voluntarism

Prior to the start of the Cultural Revolution, Lin Biao, the Defense Minister, who was the major ally of Mao during the period, began to circulate three articles written by Mao in the armed forces. These three articles were called *Lao san pian*, (*Three Old Articles*, meaning that they have to be studied again and again). Emphasis on studying *Lao san pian* was carried on the media all the time and these three articles were often printed together in one volume and in pocket size for people's convenience. Lin said that the People's Liberation Army (PLA) should become a big school to study Mao Zedong Thought. Showing his support of Lin, Mao called on the whole country to "Learn from the PLA." Soon, the *Lao san pian* became the bible of the country.[21]

One of these three articles, entitled "The Foolish Old Man Who Removed the Mountains" ("Yu Gong yi shan"), reveals the voluntaristic nature of the Cultural Revolution. In the article, Mao uses a fable to make his point: sheer human determination can make anything in the world happen. In ancient times, the fable says, there were two big mountains in front of the door of an old man named Yu Gong, or the foolish old man. Yu Gong was determined to remove the mountains, which were causing inconvenience to his family. Using primitive tools, the old man removed the dirt and rocks of the mountains bit by bit every day. Finally, God was touched by the old man and he sent angels down who removed the two mountains for the old man.

People were encouraged to believe that with sheer determination, anything can happen. This spirit is in a sense a continuation of the Great Leap Forward when the party decided that China should surpass Britain in terms of steel production and other major industrial indexes within 15 years.[22] However, the Cultural Revolution voluntarism was different from that of the Great Leap Forward in the sense that while the latter focused on material production, the former concentrated on transformation of human consciousness. Actually, the very name of this movement suggests that Mao hoped to transform society through ideological means, rather than waiting for the ripe time for revolution produced by economic development. The Party Central Committee claimed that this was to be a movement to "touch men to their very souls," to "put daring above all else and boldly arouse the masses."[23]

Jiang Qing's "Eight Revolutionary Operas" were also aimed at the transformation of human consciousness. The ballet "The White Haired Girl" (Baimaoniu) teaches the lessen that the old society, the one before 1949, turns humans into ghosts, while the new society turns ghosts into human beings. The story says that Yang Bailao, the debt-ridden father of

Xi Er, commits suicide because of the landlord's pressure for the return of the debt. Xi Er, the heroine of the opera, is taken by the landlord to his home to be a housemaid. She is subsequently raped. Xi Er then escapes from the village and runs into the mountains and survives by eating wild plants. Because she has no salt to eat, her hair turns all white. The Chinese believe that if one does not eat salt for a long time, his or her hair would lose color to become white. The villagers who bump into her think that she is a ghost, because of her strange color of hair and her shabby clothes. When the PLA comes, the soldiers and the villagers find her in the mountains and save her. Her white hair gradually turns black, the usual color of a Chinese. Thus she looks like a human being again. The opera was first put on stage in Yenan in the 1940s and ran through the Maoist years after liberation. It was so touching that a communist soldier reportedly almost killed the actor who played the role of the landlord by aiming at him with his loaded gun.

Spirit of the Cultural Revolution 2): Ethic-Purism

As the article "The Old Man Who Removed the Mountains" reveals the voluntaristic nature of the Cultural Revolution, the other two of the *Lao san pian* focus on communistic altruism, that is, ethic-purism. One of the articles is "To Serve the People" ("wei renmin fuwu"), which was written by Mao in memory of a unselfish communist soldier during the Anti-Japanese War (1938–45). In fact, every store and restaurant during the Cultural Revolution had the slogan "To Serve the People" in front of its door. This slogan also appeared on the Mao badge that Zhou Enlai wore all the time. As a legacy of the Cultural Revolution, the handwriting by Mao of this slogan is still at the front gate of Zhongnanhai, the central government's residence where the Beijing demonstrators wanted to break into during the 1989 Tiananmen incident. The third article, "In Memory of Dr. Bathune" ("jinian baiqiuen"), was written by Mao to praise a unselfish Canadian medical doctor who helped the Chinese communists during the Second World War. The Chinese people are probably more familiar with this Canadian than most of his countrymen are.

In line with Mao's idea that the power of examples is inexhaustible, a contemporary altruistic hero was created. His name was Lei Feng, a PLA soldier. Mao called on the Chinese people to learn from Lei Feng. His name was known to everybody. Lei Feng cared for everybody else, except for himself. He donated 100 yuan (50 US dollars then) from his savings that were from his monthly allowance (6 Yuan, or 3 dollars) without leaving his name, and he participated in voluntary labor work without leaving his name.

The theme of "The Red Lantern" ("Hong deng ji"), Jiang Qing's another opera, is that revolutionary concerns should take priority over family ties that are a central notion of Chinese tradition. In this Beijing Opera, three characters form a family based on revolutionary connections, not on blood linkage: Li Nainai, the grandmother, did not give birth to Li Yuhe, the father. She is the wife of Li Yuhe's colleague. Li Tiemei, the granddaughter of the family, has blood connection with neither Granny Li nor Li Yuhe. She is the daughter of another colleague of Li Yuhe. Both the colleagues of Li Yuhe were killed earlier in a workers' strike. Li Yuhe, the hero of the opera, takes the responsibility of taking care of the infant daughter Li Tiemei and the old widow Granny Li out of pure revolutionary sentiments, not blood connections or ordinary sympathy. This family devotes itself entirely to the revolution led by the party.

The political slogan to justify this transformation of people's consciousness towards ethic-purism can be summarized as *Dou si pi xiu*, or to struggle against one's selfishness and to criticize revisionism. In the first three years of the revolution (1966–69), teaching in China's colleges and universities was practically stopped. Reporting on how one had learned something from Mao's works in order to become less selfish (*dou si*) and criticizing the ideas of Liu Shaoqi (*pi xiu*) were the order of the day. This is especially true in China's educational system because the intellectuals and students were supposed to be the ones who needed this transformation of consciousness the most. This practice continued even after the Cultural Revolution largely passed its zenith. For instance, even after the Lin Biao Affair (1971), high schools in Tianjin still devoted a quarter of their time to *dou si pi xiu*. Out of the four hours each morning, one hour had to be devoted to political activities.

Another way of building up altruism was to fight revisionism (*pi xiu*), a term that has unique Chinese connotations. Originally, revisionism was a school of thought developed by Eduard Bernstein during the Second International period. By challenging some aspects of orthodox Marxism, such as the breakdown theory, revisionism mainly called for realistic strategies such as parliamentary politics on behalf of the working class in their struggle against the bourgeoisie. In the Chinese context, the bourgeoisie became the bureaucrats. During the Cultural Revolution, Mao believed that the bourgeoisie was within the party. That is to say although the means of production were in public hands, the bourgeoisie still existed. The irony is that during the Cultural Revolution, everything bad became revisionism. So when somebody wanted to live a more polished lifestyle, others would quite often say, "This guy has become revisionist."

Economic Origins:
The Country Has Become Richer, The People Have Become Poorer

Deng's reform started with a restoration of the Four Modernizations program first put forward by Zhou Enlai. The people responded to this calling enthusiastically. The people's ready acceptance is directly connected with the economic situation in China at that time. Not long before his escape from China in 1971, Lin Biao complained about the economic situation in the country by saying that the country had become richer, the people had become poorer (*guo fu, min qiong*). Whatever the nature of the Lin Biao Incident, there is certainly much truth in his judgment of China's economic situation at that time.

Many Western Sinologists seem to believe that China has done comparatively well in providing the basic needs for the Chinese people. This was supported by statistics by such respected international organizations as the World Bank. By the early 1980s, statistics from the World Bank reveal that China's social profile bore resemblance to that of countries with far higher income levels in terms of literacy, health care, average daily diet calories and life expectancy.[24]

The data is apparently solid. According to Li Jingwen, Director of the Metrological Economics Institute of CASS, statistics gathered by the World Bank are generally not only more accurate, but also more up to date than Chinese government's data. The Chinese government has some regulations that require various official departments to cooperate with the international organization. Because of this situation, various official research institutes were reportedly blamed by Deng Xiaoping for their inefficiency in gathering data.[25]

The achievements made by the regime concerning the literacy, health care, average daily diet calories and life expectancy for most Chinese people certainly deserve credit. In addition, these achievements are in accordance with the fact that from 1957 to 1976, China's annual average growth in industry had been over 10 percent, in spite of the disastrous Great Leap Forward and the Cultural Revolution.[26] "The overall GNP had a long-term growth rate from 1949 to 1984 of about 6 percent per annum. Other data could be presented, but they would no doubt be just as misleading as these unqualified figures. . . . Although this (growth of population) reduces the actual annual percentage increase in the GNP per capita to just about 4 percent, compared to most developing countries, this still is quite good."[27]

However, other data show that the other side of the picture is not that good for the Chinese people. Sources from China reveal that from 1953 to 1978, the wages of government employees had risen by only

1.4 percent annually. If we do not include the First Five-Year Plan period (1953–57) when the wages rose quite rapidly, the annual average wage increase for government employees from 1957 to 1978 was only 0.1 percent. Meanwhile, the annual inflation rate during this period was higher than the average wage growth, 0.3 percent.[28]

We have to use other statistics to interpret this seemingly self contradictory situation in which the average wages for Chinese workers did not rise, but the production did. We have found that although the average wage of workers did not rise much, the total volume of wages increased substantially during this period due to an increase of the number of workers. In 1952, the total volume of wages in China was 6.8 billion yuan. In 1976 when Mao died, it had been raised to 40.6 billion yuan. In 1978, it jumped again to 57 billion yuan.[29] That is to say that in addition to an overall rise in population, a higher percentage of the population was working in 1970s than in 1950s.

Another factor that explains this situation is that parents in recent years supported fewer number of children. In 1950s, the Chinese government followed the practice of the Soviet Union of encouraging births. From the late 1960s, birth control was practiced, an attempt adopted by the regime to improve people's standard of living. In the early 1950s, usually only the husband worked. The wife stayed at home to take care of the often multiple number of children. In the 1970s, for most families, both husband and wife had to work. In addition, they began to have fewer children, either because of government policies, or out of their own considerations. The fact that Chinese workers had a decent life, a situation that is even recognized by the World Bank, is largely due to the equalitarian policies adopted by the government to spread the wealth of the nation as much as possible by giving jobs to everybody and discouraging births of new babies.

We also have to realize that rapid national development at the expense of improvement of people's standard of living cannot be sustained very long. This has been shown by both the experiences of China and the former Soviet Union. Towards the end of the Cultural Revolution, both the Chinese workers and peasants were demoralized. Going slow at work was characteristic in China's factories and communes.[30] This situation definitely called for change. It has been pointed out that China was behind even western Africa in per capita income, a situation which may disfranchise her as a player in the international game.[31] The people do not want to be treated as slaves or children, for whom survival is the most important, if not the only, concern. Actually, this is exactly the charge against communism by Havel.[32]

PART II

Three Versions of Scientism

CHAPTER 3

Marxist Scientism—Hu Qiaomu

Life and Experience

Intellectually, Hu Qiaomu's science, which focuses on historical materialism, is in line with materialistic scientism. Although historical materialism and dialectical materialism, which form orthodox Marxist philosophy, cannot be separated, each has its own focus. Historical materialism is mainly a science of history. Dialectical materialism as a philosophy distinguishes itself not only from mechanical materialism but also from the dialectical idealism of Hegel. The disastrous Cultural Revolution made Marxism so unpopular among Chinese intellectuals that many intellectual leaders, especially those who are junior in age, are reluctant to take Marxism seriously, although they are probably significantly influenced unconsciously by a Marxist way of thinking.

The political connotation of Hu's historical materialism in the current Chinese context is its promise of the inevitable success of communism and its defense of one-party rule, the agent that is supposed to ensure the transition to communism.

As a person, Hu was probably closer to the center of power than any of the other intellectuals studied in this book. Because of Hu's sophistication in interpreting the orthodoxy and his consistency in upholding it, Hu has acted as one of the most important spokesmen for the regime, under both Mao and Deng. Actually, Hu probably has been one of the most enduring high level establishment intellectuals in PRC history. An analysis of Chinese Marxism in the post-Mao era loses coherence if Hu's role is neglected. In two of the most important articles he wrote in this period in which he attacked the trend of "liberalization" in 1980 and the theories of humanism and alienation in 1984, Hu declared that he was representing the "center," the Central Committee of the CCP.[1]

Hu's intellectual orientation is connected very closely with his intellectual and political background. Generally speaking, the attitudes towards Marxism of the theorists discussed in this study roughly correspond to their ages and experiences. The younger they are in age, the less likely they are to stick to Marxism. Hu Qiaomu, born in 1912, who has more intellectual and revolutionary experiences than any of the other five, is the most senior. Su Shaozhi, Wang Ruoshui and Li Zehou, now all in their sixties, fall in the middle. The last group with Jin Guantao and Gan Yang, now in their forties, is the youngest. This situation perhaps shows a declining trend of influence for Marxism among Chinese intellectuals.

Hu was born in Yancheng, Jiangsu Province into a wealthy landowner's family in 1912. He studied physics at the Qinghua University from 1930 to 1932. It should be noted that all of the three Chinese intellectuals that I have chosen for this sample study, who represent the three versions of scientism, have backgrounds in areas other than the humanities: Hu, physics; Su Shaozhi, economics; Jin Guantao, chemistry. Economics has long been regarded by positivists as one of the most successful disciplines in social sciences to adopt a scientific approach. Hu joined the CCP shortly after college in 1935. He then became primarily engaged in journalism and publishing work in the then CCP headquarters in Shaanxi Province. This earned Hu the crucial credits of belonging to the first-generation revolutionaries, because 1938, when the Anti-Japanese War broke out in China, was the dividing line that separated the first-generation Red Army cadres (*hongjun ganbu*) from the second-generation anti-Japanese cadres (*kangri ganbu*).

The event that decisively shaped Hu's career was his replacement of Chen Boda as Mao Zedong's secretary in 1945.[2] After the founding of the PRC, both Hu and Chen were appointed by the party as among the so-called Five Big Secretaries (*wudamishu*) of the party Chairman. Among the five, these two were mainly responsible for drafting documents and doing research for Mao.[3] The importance of being the secretary of Mao can be seen in that Hu was the vice director of the Central Party Committee's Propaganda Department, which supervised China's ideological work, and was simultaneously an alternate member of the Secretariat, which was in charge of the day to day work of the CCP. Hu held these two positions from 1956 to 1966. The importance of being the secretary of Mao can also be seen in that Chen became the Head of the Leading Group of the Cultural Revolution, which, directly under Mao, controlled the whole process of the Cultural Revolution.

Hu did not spare efforts in exerting influence on China's political agenda to meet his own intellectual and political beliefs. In the late 1950s and early 1960s, Hu was responsible for supervising the compilation of the first four volumes of *Selected Works of Mao Zedong*, the articles written by Mao prior to the founding of the CCP. This was an extremely important position in that Hu acted as a main interpreter of Mao's ideas. Hu later admitted that sometimes he took too much liberty in changing the content of Mao's original works.[4] Recent evidence shows that some of the changes, either by Mao or Hu, have proved to be of decisive importance in understanding Mao Zedong thought. For instance, Mao's early remarks that ideas sometimes had to come before revolutionary actions were omitted in the post-liberation version of Mao's works in the *Selected Works of Mao Zedong*.[5] Considering the fact that Hu, as a "liberal intellectual,"[6] was closer to orthodox Marxism, while Mao was sometimes voluntaristic, this vitally important change could very well have been done by Hu.

The selection by Mao of Hu Qiaomu, as a leader of the liberal intellectuals prior to the Cultural Revolution and of Chen Boda, the chief leader of the radical intellectuals during the Cultural Revolution, to be his secretaries may reflect Mao's ambiguity in thinking. Mao seemed to be caught between orthodox Marxist economic determinism and unorthodox voluntarism. The fates of Hu and Chen may also serve as a barometer of China's political atmosphere. Prior to the Cultural Revolution, the liberal Hu seemed to be more prominent than the radical Chen as a spokesman for Mao. During the Cultural Revolution, Hu was purged, while Chen rose to prominence as a major spokesman for Mao. After the Cultural Revolution, Chen fell. Hu again became the main spokesman of the regime and a chief interpreter of Mao's thought.

Besides alteration of Mao's works, Hu also intervened in China's academic and literary world to suit his own intellectual convictions. In 1950, in defiance of the protests of Jiang Qing, and possibly Mao, Hu approved the showing of the controversial movie, "The Inside Story of the Qing Court" ("qing gong mi shi"), which was later described by Mao as "treasonable—out-and-out treason."[7] This event is significant in that important political struggle in China is often reflected in the form of different treatments of historical stories, such as this movie. This is in the Chinese political tradition where political actors are often unwilling to settle political disputes in public. Politicians like to use such indirect means to attack each other.

On another occasion, Hu threw himself behind the party-bureaucracy faction again, perhaps to the distaste of Mao. Hu was believed to have been behind Wu Han when the former historian wrote the famous play "The Dismissal of Hai Rui" ("hai rui ba guan"). Hai Rui was a Ming official, who, in true Confucian fashion, had been loyal to the emperor while at the same time criticizing his shortcomings. Wu Han wanted to criticize Mao for his harsh treatment of the former Defense Minister Peng Dehuai, who criticized Mao's Great Leap Forward policies.[8]

With all this as part of his record, Hu was relieved of all his posts at the beginning of the Cultural Revolution, along with most of the liberal intellectuals. He was humiliated in mass criticism meetings, a common practice of the Cultural Revolution, where victims were not only criticized for their wrong ideas, but also often beaten physically. Some victims died as a result. Hu was charged with the crime of being against the party, socialism and the people (*sanfanfenzi*).[9]

After the zenith of the Cultural Revolution (1966–69), Mao tried to correct some of the leftist tendencies by targeting Lin Biao, his chief radical ally in the movement. Mao first removed Chen Boda, who had become the main adviser of Lin, from all his positions. Lin Biao's death paved the way for Deng Xiaoping's ascendance in 1974. Deng brought with him Hu Qiaomu, his former close associate in the Secretariat. Hu again was put in charge of compiling Mao's works by Deng, and almost certainly with the approval of Mao.

Hu played a minor role in helping Deng restore some of the practices adopted by the party-bureaucracy faction. Hu Qiaomu and Hu Yaobang were ordered by Deng to draft the famous *The Report of the Chinese Academy of Sciences* (*zhongguo kexueyuan huibao tigang*), which stressed the role of science and technology and, consequently, the role of intellectuals. This document, which was clearly an attempt to restore some practices of the party prior to the Cultural Revolution, had been perceived by Mao as falling far beyond the boundaries. As a result, Deng was removed again. Hu Qiaomu wrote a self-criticism to the party upon Deng's falling into disgrace, not only criticizing himself, but also exposing Deng. Hu said it was wrong for him to have taken too much liberty in changing some content of Mao's works and to have drafted some bad documents such as the report. But he cleared himself by implying that it was Deng who encouraged or forced him to do so.[10]

With the triumph of Deng after Mao's death, Hu appeared in his third ascendance. He was made a member of the Politburo at the CCP 12th Central Committee, the highest position he had ever held, and the president of the newly founded Chinese Academy of Social Sciences (CASS) (1978–82). By becoming the Director of the Committee for the Editing and Publishing the *Selected Works of Mao Zedong* (1979), he was again put in charge of compiling Mao's works. Hu's third ascendance to power and the reemergence of orthodox Marxism in China in the 1980s were responses to Mao's voluntarism during the Cultural Revolution.[11]

Science As the Philosophical Starting Point

Given this situation, it is not surprising that Hu considered Leninism, which was in his words the "development of Marxism in the twentieth century," the main source from which the Chinese revolutionaries drew intellectual strength.[12] Hu's Marxism excludes the ideas expressed by the young Marx who wrote *The Manuscripts*, which, according to Hu, was immature. Hu listed the following aspects of Marxism and Leninism as of particular relevance to China:

> historical materialism and the theory of class struggle, armed struggle, the theory of the party which is composed of advanced elements of the proletariat, the October Revolution, the theory that the proletariat should form alliance with other revolutionary classes, the theory of the dictatorship of the proletariat, and the theory that the development of the productive forces is important.[13]

Hu's remarks did not come from casual talks. They were from an important article he wrote to celebrate the 70th anniversary of the CCP in 1991. Therefore, it is worthwhile for us to break down these statements to see where the components belong. Among the concepts mentioned in the above paragraph, "historical materialism," "the theory of class struggle," and "the theory to develop the productive forces" probably have more to do with the Second International Marxism[14] than with any other school of thought. Armed struggle, the theory of the party which is composed of advanced elements of the proletariat, the October Revolution, the theory that the proletariat should form alliance with other revolutionary classes, the theory of the dictatorship of the proletariat were probably more related to Lenin and Stalin than with any one else.

Hu was not alone to have adopted this orthodox Marxist position. The early generations of Chinese Marxists learned Marxism first through the Japanese and then through the Russians. The Chinese communists were by and large the students of the Russians. Bolshevism has left a deep mark on most of the first generation Chinese revolutionaries, including Hu Qiaomu. The texts by Lenin read by Mao the most frequently included *The Two Strategies, Left-Wing Communism: An Infantile Disorder?*,

The State and Revolution and *Imperialism Is the Highest Stage of Capitalism*.[15]

Mao's own attitudes were clearly reflected in the party's ideological orientations in various periods of time. For instance, the party listed twelve books as musts of Marxism-Leninism for party cadres in 1949. These twelve books remained the top required reading lists for cadres for quite a long time. Among the twelve books, only one was by Marx and Engels: *The Communist Manifesto*; three were by Lenin: *Imperialism Is the Highest Stage of Capitalism, State and Revolution, Left-Wing Communism: An Infantile Disorder?;* one was by Stalin: *A History of the Communist Party of the Soviet Union*; three were by others who wrote about the theories of Lenin and Stalin.[16]

Marxist Science versus Idealistic Humanism

In the 1980s, the most important theoretical battle within Marxist discourse in China was the one between Hu Qiaomu and Wang Ruoshui over the latter's theories of socialist humanism and alienation. Although these two concepts are familiar topics among Western Marxist theorists, they were new in the eyes of most Chinese Marxist intellectuals. Chinese intellectuals' world outlook was by and large influenced, if not shaped, by orthodox Marxism, in spite of the fact that most intellectuals have complaints about the regime, some even have hostility. Humanism and alienation are even more unfamiliar to most ordinary people. Most people meet the phrase of humanism only on the walls of hospitals which, as a slogan, is from Mao's quotation: Uphold Revolutionary Humanism. This is a remark made by Mao during war time, when he encouraged the revolutionary soldiers to treat captives nicely. It has no social connotation whatsoever for common people. The word alienation is even more strange for most people.

Thus, the fact that the regime was so concerned about Wang's introducing and Sinocizing the concepts of humanism and alienation and the Chinese intellectuals were so ready to respond to the debate is truly significant. Why did Chinese intellectuals, especially Hu Qiaomu and Wang Ruoshui quarrel over the two concepts? It is because the debate carried very significant political implications. Before finding out the social and political connotations of the debate, let's take a brief look at Hu's argument during the debate.

In an important article Hu wrote in 1984 entitled "On Humanism and Alienation," Hu spent about 20,000 Chinese characters (equivalent of about 10,000 English words), or about half of the length of the article, explaining the scientific answer to the issue of what was the driving force of history and attacking the various unscientific versions of humanism. The scientific character of Hu's theory, that is, historical materialism, has two key dimensions: 1) the existence of the objective world is independent from human will; 2) this objective world has a law of development which cannot be changed by human will. The first dimension is concerned with the ontological issue of materialism versus idealism in philosophy, while the second dimension is concerned with the issue of dialectics versus metaphysics.

Apparently, Hu's science is different from the commonly held view that science is basically a method. Hu's conception of science has strong ontological concerns, while conventional conception of science is chiefly concerned with methodology. According to Hu, the touchstone for real science versus pseudo science is whether it is materialistic or idealistic. He said:

> In contrast to historical idealism, historical materialism does not start from such abstract concepts as man, human nature and the essence of man. It explains history from the view point of concrete social material living conditions.[17]

By grasping the scientific answer to the driving force of human society, according to Hu, the proletariat and the people have found the scientific guidance with which they have been able to achieve great success.[18] Nevertheless, history has proved that the laws embodied in historical materialism are false. It was the underdeveloped countries that became socialist countries, not the industrialized ones; Eastern European socialist countries and the former Soviet Union have not advanced to communism, but gone back to quasi-capitalism.

How is Hu's historical materialism related to Marx? His main charge against Wang Ruoshui's claim "The starting point of Marxism is man" as "non-Marxist" is perhaps based on the following frequently quoted paragraph by Marx: "Wagner has not even noticed that my analytic method, which does not start from man, but from the economically given period of society. . . ."[19] But this does not lead to economic determinism, because, as we will show, Marx made many statements denouncing economic determinism.

Hu took the trouble to cite whole paragraphs from Marx and Engels to support his science, or his historical materialism. One of the key sentences comes from the Preface to *The Critique of Political Economy* (1859) by Marx: "It is not the consciousness of people that determines [*bestimmt*] their existence, but their social existence that determines their consciousness."[20]

However, the ambiguity in the translation of this sentence by Marx has been noted. Peter Manicas suggests that the German word *bestimmt* could be either translated into "determine," "influence," "constraint," or "conditioning" each of which has quite different meanings.[21] This interpretation has been confirmed by remarks made by Marx and Engels on numerous occasions.

Faced with many clear evidences that Marx may not have been as reductionist as orthodox Marxists believed, Hu Qiaomu argued that the mature Marx, who wrote *Capital*, held different views from the young Marx who had produced the "immature work" of *The Manuscripts*.[22] *The Manuscripts* is one of the main texts from which various kinds of neo-Marxists in the West drew strength in their debates with orthodox Marxists. It was also the chief text used by Eastern European unorthodox Marxists in their fight against orthodoxy before the collapse of the communist governments in 1990.[23] Not incidentally, Wang Ruoshui also uses the text as a weapon against Hu Qiaomu.

It is not my intention to make a final judgment as to what Marx really believed regarding these orthodox and unorthodox interpretations as offered by Hu, Manicas, Ollman, Sayer and others. Although many people may share Max Weber's complaint that Marx is often treated like a taxicab that one can drive where one will, it is hard, if not impossible, to determine his real intentions, given the complexity of his thought. Some went so far as to suggest that it may not be possible or desirable to find a definitive or a disinterested interpretation of Marx's thought.[24]

People have good reasons in not believing a definitive interpretation of Marx's thought. Among the three main aspects of Marxism, Marxist philosophy, Marx's views on socialism, and Marx's ideas about capitalism, he was never systematic and specific on the first two aspects. The central concern of Marxist philosophy, as posed by Hu, has been the extent to which the economic realm influences politics and ideology, and how independent politics and ideology can be from this influence as they develop historically. It seems that within the tradition of Marxism that became orthodox under Stalin, the solution to this problem has been cast largely in terms of economic determination of political and ideological superstructure. Marx's not-so-serious picture of communism—instead of working at the machine all the time, people should be free to do whatever they like such as to fish in the morning and to compose poems in the afternoon—has served as something to ridicule Marxism for its utopianism.

Marx's critique of capitalism is perhaps the only aspect of Marxism that is now still considered valid among Western scholars. Nevertheless, people can still find ways to legitimize their current doings by citing Marx, whether his words or his deeds. For example, in order to justify China's recent establishment of stock exchanges, a Chinese official circulation speculates that Marx made a fortune of 400 Pounds in 1864 by selling stocks.[25]

Marxist Science Versus Metaphysical Alienation

In addition to his claim that one touchstone to distinguish science from pseudo-science is materialism versus idealism, Hu Qiaomu's second touchstone is whether one sticks to the method of dialectics or not. His charge against Wang Ruoshui is that alienation as a method belonged to the young and immature Marx, while dialectical method belonged to the mature Marx.

For Hu, it was the immature Marx in *The Manuscripts*, influenced by Feuerbach's analysis of religion, who talked about the alienation of labor. Marx used this concept as a basic category to explain the development of history, to criticize capitalism and to explain the inevitability of the demise of capitalism and the triumph of communism. However, according to Hu, in the mature works of Marx such as *The German Ideology* and *Capital*, Marx only used this concept for convenience, not as a basic category.[26]

Hu believves that the mature Marx used dialectics as his method of analysis, not alienation. According to Hu's historical materialism, the engine of change is a dialectic between the mode of production and superstructure. The dialectic takes the straightforward form of deepening and resolving the functional contradictions in which old relations fetter the emergence of new forces of production. Societies, through their innate dynamics, progress from the primitive stage to slavery, to feudal, to capitalist, to socialist and finally to communist society.[27] Hu attached much emphasis on this position by saying that the scientific character lies in the fact that it cannot be changed by human will. "If something is called a 'law,' it refers to something that cannot be overcome by human will. Otherwise, it won't be called a 'law,' " he said.[28]

We have found that Marx made some remarks which are in direct opposition of Hu's interpretation. Marx said, my critic "feels that he absolutely must metamorphose my historical sketch of the genesis of capitalism in Western Europe into a historico-philosophic theory of the general path every people is fated to tread, whatever the historical circumstances in which it finds itself. . . . But I beg his pardon."[29] Marx also made it clear that there was no "general historico-philosophic theory."[30] Like the issue of materialism/idealism, the claim that dialectics belongs to Marx is also open to dispute. This is not only because "dialectics" was used not only by Marx but also by Hegel, but also because Marx himself may not regard it as the only, or the best, reliable method for scientific pursuit. For instance, Marx never used the term "dialectical materialism."[31]

Application of Marxist Science

Based on historical materialism, the political implications of Hu's theory are concerned with 1) the firm belief that the ultimate success of communism cannot be doubted; 2) the role of the party to ensure this success cannot be doubted. In line with the argument by Karl Kautsky, Hu believes that socialism is the inevitable product of capitalist development, because of the economic effects of that development and their political consequences. The economic tendencies of capitalism involve an increasing polarization of wealth, the decline of the peasantry and urban petty bourgeoisie, the concentration of capitalist production, and the growth of the organized working class to that it finally encompasses a majority of the population.[32] Hu argued:

> It is wrong to doubt the eventual success of communism, because the concept of communism has two aspects: communism as a social system in the future and communism as ideas which show why and how to realize this system. The fact that communist movements have been moving forward shows that the Marxist theory about the law of social development is correct.[33]

The second political connotation of Hu's science, historical materialism, is one party rule. Hu holds that the revolutionary party is the agent to ensure this inevitable success of communism. This is because, according to the theory, the conflicts between the old mode of production and the new one are reflected in the class struggle between the bourgeoisie and the working class. The working class, by representing the new mode of production, is the most advanced class. The party, which is formed by the most advanced elements of the most advanced class, has on its shoulders the task to ensure the ultimate success of communism. He says:

> only the party which embodies the most advanced political forces is able to represent the long term interests of the people. The adjustments of interests among various sectors of society, the interests between sectors and the whole society, people's long

term interests and their short term interests and the unity of all
nationalities within the country can be realized only by the
leadership of the party. The establishment, development, con-
solidation and improvement of socialist democratic system are
not possible without the leadership of the party.[34]

Hu was frank to point out that among Deng Xiaoping's Four Cardinal
Principles: socialist road; the Marxism-Leninism Mao Zedong Thought;
dictatorship of the proletariat; the leadership of the party, the most
important is the last one. He was also correct in pointing out that the thrust
of the bourgeois liberalization which emerged in the late 1970s and early
1980s, was against the party monopoly.

Marx and Engels said precious little about the nature of a revolutionary
party. Marxist party theory was mainly developed through the practices
of communist movements worldwide, especially in the Soviet Union and
in China. Compared with other aspects of Marxism, Marxist party theory
is more a result of historical contingencies. Hu's ideas about the party
certainly remind us of Lenin's remarks concerning the Russian party. But
sticking to some words of Lenin does not necessarily equal to acting in
line with the ism of his. We have to remember that Lenin stressed the
importance of having a party composed of reliable, experienced and
hardened workers under the condition of Czarist Russia. This party could
not possibly have exercised democracy within the organization. Thus, as
Lenin candidly admitted, the party was not democratic.

One may indeed argue that under the conditions of Czarist Russia,
this was the only thing possible for the communists. One may also argue
that before the founding of the PRC, the Chinese party had to follow the
model of the Russian party. However, after seven decades of socialism in
the former Soviet Union and after four decades of socialism in China, it
is hard for people to be persuaded that the time is still not ripe for people's
participation in the country's democratic process.

If the problem of the ruling party cannot be solved properly, Hu
Qiaomu, by logic, had to make some outrageous arguments concerning
democracy. In the following paragraph, he not only implied that the
current Chinese system was not democratic, but also seemed to hint it
was unnecessary to implement democracy now. He said:

It is absurd to worship democracy one-sidedly to the neglect of
concentration of power (*jizhong*) and authority, or to assume that
democracy itself is concentration of power and consequently to
oppose "democratic centralism." This is equal to believing that

any problems, no matter whether significant or trivial, have to be settled through the ballots. If we believe this, we would have to assume that every person is an encyclopedia, thus having the capacity for correct judgement. Consequently, the masses would be buried in ballots by this kind of democracy. . . . This absurd "democracy" is not only inconceivable now, but also unimaginable in the future.[35]

We get several messages in this paragraph. First, democracy seems to be treated as the opposite of concentration of power. Thus it is wrong to give too much credit to democracy. Then Hu seems to use the term democracy in a conventional sense, that is, a Western political system, which is characterized by settling disputes through ballots, is democracy. Then, we have the most important rationale for undemocratic systems, which is shared not only by people like Hu Qiaomu, but by Fascists as well: People are not intelligent enough to know their own interests; therefore, they have to be led by supermen, the communist leader or the Führer. Finally, democratic centralism seems to Hu to be a better form of democracy.

The last two points are the core of Hu's political agenda. Hu rejected the idea that holds "that the people know their long term interests under any circumstances and that the party is not the most advanced troop of the proletariat and the people."[36] For Hu Qiaomu, it is not the people who should master Marxism, but it is Marxism that must master the people.[37] Hu's views on this are not only in opposition to Western liberal democracy, but also to populism. This position is in line with the Leninist tradition that the party, which is supposed to be formed by the advanced elements of the proletariat, should be the vanguard in the revolutionary cause.[38]

What, specifically, is Hu's democracy? It is the so-called people's democratic dictatorship. This system, which was founded upon the establishment of the PRC, was originally a product of historical contingencies, such as World War II, the Chinese Civil War, the Korean War and the simulation of the Russian model. This system runs as follows. Horizontally, the majority should take the priority over the minority. Vertically, lower level organizations should obey higher organizations and the whole party should obey the Central Party Committee.

In spite of Hu Qiaomu's insistence on historical materialism, his theory is not simply a restoration of the party ideology as endorsed by the party-bureaucracy faction headed by Liu Shaoqi before the Cultural Revolution. His ideas have witnessed some changes too. This is especially visible in the area of economics. Hu's ideas on economics are very much in accord with the ideology of the current regime: in terms of philosophical orientations, the official guiding thought is still very much within the framework of the orthodoxy, at least in theory; politically, the structure copied from Stalin's Russia has remained largely the same; economically, however, the policies adopted by the Dengist regime have shown much more flexibility.

Hu remarked that some viewpoints and predictions by Marx, Engels and Lenin had been treated by the Maoist regime rather dogmatically. These viewpoints included a number of key points: 1) socialism is a rather short period of transition to communism; 2) the means of production of socialism have to be owned totally by the public; 3) socialist production has to be directly planned; 4) the socialist economy does not allow commodity production. But according to Hu, this had resulted in an over concentration of economic power by the central government, a lack of vigor in the country's economic structure, too tight control of the government's budget, and a serious hindrance of productive forces.[39]

However, Hu did not believe that the dogmatic attitudes towards the words of Marx, Engels and Lenin were solely responsible for the problems created by China's old system. According to Hu, these attitudes and practices were the result of historical conditions. First, under the condition of widespread social turmoil and disasters at the beginning of the PRC, these practices worked well. Second, because of the hostile international environment before 1972, when Nixon visited China, what had been produced was the best possible system that could have been produced.[40]

Whatever the views of Marx on humanism and alienation, these two questions are central in assessing the socialist revolution and socialist construction of China, and in other countries. This is because on the way to the wonderful world of communism promised by Marx, communist movements throughout the world are haunted by two problems they cannot fail to face: the sacrifices of the people and the dictatorial regime that enabled the servants of the people to become masters. That's why humanism and alienation are not only a weapon used by Chinese Marxists to question the practices of the leadership, but were also used by Marxists in other countries, especially in Eastern European countries before the collapse of communism there.

CHAPTER 4

Technological Determinism: Su Shaozhi

Life and Experience

Although his theory was put forward in the name of "scientific socialism" and his writings are always full of Marxist language, it is hard to put Su Shaozhi in any category, because of his selectivity in using Marxist theories. Su differs from Hu Qiaomu, who consistently advocates the Marxist scientism of historical materialism, and Jin Guantao, who endorses empirical scientism.

Probably because of this situation, the various interpretations offered by Western Sinologists regarding the philosophical and political orientations of Su often contradict one another. For instance, Maurice Meisner sees Su as an orthodox Marxist, or one attempting to follow the models of Eastern Europe.[1] Ding Xue-liang, however, classifies Su as a Neo-Marxist who tries to provide theoretical support for government reform policies.[2] Andrew Nathan believes that "what the party democrats (including Su) had in mind was not the overthrow of socialism but democratic socialism."[3] Bill Brugger and David Kelly feel that, in criticizing feudalism and Mao's conception of democracy, the Marxist Su Shaozhi and the non-Marxist Fang Lizhi "are so close as to be virtually indistinguishable."[4]

For the purpose of analytical convenience, I have used the term technological determinism to describe Su's main intellectual orientation, given the fact that developing productive forces is at the center of his theory. This approach is not only in accordance with the traditional Chinese way of thinking of not viewing the pursuit of knowledge for its own sake but for solving problems of this life, in this world, but also in line with some aspects of Chinese tradition on science; its belief in technology and its use for political purpose. Therefore, I categorize technological determinism as a species of Chinese-style scientism, again for analytical convenience.

Although Su's theory does not belong to any established intellectual category, it is extremely significant politically. Su is believed to be the first to put forward the concept of "elementary-stage socialism," which since the Thirteenth National Party Congress in 1987 has been accepted by the government as the central idea of the official philosophy for reform.[5] This is so in spite of the fact that many of Su's ideas on political reform may not be favored by the ruling elites.

Su was born into a Manchu nationality family in Beijing in 1923. He graduated with a major in statistics from Chongqing University in Sichuan Province in 1945 and earned his masters in economics from Tianjin's Nankai University in 1949. Although basically an academic, Su became actively involved in politics very early in his career. Su joined the CCP in 1953 before becoming an Associate Professor in economics in Shanghai's Fudan University in 1956. In 1959, he held joint appointments as an editor of the party magazine, *Jiefang* (*Liberation*) in Shanghai, and as a member of the powerful Propaganda Department of the CCP's East China Bureau (*huadong jiu*), which was in charge of the several eastern China provinces.

Su was a coauthor of *Textbook of Political Economy: (Socialist Part)* (*zhengzhi jingjixue jiaocai*), which was written mainly for college students and cadres. This book, which was published before the Cultural Revolution, sold more than 500,000 copies. The publication of this book has a number of important implications for understanding Su's early intellectual and political career.

First, in Maoist China, colleges and universities quite often used only one or two standard text books in each discipline. They had to be authorized by high authorities. Thus Su must have been very highly regarded in his area by his colleagues, and he was trusted by the party. In addition, Maoist China did not recognize Western-style economics. Economics and political economy then were considered identical, meaning in the Western sense, political economy. This is different from the Western context where economics means pure economics and is considered scientific. Whereas political economy is often associated with Marxism and is often considered by many to be unscientific. China's political economy during the period was basically a copy of Stalin's version of Marxism. Su was probably more of a political economist than an economist in the Western sense, although he may be competent in both.

Although Maoist voluntarism dominated China's ideology during the Great Leap Forward in 1958 and the early period of the Cultural Revolution, orthodox Marxism has been the official ideology in China throughout the four decades of CCP rule. Su's textbook, which was closer to Liu Shaoqi's policies than with those of Mao, was criticized during the Cultural Revolution by the radicals for having right tendencies; the other authors of the book, Jiang Xuemo and Yong Wenyuan, were purged as a consequence. Su was not purged, perhaps because he was transferred from Shanghai to Beijing to work as a *Renmin ribao (People's Daily)* editor in 1964.[6]

After the Cultural Revolution in 1978, Su settled accounts with the Maoist radical intellectuals. In an important article, he fervently criticized the idealism and metaphysics of Chen Boda, the Maoist radical leader during the Cultural Revolution. By "idealism," Su referred to the notion of "putting politics in command"; by "metaphysics," he referred to the practice of dogmatically sticking to some words by Marx, Lenin and Mao. Su argued that leftism turned Marxism upside down.[7]

Meanwhile, Su shocked China's academic and political circles by putting forward his theory that although China was "within socialist category *(fanchou)*, it had not become a real socialist society."[8] This was the embryo form of his elementary-stage socialism. The Chinese power structure was so concerned that Deng Xiaoping reportedly ordered the matter investigated. As a result, Su was criticized.[9]

Su suffered another major criticism in the 1983 Anti-Spiritual Pollution Campaign for his liberal theories. Some conservatives such as Deng Liqun wanted to fire him from his post. It was reported that Su was saved by Hu Qiaomu, not so much because Hu liked Su, but because it was hard to find respected Marxists like Su to head the Marxism-Leninism-Mao Zedong Thought (MLM) Institute in the Chinese Academy of Social Sciences (CASS).[10] In the following discussion, however, we may find that as former liberal intellectuals who lost favor during the Cultural Revolution, Hu and Su shared many things in common, at least on the surface.

Su suffered his third, and worst, setback in 1987 shortly after he got his first chance to come to the center of power to join the five-member Staff Office of Zhao Ziyang's Political Reform Consultation Commission, established to provide a platform of political reform for the Thirteenth National Party Congress held in October 1987. The importance of this commission can be seen from its membership of Zhao Ziyang, Bo Yibo, Hu Qili, Tian Jiyun, and Peng Chong. The Staff Office, which included

Bao Tong, Zhao's top adviser, was believed to be the core of Zhao's "brain trust."[11] Su was expelled from this commission and lost his job as the director of the MLM Institute.[12]

His purge was believed to be a result of political struggle within the party rather than a consequence of theoretical disputes. The theorist's loss of favor in August 1987 was believed to be part of the price Zhao was forced to pay to the conservatives to have Su's "elementary stage of socialism theory" adopted as policy in October.[13] Zhao's invitation of Su to join the commission may have been approved by Deng Xiaoping. This may indicate that Su's expulsion from the commission may not have been the intention of Deng.[14] The event may also indicate that while the embryo form of the theory of elementary-stage socialism shocked China's academic and political circles in 1978, the mature form of this theory was no longer so shocking for these circles ten years later. The irony is that in 1978 Su was criticized because the party felt threatened by his theory, but his 1987 purge was the result of the party's acceptance of it.

Science As the Philosophical Starting Point

Su Shaozhi's philosophy is created in the name of scientific Marxism. He complained in 1986, "We have often emphasized Marxism as an ideology while neglecting it as a science."[15] It seems that two aspects that are said to be parts of Marxist science are stressed by Su: 1) The development of history has an objective law of its own, which is not only independent from human will but also is determined by productive forces; 2) The dialectical concepts of quality/quantity are especially valuable in dividing socialist development in China into stages.

In promoting his stage theory, Su draws heavily upon some aspects of historical materialism. He declares that China should follow objective laws. He says that "the basic tenets of Marxism are a scientific generalization of the objective laws of historical development."[16] He says that the Third Plenary Session of the CCP held in late 1978 is a renewal of the Marxist [ideological] line of dialectical materialism and historical materialism, opposed to taking Marxism as dogma, approaching Marxism in a creative way.[17]

The view that people should follow objective laws in history, of course, was shared by some famous Marxists. For instance, Plekhanov, the Russian Marxist philosopher, believed that "man's activity now appears as an activity subordinated to the law of necessity."[18] Freedom, for Plekhanov, repeating Engels, and through Engels Hegel, was the recognition of necessity. In other words, human freedom was the consciousness of being determined. However, the notion that society has a dynamic of its own, which is a critique against Mao's voluntarism, does not belong to orthodox Marxism alone. It is shared by such Western liberals as F. A. Hayek. Hayek argues that human society is the "result of human action, but not of human design," because people know less than they realize.[19]

For Su, the key to this objective law is the notion of base/super-structure with productive forces as the most decisive forces. Su cited Marx as saying: "Social relations are closely bound up with production forces. In acquiring new productive forces, men change their mode of production; and in changing the way of earning their living, they change all their social relations. The hand-mill gave a society with feudal lords; the steam-mill, society with industrial capitalists."[20] Su remained with this position even after the 1989 Tiananmen incident:

> I think one of the basic ideas of Marxism—historical materialism— is still valid. The essence of this, as Marx said, is that "No social order ever perishes before all the productive forces for which there is room in it have developed; and new, higher relations of production never appear before the material conditions of their existence have matured in the womb of the old society itself."[21]

However, this economic determinist analysis as adopted frequently by Su Shaozhi was perhaps not the intention of Marx, not even of Engels. Let's take a look at Engels' following statement:

> Marx and I are ourselves partly to blame for the fact that the younger people sometimes lay more stress on the economic side than is due to it. We had to emphasize the main principle vis-a-vis our adversaries, who denied it, and we had not always the time, the place or the opportunity to give their due to the other elements involved in the interaction.[22]

But Engels added that if somebody twists this into saying that the economic element is the only determining one, he transforms that proposition into a meaningless, abstract, senseless phrase.[23] How to understand Marx's above statements as quoted by Su in support of his stage theory? There might be two possibilities: 1) Marx and Engels were not consistent; 2) Marx's statements could be interpreted differently as compared with the one offered by Su. For Marx's first paragraph, the sentence of "The hand-mill gave a society with feudal lords; the steam-mill, society with industrial capitalists" could be figurative. Marx's second paragraph does not lead automatically to historical materialism, because on numerous other occasions, as we mention from time to time going through this book, he made remarks contrary to historical materialism.

Based on his interpretation of Marx's remarks, Su emphasizes the role of productive forces:

> In the tides of change in the present world, the qualitative change of the social productive forces—a new scientific and techno-logical revolution—is the basis of the entire transformation. Without a doubt, the new technological revolution will certainly exert a deep and extensive influence on society, economy, politics and culture.[24]

Su said that the following are the effects of the newly-emerged scientific and technological revolution on society: 1) the change of indus-trial structure; 2) the change of labour force structure; 3) the change of resource structure; 4) the change of social axis.[25] The notion that advances in productive forces will inevitably bring about changes in social relations is not only in line with Eduard Bernstein's revisionism in the early stage of communist movement,[26] but also similar to the so-called convergence theory in modern times.[27] All these arguments are aimed at discrediting the orthodox Marxist class theory.

In addition to the materialistic notion of base/superstructure, the second element of Marxist science emphasized by Su Shaozhi are some notions in dialectics. According to Chinese text books about Marxist philosophy, it was Engels who gave a good summary of Marxist dialectics. Indeed, Marx never discussed dialectics in detail. According to Engels, there are three laws in Marxist dialectics: 1) transformation between quantity and quality; 2) unity of opposites; 3) negation versus negation.[28] Drawing upon this interpretation of Marxist science, Su argues that while the two dialectical categories of quantity and quality are related, they should not be confused with each other. Su argues that failure to distinguish stages of social development violates dialectics:

> The development of matter is always from changes in quantity to changes in partial quality, then to final changes in quality. The final changes in quality are big stages of development, while partial changes in quality are only small stages of development. Therefore, after the proletariat seized power, socialist develop-ment has to undergo changes in quantity, to partial changes in quality and to complete changes in quality.[29]

Su's science is not only intriguingly connected with some key notions of orthodox Marxism such as base/superstructure and dialectics, it is also unclearly related to the Western experimental scientific tradition. In order to challenge, or avoid some key notions of Marxism, especially some notions in Marxist political economy, Su challenges the notion that Marxism is "the science of all sciences" by saying that Marxism is only one science among many:

> Marxism is only a science, not an all-inclusive "science of sciences." As one of the sciences, it must follow the rules and characteristics of science in general. Science, which lays stress on practice, development, and new creation, has no final end, no absolute authority. Science, which never fears criticism, is developed through debates. Any science, confined by its own special conditions and limitations, can be applicable only over a certain range. So, a particular science can be imperfect, surpassed, and falsified. Marxism cannot become a science while these basic characteristics and rules are neglected and despised.[30]

However, people need to be informed about the characteristics and rules of science in general. As discussed in chapter one, the rules and characteristics of orthodox Marxism, Baconism, historicism and postmodernism are drastically different. For instance, historical materialism from which Su has borrowed heavily cannot be falsified by Baconian experiments, although historical events such as the October Revolution, the Chinese communist seizure of power and the more recent collapse of communism in the former Soviet Union and Eastern Europe have all discredited it. Therefore, the rules and characteristics of science in general really do not tell much.

Application of Marxist Science

Su Shaozhi's political theory is created in the name of scientific socialism. From the notion of base/superstructure, it was deduced that developing productive forces not only can ensure socialism in the end, but also can prevent the restoration of capitalism at present; from the notion of quantity/quality, it was deduced also that social development in China has to undergo several stages, including making up some of the lessens of capitalism.

According to Su, "The socialism practiced in China is, in the final analysis, to develop productive forces and to develop China's economy gradually."[31] "Therefore, we have decided to concentrate all our efforts on economic construction. Only with material civilization can we have spiritual civilization. Only with highly developed productivity and abundance of materials can we speak of communism."[32] But does developing productive forces have to belong to socialism? Probably not. The argument that productive forces are the driving force of society is shared by many theorists in all contemporary developing countries, whether socialist or capitalist.

For Su, developing productive forces cannot only ensure socialism, it can even prevent the restoration of capitalism. He regards the fear as groundless that by declaring that China had not become a full fledged socialist society, a restoration of capitalism may be possible. Su's argument was based on the notion of base/superstructure. He said:

> A restoration of capitalism can be avoided only when productive forces have become so developed that the capitalist relations of production cannot let them function within capitalist relations of production. . . .This is a result of the law that the productive forces determine the relations of production.[33]

By this logic, the more developed the productive forces are, the less likely capitalist restoration occurs. Modernization thus has become a panacea, which not only solves the problem of poverty, but also ensures socialism. Su's theory is the inverted form of Karl Kautsky's economic determinist philosophy in that while the former believed that to develop productive forces can prevent capitalism from being restored in socialist countries, the latter believed that economic development would ensure the success of socialism in a capitalist society.[34]

The official theory guiding the reform, which was authorized by the Thirteenth National Party Congress in 1987, is identical to that put forward by Su. Consider the following paragraph read by Zhao Ziyang, then the General Party Secretary at the Congress:

> our country is at the initial stage of socialism. . . .We must start from this reality and cannot bypass this stage. . . .The assumption that we could bypass the initial stage of socialism without immense development of productive forces is utopianism in the realm of revolutionary development and is the root of leftist mistakes. . . .
> The fundamental task of socialist society is to develop productive forces. At the initial stage, in order to get rid of poverty and backwardness, the center of all of our work should be the development of productive forces. Whether something is conducive to developing productive forces should be the starting point for considering all problems and the fundamental criterion of all work.[35]

In spite of the 1989 Tiananmen incident, the reform faction, which has been the mainstream of the Chinese ruling elite, has largely stayed with this theory. The socialism put forward by Jiang Zemin, who became the General Party Secretary after Tiananmen, sounds similar as that of Su Shaozhi: "The basic task of socialism is to develop productive forces. The superiority of socialism is reflected in the fact that its productive forces develop faster than that of capitalism."[36] As will be shown throughout this book, the conflicts between many dissidents including Su and the Chinese government can be seen as more of a battle in real world politics than a confrontation in terms of theories.[37]

Nevertheless, the base/superstructure notion not only can ensure socialism and prevent a (full fledged?) capitalism, it can also justify doing (some elements of?) capitalism. Su believes that it is necessary to make up the missing experience of capitalism, because China skipped over this stage of development. He argues that China is still in a transition period from pre-socialist to socialist society, still catching up with the missed lessons of capitalism.[38]

> Socialist revolution can occur and win victory before the social productive forces have reached very high levels of development. But a socialist society cannot be built in its complete form before the productive forces have reached a certain basic level. . . . If New Democracy had been more fully developed and the trans- formation of the means of production had been carried out in more steady steps, the situation would have been different today. The reform in ownership and the emergence of the various sectors of the economy at the present stage show that it is not unreasonable to say that we are making up for lost lessons.[39]

Indeed, Su had many favorable comments about Western democracies. If it was evil at all, it was a necessary evil. Su said, such values as liberty, equality and universal fraternity, and such systems as checks and balances of power, universal suffrage do not belong to the bourgeoisie alone. "Such democratic rights were demanded even more urgently by the working people at the time of the bourgeois revolution in Europe."[40] Although Su has not laid down systematically what democracy means, he sometimes was positive about some features of Western society. Su remarked on another occasion, "Under a democratic system, such as the United States, the role played by individuals is quite limited."[41] It is also interesting to note that Su made it explicit that capitalist ideas as part of the super- structure were not as serious a problem as feudalist ideas. On the contrary, he seemed to suggest that because of the absence of a stage of capitalist development, China does not have a democratic tradition.[42] These overt pro-West remarks were probably the reason that Hu Qiaomu did not like Su's stage theory from the very beginning.[43] They may also explain the final split between Su and the Chinese government.

Su's ideas became increasingly pro-West after the 1989 Tiananmen incident. As a member of the Board of Directors of the Center for Modern China, a research institution based in Princeton, Su Shaozhi aimed at contributing to "China's course toward democracy and a free economy," as the guideline of the Center reveals.[44] This is certainly a departure from his earlier views concerning socialism. Thus, Marx would be turning in his grave if he learned that one of his influential disciples, born in China but now based in the United States, is now using his ideas to promote a free economy.

In addition to his emphasis on developing productive forces and his advocacy of catching up with the missed lessons of capitalism based on the base/superstructure notion, Su Shaozhi also uses the orthodox Marxist dialectical notion of quantity/quality to advocate the idea that it was necessary to divide the whole process of socialism going to communism into stages. Su's stage theory is consistent with his advocacy of catching up with the missed lessons of capitalism. He remarks,

> We believe there are several stages during the whole process of going from capitalism to communism. The first stage is from capitalism to socialism. This stage can be further divided into two sub-stages: (1) that from the success of the proletarian revolution, i.e., seizure of power, to the accomplishment of the public ownership of the means of production, (2) that of underdeveloped or incomplete socialism. The second stage is developed socialism or complete socialism. The third is communism.[45]

Failure to distinguish underdeveloped socialism from developed socialism can have grave consequences, according to Su. It would lead to premature elimination of private economy, family plots, household sideline production, the practice of to each according to his work, commodity production, and personal material interests. It could even lead to a premature transition to communism.[46] Here, Su was apparently referring to the Maoist practice during the Great Leap Forward and the Cultural Revolution.

Based on this understanding, Su defines the nature of Chinese society. He believes that since 1956 when China finished the nationalization of the main means of production and collectivization of agriculture, the country had entered a socialist category (*fanchou*), which is a broad category. Three conditions were necessarily but not exclusively required for the entitlement of this category: 1) the establishment of the proletarian dictatorship; 2) public ownership of the means of production; 3) collectivization of small producers. Su argues that by possessing these three conditions without others, for instance, the elimination of commodity production, China can be called "underdeveloped, or incomplete socialism."[47]

Su goes on to say that this "underdeveloped socialism" is different from socialist society in the sense that the former, having capitalist legacies, can produce capitalist elements, while the latter, without capitalist legacies, does not produce capitalist elements.[48] This classification leads to the conclusion that from 1949 to 1956, China was in the first sub-stage of the first stage, the establishment of the PRC to the accomplishment of the public ownership of the means of production. From 1956 to 1980 when Su made the remarks China had been in the second sub-stage of the first stage, underdeveloped or incomplete socialism.

But what are the specific characteristics of socialism? In 1985, Su was unclear. On one occasion, Su explicitly said that he did not want to talk about socialist political economy systematically, although he discussed in details some of China's specific economic policies.[49] Su says:

> Today, we cannot find the typical socialist mode of production, nor do we know if there is one. . . . Comrade Deng Xiaoping once said, "What is socialism and what is Marxism? We were not quite clear about this before." What he said still has an immediate significance today.[50]

This downplaying of the relations of production is consistent with his emphasis on developing productive forces. It is a kind of technological determinism.

When he finally came to define socialism in 1988, Su seemed to be talking about China's future. He listed five characteristics of socialism: 1) public ownership; 2) the distribution formula, to each according to his work; 3) government of the working people, especially democracy at a high level; 4) a planned economy; 5) an emphasis on spiritual civilization in addition to material civilization. He goes on: "These considerations apply, or should apply, to all socialist countries."[51] Apparently, these five characteristics belong to real socialism, not to underdeveloped socialism or incomplete socialism as is the case for China.

Selective Adaptation of Marxism

It is interesting to note that Su as a Marxist has advocated a free economy. In order to make these two incompatible things, Marxism and a free economy live together, one probably has to treat Marxism in a very special way. The most intriguing treatment of Marxist theory by Su was that he sometimes failed to distinguish the two components of the economic base: productive forces and relations of production. This situation relates to the fact that he seems to emphasize historical materialism to the neglect of Marxist political economy, although Su believes, following Engels, that Marx's two discoveries lead to the creation of scientific socialism: historical materialism and surplus value.[52] If one stresses productive forces to the neglect of relations of production, then he becomes a technological determinist, not a historical materialist.

This situation casts doubt on Su's Marxist rationale in advocating developing productive forces in China, because Marxist political economy is crucial to determine whether productive forces and relations of production suit each other. Su's rationale is: In capitalist society, the development of new science and technology would not save capitalism, because it does not ease the basic contradiction of capitalism;[53] in socialist society, the development of new science and technology suits the relations of production, which are generally more advanced than productive forces.

Nevertheless, Su's position on Marxist orthodoxy was not firm on all occasions. He mentioned that the advance of human civilization had drastically changed the class structure of capitalist society. Thus, the orthodox Marxist class theory was called into question. Secondly, he mentioned the fact that modern capitalism had adopted some measures, such as welfare programs and the nationalization of sectors of the economy and intervention in market mechanisms, which raised questions for him about the orthodox Marxist break-down theory. Finally, in his discussion of the international communist movement, he raised the question of whether it was possible for different countries to adopt different roads to socialism.[54]

The political implication of this selective adaptation of Marxism is significant. If one argues that Western capitalism may not be doomed, as Su suggested by questioning the orthodox Marxist breakdown theory, but insists that a pre-capitalist society such as China has necessarily to progress into some kind of quasi capitalist-socialist society first, as Su held by resorting to the orthodox stage theory, then the logical conclusion is to postpone socialism into the indefinite future.

An easy escape for Su from this contradiction would be resorting to Engels' "in-the-last-instance"[55] rhetoric. That is to say, one could argue that although sometimes superstructures affect the economic base, "in the last instance" it is the latter that has the final say. Thoughtful analysis suggests that this is meaningless rhetoric. Alan Hunt observes that there is no general mechanism of connection between the economic relations of a society, the relations between classes and whatever objective interests may be ascribed to them, and the formation of arenas of struggle in that society, the organization of forces engaged in them and the issues and ideologies on which they divide.[56]

Here are some more examples to show Su's selective adaptation of Marxism. It seems that although his theory of the elementary stage of socialism is based on historical materialism, on numerous other occasions Su was not so deterministic. He once remarked that "almost all those countries which underwent revolution resulting in the birth of a new regime after World War II are underdeveloped ones. This seems to have forecast a historical trend having the character of a law."[57] According to historical materialism, the successes of socialist revolution in underdeveloped countries should be regarded as exceptions, not the law. If Su upholds this phenomenon as a law, then he is arguing against the historical materialist stage theory, at least as far as it has always been articulated.

Although Su justifies the making up for the missed lessons of capitalism by resorting to historical materialism, he uses unorthodox Marxism to criticize the evils of Chinese society. What aspects of the superstructure of China are not compatible with the socialist economic base? Su said, "What are the obstacles to our country's advance towards modernization? The chief one remains the feudal autocratic tradition and the ignorance that goes along with it."[58] If he upholds the base-superstructure logic, he cannot possibly say that after 40 years of socialist construction, the chief obstacle is still the feudal tradition, even if he resorts to the "in-the-last-instance" argument of Engels.[59] This is because the mode of production in China from 1957 to 1979 was totally different from the feudal one prior to the founding of the republic in 1949, no matter whether you call this new mode of production socialist or not.

Although Su's theory may not have necessary connections with Marx and science, it may be in accordance with the Chinese tradition on science: its stress on technology and to use it for political purpose. This pragmatic attitude of not viewing the pursuit of knowledge for its own sake but for solving problems of this life, in this world, can be traced to ancient times. Western analytical rationality is new to the Chinese who have their own practical rationality.

CHAPTER **5**

Empirical Scientism: Jin Guantao

Life and Experience

Jin Guantao is one of the most sophisticated scholars, not only among the six intellectuals under study, but also in contemporary China. In addition, he has always consciously tried to distance himself from real world politics, although his ideas have important political implications that are liberal and pluralistic in a general sense. Born into an intellectual's family in Yiwu, Zhejiang Province in 1947, Jin did not care very much for philosophy in his teenage years, even less so for politics. Jin describes his early philosophy as inheriting the traditional Chinese way of thinking characterized by direct perception of the world through senses. He buried himself in books of natural sciences in high school and his early years in college. According to Jin, he would probably have inherited his father's career to become a chemistry professor if the Cultural Revolution did not break out in 1966. He was then a student of chemistry at Beijing University.

There were three kinds of students in terms of political attitudes at Beijing University when the revolution started: those involved in criticizing and purging the others; those criticized and purged; those who were outsiders. However, even the outsiders were emotionally involved: they were watching the great event intensively. Jin was one of the outsiders. One incident had a profound impact on his life. In a summer day of 1966, he was discovered studying English in private, a crime that contradicted the Red Guards' enthusiastic participation in the revolution. He was criticized as a result. From that time on, Jin turned more of his attention to the event.[1]

Jin began to think about what was going around him and began to study philosophy. This is because he found that Marxist philosophy was unable to interpret the chaotic situation for him. He sensed that either the (Marxist philosophical) theory or reality has to be wrong. Jin also started his self reflection and evaluation of the events while reading Marx's works including *The German Ideology* and *Capital*. This is not only because that Jin was aware of the incongruity between reality and official theory, which was said to have originated from Marx, but also because Marx was Jin's most admired person at that time. Jin was impressed by the fearless character of young Marx. Then Jin read Hegel, from whom Marx's dialectical materialism was said to have partly originated. He was so obsessed with the Hegelian philosophy that he earned himself a nickname, Jin-gel.

After two years' study, Jin came to an intellectual crisis in 1968, which, in his own words, made him feel that he was in a state of virtual insanity. This crisis happened when he discovered that dialectics, to which he had devoted so much, either had to carry metaphysics traits, or had to be confused in nature. In 1970, Jin graduated from Beijing University and became a worker in a factory which produced plastic products in his hometown Hangzhou, Zhejiang Province. The research conditions in Hangzhou were not as good as that of Beijing for Jin. Furthermore, Jin's intellectual crisis got worse, because he found that his discoveries, which took him five years of study and caused him so many pains concerning philosophy versus science, were nothing new, a situation that resulted from his ignorance of Western literature. Jin found that his "discoveries" were very much in line with mainstream Western philosophy and had been circulated in the West for more than 100 years.[2] He recalled:

> From those days, I woke up from my youth dream of philosophy. I realized that I am not a philosopher. I will never be. It is meaningless even if I can become one. At the time of my youth, philosophy was the truth of the universe, i.e., the summary of the wisdom of both natural and social sciences. Now this dream was smashed, thus putting an end to philosophy and "isms." What was left was a conglomeration of concrete problems.[3]

This intellectual conviction compelled Jin to retreat to science, an involuntary step that benefited him much in his later career. The period from late 1968 to 1974 was the time when Jin, having become disillusioned with dialectics, was having a deep reflection of the whole range of issues of philosophy and science. From that time on, Jin tried to use science to improve philosophy.

Science As the Philosophical Starting Point

Against Reductionist Materialism

Jin Guantao wrote two books and a long article dealing specifically with philosophy. These three pieces are entitled respectively *Philosophy of Man (Ren de zhexue)*, "Philosophy of Development" ("Fazhan de zhexue"), and *Philosophy of the Whole (Zhengti de zhexue)*. The first book departs from Newtonian mechanics, which often lends a hand to reductionist ways of thinking. The article deals with dialectics from the point of view of cybernetics and systems theory. The other book presents the author's own view on philosophy in general.

Philosophy of Man devotes an extremely small proportion directly to the issue of man itself. Rather than commenting on what man is or what man should be, this book spends much of its volume in refuting reductionist, mechanical materialism. Jin believes that philosophy is nothing without man. Being is not objective in the mechanical sense, but is conditioned by other things. He says:

> It is precisely because of the observation of human beings that cause the irregular movements of the electrons. When humans measure their positions. . .[humans] will inevitably interrupt their movement, thus causing uncertainty of their momentum [of pace]. . . . It does not make any sense to talk about electrons when one is not observing them. . . .The fact that electrons possess certain qualities is because we observe them. We cannot talk about the quality of matter without resorting to man's sensing. The belief that matter or quality can be independent from human sense and consciousness is ridiculous. . . .Similarly, the moon does not exist when nobody looks at it. . . .Materialism has been falsified.[4]

Jin's awareness of the limitations of the mechanical Newtonian physics is not new. Even Second International Marxism recognizes the problems of mechanical materialism. Engels, among other leading Marxists at that time, tried to solve the problem by creating the so-called dialectical materialism. Actually it has been the classical practice of many orthodox

Marxists to distinguish themselves from mechanical materialists by claiming
to be dialectical. Jin, however, does not believe this has solved the problem.

New Explanation of Dialectics

In "The Philosophy of Development" (1986), Jin tries to replace dialectics,
which explains development of matter, with systems theory. He said:

> Can the philosophic thought previously expressed by "internal
> contradiction" and "unity of opposites" [in dialectics] be ex-
> pressed using concepts of systems theory? That is, can we inter-
> pret contradiction as the instability of a system, its being placed
> in a state of uncertainty by breakdown of internal regulation?
> I maintain we can equate contradiction with instability and
> uncertainty.[5]

Jin said that his concept of instability is actually borrowed from
American scholar W. B. Cannon. Cannon argued that any living system
has a basic characteristic: the state of stability. For instance, the body
temperature of animals remains basically the same regardless of the
external condition. If the temperature goes too high or too low, the
breakdown of internal regulation would occur and the animal would die.[6]
Apparently, the concept of instability in Jin's theory certainly carries
different connotations than that carried by contradiction in dialectics.

In fact, the fact that Jin equates instability with contradiction may
be political. That is, in order to sell his systems theory in the Chinese
context, he had to borrow Marxist rhetoric. In this case, he equates systems
theory with dialectics. The political situation in China changed very fast
in the 1980s. By 1988, two years after Jin made the above equation, he
felt that there was no longer a need to say good things about dialectics.
In his intellectual autobiography, he openly discarded "dialectics:"

> As a method, the purpose of dialectics is to find the law of
> development. In line with the principle of dialectics, the dual
> nature of matter, existence and its negation of nonexistence, has
> to be introduced in order to discover and articulate development.
> That is to say that the matter has the elements which could negate
> itself, i.e., existence versus nonexistence. . . . Problems arise here.
> Not only is it impossible to use language to express development,
> but also development theory which is in line with dialectics, has
> to exist simultaneously with its opposite, the non-development

theory. This results in absolute confusion of concepts and intellectual void.[7]

Jin criticizes mechanical materialism and has abandoned dialectics. Does he advocate idealism, as a Chinese philosopher He Zhama charged?[8] Or, does he advocate a kind of pseudo-scientific mysticism as implied by Brugger and Kelly? The situation may be more complicated than these two interpretations. He Zhama's viewpoint is apparently in line with the philosophy of the current conservative faction within the Chinese government, which is similar to Second International Marxism. It is the standard practice among orthodox Marxists to identify those who function within the Baconian science tradition as idealists.

The interpretation offered by Brugger and Kelly has to be enriched by more recent literature. Brugger and Kelly's research on Jin, as represented in *Chinese Marxism in the Post-Mao Era*, was completed in late 1988 although this book was published in 1990. They originally wanted to cover only the period 1978–85. Consequently, some important works by Jin and Liu either did not receive sufficient attention by Brugger and Kelly or had not been published when the two completed their research. For instance, Brugger and Kelly commented intensively on "Philosophy of Development," which was published in 1986. They spent lots of effort in trying to prove that although Jin still upheld dialectics, what he really wanted was cybernetics and systems theory. They probably did not have a chance to read carefully *Philosophy of the Whole* (1987), in which Jin did not resort to Marxist rhetorics while presenting his own philosophy. Although *Philosophy of the Whole* is in the bibliography of *Chinese Marxism in the Post-Mao Era*, Brugger and Kelly made few references to this book, if any at all. In addition, if Brugger and Kelly had a chance to read Jin's intellectual autobiography published in 1988, they would not have tried so hard to prove that Jin's theory has little to do with Marxist dialectics, because Jin made it explicit in this article that this concept is useless in philosophical discussion. This intellectual autobiography of Jin is not in the bibliography of *Chinese Marxism in the Post-Mao Era*.

A New Philosophy

Jin has rejected materialism as an ontological approach and dialectics as a method. What is his own philosophy? It seems that Jin has taken steps towards what was described by Tom Sorell and Hohn Wellmuth as empirical scientism, which not only intends to replace humanities and social sciences, but also to replace philosophy. Regarding the nature of science,

Jin Guantao and Liu Qingfeng[9] lay out the norms of scientific inquiry as
follows: 1) Natural science has to be based on experience and experiments
which are then summarized and analyzed; 2) Theories of natural science
must be logical and subject to verification and falsification; 3) From the
theories in natural science, conclusions beyond these experiences and
experiments can be reached by deduction.[10] The norms of natural science
as laid out by Jin and Liu are identical to Baconian science.[11]

For Jin, the social sciences and natural sciences are an integrated
whole. He quotes Marx's remarks in support of his approach: "Natural
science will in time incorporate into itself the science of man, just as the
science of man will incorporate into itself natural science: there will be
one science."[12] However, Marx's belief in the unity of natural sciences and
social sciences does not lead to Baconism. To the contrary, Marx's attempt
could be viewed as an attempt to refute the idea of taking Baconian science
as the science. Marx's approach is closer to a historicist position.[13]

Regarding the relations between his science and philosophy, Jin argues
that the starting point of philosophy should be the same as the starting
point of science: it should start from the most common concept, that is,
the conditions on which matter or substance is based and consequently
can be verified.[14] Benedict Spinoza (1632–1677) borrowed principles in
geometry to spell out his ethics. The generally acknowledged truth in
philosophy has to be subject to falsification. A philosophical system that
is not based on science will be challenged by science and its basic concepts
will be smashed by the rapid development of science. In refuting paradoxes, Jin cites Karl Popper (1902–) as saying that the opposite of super-
ficial truth is fallacy. But the opposite of profound truth is still truth.[14]

Jin regards science as a tool to liberate philosophy. He feels that if
one does not understand the methodology of natural sciences, which in
the twentieth century has been characterized by sophisticated mathematics,
one would not be qualified as a philosopher.[16] By saying that some methods
of natural sciences, such as sophisticated mathematics can liberate philosophy and that truth in philosophy has to be subject to falsification, Jin
seems to have treated Baconian science and philosophy as identical. This
is scientistic, because philosophy always has value connotations which
can never be falsified.

Nevertheless, Jin's other remarks that seem to negate scientism have
also been noted. In the following paragraph, Jin seems to have embraced
philosophy not as a scientific philosophy as was discussed previously:

> It does not matter whether a philosophical discussion is right
> or wrong, has meaning or does not have one. The touch stone
> of real philosophy is whether it is fearless in thought and thor-

oughly deep. . . . A philosophical theory has to be one's self reflection of the soul. If not, this so-called philosophy is no different from a high school student's copy of other people's great ideas. Philosophical enlightenment has to be realized only by one's embracing it with his soul. Real philosophy requires that one not only has to study the universe with it, but to create one's own philosophy. . . .[17]

The message carried in this paragraph is closer to a description of religion, which is a combination of mysticism and values, or, to a lesser degree, to an ideology that is largely a marriage of values and theories. It is less close to Jin's previous discussion about philosophy which has to be subject to falsification. How can we interpret this seeming inconsistency? It seems that although he does not openly advocate scientism, given the apparent limitations of this approach, Jin embraces it when doing concrete research. That is to say that on an abstract level, he would probably say that scientism is not the way or the only way to approach truth. On a concrete level, that is, when he does specific studies, he does believe that Baconian science is the way. In the following, we will see that Jin in his study of Chinese history intends to replace humanities such as history with his science.

Application of Empirical Science

The Book: The Cycle of Growth and Decline[18]

In his introduction to both the 1984 and 1992 editions of *The Cycle of Growth and Decline*, Chinese philosopher Bao Zunxin remarks that Jin's work is the first attempt to introduce the methods of the natural sciences, including cybernetics, systems theory and mathematical models, into the study of Chinese history. This is a good summary of the methodology of Jin's concrete studies. In the book, Jin Guantao [and Liu Qingfeng] argue that the official explanation of Chinese history cannot answer all the questions regarding the fact that China's feudal society lasted so long. For instance, some attribute the failure of social transformation from feudalism to capitalism to the fact that the exploitation by the landlords and the state was too harsh. Consequently, the peasants were always on the verge of starvation and thus productive forces could not be developed to promote the change in the relations of production. This explanation was offered by Mao and has been the official interpretation. Jin points out that the exploitation in Medieval European countries of the serfs and peasants was more cruel than in China.

Jin argues that researchers should free themselves from the analytical method of trying to find the ultimate single cause of events such as the economic, political and ideological. Instead, attempts should be made by trying to find the cause of events by looking at the interactions among the three perspectives. Breakthroughs have to be made in terms of methodology, he insists.[19]

This method is systems theory, cybernetics and information theory. Based on his interpretation of systems theory, Jin believes that there are four models in systems functions: 1) standstill; 2) replacement of the old by the new; 3) extinction; 4) ultrastability.[20] Jin regards the transformation of European societies as belonging to the second kind. That is, primitive society is replaced by slavery society, which is further replaced by feudal society and finally feudal society is replaced by capitalist society. The mechanism for this kind of social transformation is characterized by its piece-by-piece change. The result is that a new system is gradually created from the old.

The Chinese feudal society, however, is the fourth kind: an ultra-stable structure, according to Jin. The mechanism of this kind of social change is characterized by its abruptness and totality. The deviation by any subsystem from the point of equilibrium will bring down the whole structure, and all embryonic features of the new structure are destroyed. That is to say that the collapse of any one of the three subsystems of China's feudal society—the autocratic political system, the landlord economy or the Confucian-Taoist ideology—would bring down society as a whole. Because of the fact that the Chinese feudal system was sophisticated to the point of perfection, any new society that emerged shortly afterwards will be modeled exactly after the old. From a historical perspective, the Chinese feudal society witnessed an interesting phenomenon where the feudal system was maintained for several thousand years, precisely because of this kind of periodic collapse of individual dynasties. These upheavals serve the purpose of getting rid of what Jin calls non-organizational elements (*wuzuzhi liliang*). These so called non-organizational elements are mechanisms that cause the subsystems to leave the point of equilibrium vis-a-vis the main system. The main non-organizational elements in China's feudal society are official corruption and concentration of land in the hands of the few. Jin shows that these two things always occur at the end of each dynasty.[21]

Such is Jin's application of his science [and philosophy]. Now we want to briefly examine how well he has applied systems theory to the study of Chinese history from the point of view of methodology. We want to see the scientific character of this approach. We will do so by doing a comparison between the first edition of the book, dated in 1984, and the latest edition, 1992. Not only does this show that Jin has made progress over the years in terms of theoretical sophistication, but also it can best illustrate the strong and weak points of the methodological approach of this book in general.

In the 1984 edition of the book, Jin mentions the following two points: 1) The theoretical framework of this book is based on cybernetics and systems theory.[22] 2) The Chinese feudal society is a relatively closed system and systems theory is more suitable for studies of closed systems.[23] In the 1992 edition of the book, however, these statements are gone. Jin states:

> Nowadays, the once popular structural-functional group has lost much of its influence in sociology. Although people have got used to the approach of viewing society as formed by many inter-related subsystems because of the more recent general systems theory and systems momentum theory, there has been a lack of a rigorous and logical method for macroscopic analysis.[24]

Perhaps because of this awareness, Jin briefly deals with the two general problems of systems theory when it is adopted in the study of human society: 1) it is synchronic, thus violating the common-sensible proposition that history never repeats itself; 2) human initiatives, which can play decisive roles in shaping history, can be seen nowhere. However, Bao's introduction to the book in which he says that Jin's work uses systems theory and mathematical models remains unchanged and the basic theoretical framework of the book is obviously unchanged.

As a methodological approach, systems theory as adopted by Jin has serious problems when applied to the study of China's history. Firstly, Jin is not successful in applying his central notion that scientific endeavor has to start with the "most common concepts that can be verified" in this study. Throughout the book, I have not found that Jin starts from the most common concepts that can be verified as he promised. The autocratic political system, the landlord economy and the Confucian-Taoism ideology, from which Jin's analysis of China's feudal society starts, are no more, and no less, verified than most other historical approaches which focus on the three aspects of the political, economic and ideological [cultural/social].

The methodological deficiency is also demonstrated in his treatment of statistics and data. We understand that systems theory uses data in an attempt to form a sort of outline. It is more interested in the whole rather than the parts. That's why systems theory is accused of being not empirical enough. Robert Lilienfeld goes as far as to say that systems theory "cannot be described as empirical science, as there is very little that is empirical about it."[25] But we have found that even the very incomplete data are not used systematically.

Here is just one example. According to Jin, non-organizing elements enrich systems theory. When Jin talks about these non-organizing elements, he uses many statistics and data. But these statistics and data are used in an exemplary way, not systematically. Jin talks about such and such dynasty, such and such year. There is a lack of information in this respect, of course, as he points out. However, in the authors' description, there are only eight dynasties in China's history that fit the category of *da yi tong chao dai*, or grand unified dynasties. In order to implement systems theory in a thorough way, the use of statistics may be sketchy, but has to be systematic. In addition, lack of information is characteristic in the discipline of history. Using the excuse of insufficient statistics may imply that systems theory can never be implemented in the discipline thoroughly.

In addition, starting from the three subsystems of China's feudal society as attempted by the author is mechanical. In the study of society, researchers often approach the problem from the perspectives of the political, economic and cultural (sometimes, it is called "social"), because it is believed with good reasons that this approach can cover all aspects of society. But once these three aspects are called the subsystems, they seem to have some kind of reductionist quality. In fact, other factors may be just as important in sustaining the structure of China's feudal society. Family and kin system is one such factor.

Family and kin relationships are not treated as one of the subsystems as politics, economics and culture. Jin's subsystem of culture largely refers to ideology. Such cultural aspects as family and kin system are not included. However, the Chinese family and kin systems are unique in the world. They have consistently played an important role in sustaining a stable social structure. As an illustration, in the Chinese language, the word for "country" (*guo jia*) is a combination of "*guo*" which literally means country and "*jia*" which literally means the family.

A second example is China's geographical location. Jin believes that China's geographical location cannot be taken as a subsystem. He says that geographical location could be taken as a subsystem for this kind of analysis in the context of ancient Egypt. The Nile's periodic floods could make civilizations prosper and die easily. Such is not the case in China. Jin argues against Karl Wittfogel's famous thesis that China's oriental despotism is largely due to geographical location. His argument is unjustified. We remember that theoretically the thesis of this book (1984 edition) is largely based on the assumption that ancient China is a relatively closed system.[26] China's geographical location is linked to this assumption.

Another issue of methodology is also linked to the relative isolation of Chinese feudal society. In the 1984 edition of the book, Jin says that the Chinese feudal society is a relatively closed system and systems theory is more suitable for studies of closed systems. In the 1992 edition, however, this sentence was deleted. If Jin still sticks to this position, we can conclude that he implies that systems theory may not suit open systems. There are two problems here. Firstly, an open system may not be that bad for systems theory. According to Ludwig von Bertalanffy, who is widely believed to have invented systems theory, the emergence of systems theory is partly due to the fact that the characteristic state of a living organism or cell is that it is an open system, but classical physics for the most part deals with only closed systems.[27] Secondly, the readers need to know how to define whether a system is open or closed. For instance, should we label a Hong Kong import and export company as open or closed? Apparently, for Hong Kong, it is a open system; for the world, it is part of the relatively closed system of the earth.

We do not know exactly why Jin has treated science and his own study in this way. But we do know that even in the Western academic world, it is not uncommon for people to reject scientism on an abstract level, but do research in a scientistic way. In addition, If one does not do research scientistically, he or she could slip into the relativism of irresponsibility. Jin has noticed this situation in China's academic circles. Given the fact that history seems to have convinced most academics that no absolute truth exists, many intellectuals have ceased to be more responsible even in presenting their own perspectives, because they have realized that no matter how serious they have tried in this research, the result would inevitably have limitations. In the words of Jin, this attitude encourages sloppiness and superficiality in scholarship.

The Political Connection

Factors other than academic ones may also be involved in causing Jin's ambiguity in treating science and philosophy. While it may be impossible for us to identify all these factors, we may be able to sort out the more important ones by looking at Jin's other remarks related to the philosophy-science issue. If one only rejects scientism on an abstract level but endorses it in concrete studies like many academics do in the West, we may call him or her scientistic. But if one consciously endorses scientism for political purpose, no matter how holy the politics is, the situation is different.

Commenting on why he decided to write his masterpiece, *The Cycle of Growth and Decline*, Jin Guantao said that the survival and revitalization of the Chinese nationality takes priority over all other philosophical values.[28] Under the current situation, what is good for China? For Jin, scientism could be good for China. In the book, *The Cycle of Growth and Decline*, he noted that pseudo-science under certain circumstances can be good for the spread of real science, because it can popularize the worship of science in society. For Jin, the support of society is indispensable for the development of science. He cites the example of Augustas who interpreted religion in the scientific way. It was through this popularization of pseudo-science, the Europeans gradually got to know the real science.[29]

Liu Qingfeng also explained this situation. Although she has realized the limitations of scientism that has surged in China in recent years, it has to be encouraged because given the current situation in China, scientism is most urgently needed for national revitalization. However, Liu is unsure whether scientism can fulfil this task.[30]

Compared with Marxist scientism of Hu Qiaomu, which politically provides intellectual resources to state socialism, the systems theory as embodied in Jin's works lends a hand to pluralism and liberalism in the long run. This is so in spite of the fact that in the short run, systems theory seems in accordance with more state control. That is probably why not only some Eastern European countries and the former U.S.S.R. carried out the experiment of systems theory in the early 1960s, but also why the Chinese government seems to have endorsed it. There has been much discussion about the relations between systems theory and Marxism in China's academic circles. Most of the opinions, even after Tiananmen, seem to support the notion that systems theory is in accordance with Marxism.

However, things on the surface can be deceiving. Systems theory on a philosophical level actually encourages pluralist thinking. This is clearly demonstrated in Jin's discussion about the totality approach in philosophy. Jin says,

> we will find that as philosophical concepts, possibility is more basic than reality. We should not deduce possibility from reality, but the other way around, from possibility to reality. . . . Our universe may be just one of the millions of possible outcomes after the Big Bang. . . . life could be only accidental. Evolution may also be accidental. . . .[31]

This is certainly against the monistic nature of materialistic scientism which provides intellectual support for the notions of the inevitable success of communism in the future and authoritarianism in contemporary politics. With this flexible starting point in philosophy, nothing is inevitable, communism or capitalism.

Even on the policy making level, systems theory is dangerous for the ruler. "The state as the central control unit of society rather tends to become completely replaced by a self-regulating or self-organizing social system."[32] Given all these, it is not surprising that after about a decade's experiment, East Germans abandoned systems theory in 1971. We are not surprised at all to learn of Jin's remark that "two legacies of the twentieth century have been the experiment and failure of socialism."[33] Jin and Liu found that the communist regime established after 1949 and the Chinese feudal dynasties share many similarities.[34]

Nevertheless, ultra-stability theory implies that a piece-by-piece social transformation is better in the Chinese context, because the sudden collapse of the system will not bring about a new one but a reversal to the old system. That is probably why when *Heshang*, which was believed to have borrowed heavily from this theory, was put on China's TV network and was viewed by Taiwan author Chen Zhangjin as an attempt to support Zhao Ziyang's policies favoring one-party rule plus economic reform.[35] Indeed, Jin may not want to see a sudden collapse of the regime, although he laments about his exile status in Hong Kong after Tiananmen.[36] He said in 1993 that the policies adopted by the Chinese regime after the 1989 Beijing Spring are closer to *San Min Zhu Yi*, or the Three Principles of the People, officially endorsed by the Taiwan authorities, than to Marxism.[37]

In spite of these implicit political connotations, Jin has never laid out his political platform for China's future, although he mentioned vaguely that China should transcend both socialism and capitalism. Yan Jiaqi, who shares with Jin in endorsing empirical scientism, has been specific in advocating liberal democracy for China's politics. Born in Wujin County, Jiangsu Province in 1942, Yan received his college education at China's Science and Technology University from 1959 to 1964, majoring in physics. His early dream was to become a scientist like Newton. During this period, Yan took an interest in philosophy. Therefore, in 1964, Yan became a graduate student of philosophy at the Chinese Academy of Sciences.

On entering the CAS, he found that in the realm of science the sky was always clear, while in the realm of philosophy it was changeable: sometimes clear, sometimes cloudy. After working on dialectics of nature for almost two decades, Yan found that he had enough of this area. He discovered in 1982 that it was not a valid discipline, because people working in this area do not know the object of their research.[38] His discovery apparently is linked to his earlier training in natural sciences, which, in Yan's words, can always be tested by logic, mathematics, practice, or empirical research. This has made some scholars believe that Yan, in a sense, is close to such Enlightenment figures as Francis Bacon.[39]

How can political and economic systems be arranged in accordance with science? According to Yan, it has to be done in line with rational and realistic assumptions concerning human nature. By being rational and realistic, Yan largely means that human beings by nature are self interested and are likely to make mistakes. Starting from his "rational" approach, which regards human beings as "imperfect," he argues that this realistic assumption of human nature is the basis on which democracy should be built.[40] Yan remarked that science, the rule of law, the market, and democracy that is basically a procedure to settle matters are four treasures if China is to realize modernization.[41]

Yan's position reminds us of the political theories of some of the American Founders. Drawing a comparison with the advances made by Newtonian physics, the Founders referred to the establishment of the American system as the new science of politics which is based on the assumption that "men are ambitious, vindictive, and rapacious," as revealed by Alexander Hamilton.[42] For Yan, humans are imperfect in nature and thus a just society should be based on this assumption.[43] Not surprisingly, among political theorists, the one Yan most respected was Machiavelli.[44] For Machiavilli and Francis Bacon, a political scientist describes what people do, not what people ought to do.[45]

The relationship between empirical science and liberal politics is clear in the eyes of Yan. He said that "many of my friends who major in natural sciences have embarked on the road of dissent. This is because the more we look at the society, the more we find it irrational; the more we look at natural sciences, the more we find them rational."[46] Yan added that science can solve all kinds of problems. He feel that we should solve China's problems by way of rationality.[47] Yan's scientism was demonstrated fully here.

Based on his rationality, Yan advocated the rule of law, the principle of judicature, constitutionalism, the democratic elections, party politics, and protection of private properties.[48] He believes that a political system embodied with these principles and a market economy are the basis for democracy. "Human affairs should be handled in a depoliticized way, that is, by law and regulations. For the kind of human affairs that cannot be depoliticized, mechanism of procedure should be introduced."[49] The economic system should also be based on the assumption that man has all kinds of material needs. According to Yan, commodity production is the answer to man's needs.[50] This view point is consistent with such renowned Western liberals as F. A. Hayek and L. von Mises.[51]

Yan seems to argue such principles as humanism, democracy and freedom are shared by mankind as a whole. Yan used the term *gongtong wenhua yinsu* (common cultural factors) for these general principles.[52] These remarks are very much in line with his earlier statements saying that China should adopt the mechanisms of separation of powers and checks and balances, typical attributes of the American political system.[53]

PART III

Three Versions of Humanism

CHAPTER 6

Marxist Humanism: Wang Ruoshui

Life and Experience

Taking a Marxist humanist position, Wang Ruoshui was one of the most important theorists in the 1980s. As the former deputy Editor-in-Chief of *Renmin ribao* (*People's Daily*), Wang was lower in the party hierarchy next only to Hu Qiamu among the six intellectuals under study. His personal experience was closely connected with real world politics.

As with the case of Su Shaozhi, Wang's intellectual-political orientations have an ambiguous character. That is why Sinologists often have diverse opinions in evaluating his ideas. Wang was not only characterized in 1986 as "the most important theoretician of Deng Xiaoping's faction since 1978,"[1] but also defined as a "reformed radical Maoist."[2] On another occasion, Wang, together with Su Shaozhi, was classified as a Neo-Marxist who tried to fill the gap left by the government whose "instrumental attitude" toward reform has ignored ideological elements of social transformation.[3] In terms of the political implications, Andrew Nathan put Wang in the same position as Su by saying that Wang had in mind was not the overthrow of socialism but democratic socialism.[4] Brugger and Kelly, however, viewed Wang as making himself "sound increasingly like a champion of bourgeois constitutionalism since 1985." They also noted that in criticizing feudalism and Mao's conception of democracy, the

Marxists Wang Ruoshui and Su Shaozhi and the non-Marxist Fang Lizhi "are so close as to be virtually indistinguishable."[5]

Born in Hunan in 1926, Wang studied philosophy in Beijing University under the well known philosopher Jin Yuelin. In 1949, he quit his studies to join the revolutionaries in Yenan. A few months later, Wang entered Beijing in triumph with the People's Liberation Army. He accepted an offer in 1950 to work for *Renmin ribao* by Deng Tuo, then Editor in Chief of the party paper, who later became one of the first victims of Mao's Cultural Revolution. *Renmin ribao*, known as the *People's Daily*, is the party organ. The chiefs of the paper, who are often at the ministerial level, are directly appointed by the CCP Central Committee. Journalists who work for the party mouthpiece are highly trusted by the authorities too. It is commonly known among the Chinese journalists that Zhou Enlai once said all journalists working for Xinhua News Agency (and, of course, *Renmin ribao*) should be close to the party.[6]

In the early 1950s, Wang was engaged in the party's campaigns against Hu Shi, a devoted student of John Dewey, and Liang Shuming, a Confucian scholar who refused to renounce the Chinese cultural tradition. Basing his judgment on the familiar official Marxist notion that there were only two major schools of thought in philosophy,—one was materialism, the other was idealism—Wang listed the top crime of both theorists as idealism. The intellectual stands Wang took at that time were not very far from the Soviet official version of Marxism. He attacked Hu Shi's renunciation of the objectiveness and absoluteness of truth as idealistic. Wang also charged Hu for his refusal to accept the Marxist interpretation of history of the notions of base/superstructure and class struggle.[7] Wang attacked Liang's theory of rationality for its idealism. Liang's theory asserts that not only humans, but nature, which includes mountains and rivers, has lives too.[8]

Wang's views witnessed some changes in the early 1960s as compared with those in the 1950s. This was most clearly shown in his famous "The Philosophy of A Table" published in 1963. Wang argued that the idea of the table had to come before the actual material table.[9] This was a refutation of Lenin's reductionist allegation that insisted that human perception was a direct reflection of the world.

Wang's article was a continuation of the debate on a larger scale in China starting from 1959 to 1962 about the relations between thinking and being. This debate may be perceived as a reflection by the Chinese intellectual community of the disastrous Great Leap Forward in 1958, which was mainly caused by subjective miscalculations. The Leap apparently looked odd in the eyes of many Chinese intellectuals whose views were greatly influenced, if not shaped, by the reductionist Soviet version of Marxism, which has been the mainstream of Chinese ideology since the founding of the PRC. Chinese intellectuals, who were familiar with Lenin's photography epistemology, took great interest in participating in the debate started by Wang. Within months after the publication of his article, Wang received more than 1,500 letters and articles.[10] Mao was also very much interested in the discussion. According to Wang, Mao at that time took his side.[11]

In spite of his creativity in interpreting Marxist philosophy, Wang's political stand was not always clear and this makes an evaluation of his intellectual persuasions difficult. In January 1966, Wang wrote an article entitled "Take the Challenge of Comrade Wu Han," attacking the liberal former deputy mayor of Beijing. This article was written under the instruction from higher authorities and consequently Wang did not consider this article to be his own. According to his own accounts, Wang did this because he, like millions of other Chinese, had too much trust in Mao.[12] Nevertheless, we may find in the following that the core of his theory of political alienation was very similar to Mao's perception of the Chinese society at the start of the Cultural Revolution, that is, the servants of the people had become the masters.

His political stand at that time was also consistent with this intellectual persuasion. At the beginning of the Cultural Revolution, Wang wrote:

> this movement will have a strong impact on our lives and careers. It can even decide everything, I will be free from oppression, [this movement] has not only overthrown the rule of the representatives of the bourgeoisie, but also is training thousands of new leaders. Many officials and masters have been downed. They deserved it. More new leaders are emerging.[13]

The passages had to be written by somebody who was excited by the Cultural Revolution, and who saw a very bright future for himself because of the event. However, Wang was not left enough. He was purged anyway at the beginning of the Cultural Revolution.

With the fall of Lin Biao in 1971, the faction formed mainly by radical generals from the armed forces suffered a setback. Mao added a sentence to his former slogan: Learn from the PLA. Now, it became: The people should learn from the PLA; the PLA should also learn from the people. Here Mao played the game of "1 + (-1)" which equals zero. Only two factions were left competing for power: the radical Gang of Four and the party-bureaucracy group headed by Zhou Enlai. Zhou was appointed by Mao to run the day to day work of the country after Lin's fall. Once in charge, Zhou began to correct some of the leftist tendencies. However, the radicals would not give up. This resulted in a situation where both groups gave conflicting orders to functionaries below. As a result, Wang, who was just promoted to the leading group of *Renmin ribao*, was caught between the power struggle of the two competing factions.

On August 1, 1972, Zhou Enlai gave *Renmin ribao* instructions to criticize leftist tendencies. No sooner had the excited journalists, including Wang, managed to carry out this instruction, than Zhang Zhunqiao and Yao Wenyuan imposed restrictions on the doings of the party daily. Zhang and Yao made it clear: no criticisms were allowed against voluntarism (*jingshen wanneng, wei yizhilun*). The radical leaders then ordered the Shanghai based daily *Wen hui bao* to make their views known to the public by publishing radically oriented articles. Caught between the conflicting orders, Wang took sides with Zhou by publishing a whole page of articles criticizing leftism.[14] However, *Renmin ribao*'s move was counterattacked by *Wen hui bao*. It is interesting to note that prior to the start of the Cultural Revolution, when *Renmin ribao* and the radical *Wen hui bao* were engaged in a battle over the issue of Wu Han, Wang took the side of the radical paper by attacking the former liberal historian. This time, however, Wang took the side of the liberals. Faced with the attacks from the radicals, Wang wrote a letter to Mao informing the Chairman of the conflicting orders given by Zhou and the radicals with the hope that Mao may have agreed with Zhou. Wang did not know that it was Mao who did not want to criticize the leftist tendencies. As regards Wang's letter, the party Chairman reportedly said: the author of "Philosophy of A Table" may not be that wise.[15] As a result, Wang lost favor again. Probably at this point, he came to the conclusion that the Cultural Revolution was largely a power struggle manipulated by Mao.[16]

The death of Mao in 1976 and the subsequent fall of the radicals paved the path for the return of Wang. In 1978, he was promoted to the post of deputy Editor-in-Chief of *Renmin ribao*, the highest position he has ever held. The writings he produced after the Cultural Revolution were considerably different from those which preceded the Cultural Revolution, not to say those of the 1950s. This may have been a combined result of China's recent greater exposure to Marxist writings, including of course, *The Manuscripts*, and Wang's own personal experiences, especially during the ten-year disaster.

People As the Philosophical Starting Point

Humanism

Believing that the nature of human beings is freedom, Wang Ruoshui declares that "the starting point of Marxism is man," and that "the issue of man, which should be an important part of Marxist philosophy, has been neglected. Marxist philosophy not only tells us correct methods, but also tells us the value and meaning of life."[17] According to Wang, humanism is based on the notion that the essence of man is his free and conscious action, as was described in the *The Manuscripts*.[18] He took as central texts *The German Ideology* and *The Manuscripts* and he urged young people to study them carefully.[19] Wang argues that humanism does not belong exclusively to the bourgeoisie. Marx is also a great humanist. Wang cited Marx to support his viewpoint:

> One does not have to be very smart to realize that the materialist ideas, which include the notions that humans are born good in nature, that humans are equal in terms of intelligence, that the experience, habit and education are all powerful and that the impact exerted on humans by the external world can be powerful, that the industrialization is significant, that the human indulgence is rational, are all inevitably connected with socialism and communism.[20]

However, we have found that Marx also said that communists "do not preach morality at all, such as Skiner preaches so extensively."[21] Wang goes on to argue that Marxist humanism is a belief in opposition of two other doctrines: *shendao zhuyi* (God supremism) and *shoudao zhuyi* (inhumanism). The first holds that God is the most important. Humans should restrain their earthly desire for the sake of heavenly happiness. Inhumanism holds that humans are insignificant. They are merely the instruments of history.[22]

When challenged by Hu Qiaomu that starting from an abstract "man" was no way to explain history and that this contradicted Marx's saying that "my analytic method...does not start from man, but from the economically given period of society,"[23] Wang argued that his "man" was also concrete, who lived in concrete historical environments. Wang gave the following explanation of Marx's remarks:

> First, the man, as was criticized by Marx, was an abstract man. Marx made his idea quite clear. Second, the context in which Marx made the remarks was the method by which he analyzed the value of commodities. He was not talking about his thought as a whole system. But when I mentioned "man is the starting point of Marxism," I referred to Marxism as a system. These differences should not be overlooked.[24]

In the debate between Hu and Wang, we have found that the key difference between the two regarding the issue of humanism is that while Hu restricted the definition of humanism to the area of ethics, Wang regarded the issue to be both of ethics (*daode*) and world outlook (*shijieguan*). Hu argued that it was fine to use the term humanism in the sense of ethics. It was wrong to use it as a kind of world outlook and conception of history (*lishiguan*). Wang said that although the term world outlook has the connotation of ethics, it was more than ethics. It was also a value system. Wang argued that he was not using the word in the sense of conception of history, thus he was not against "historical materialism," which was the main charge Hu held against him.[25]

Chinese text books about Marxist philosophy have different categorizations about aspects of philosophy as compared with their Western counterparts. In the West, philosophy is generally viewed as constituted by three aspects: ontology, methodology and epistemology. In Maoist China, the word "ontology" (*bentilun*) is rarely used. Instead, the term "world outlook" (*shijieguan*) is used to describe what is often called ontology in metaphysics.[26] This is perhaps an attempt to emphasize the importance of the issue of materialism/idealism in the sense that world outlook sounds more encompassing than ontology. In the Chinese context, whether an approach is materialistic or idealistic in academic research often means revolutionary or counter-revolutionary in politics.

In the Western context, more restricted terms, such as ontology, epistemology, methodology, ethics and values, are used in philosophical discussions. Although they may use the word world outlook, which literally means to view from the perspective of the world, those who are involved in the debate often know the connotations of the phrase. But the Chinese language is noted for its vagueness and its stress on symbolic meanings. In the case of the debate between Hu and Wang, *shijieguan* (world outlook) could indeed include three connotations: ontology, ethics and value, as Wang correctly argued. Hu charged Wang for using the term in the first sense, "ontology," while Wang defended himself by saying that he was using the term "world outlook" in the second and the third senses. If that was the case, the two theorists should have shaken hands and made up by saying: "Sorry, I misunderstood you." However, we know that was not what happened. Behind this debate which was more of a play on words than anything else, there were enormous political implications.

The political implication of this humanism primarily lies with its opposition to the practice adopted by the Maoist regime that forewent people's welfare for the purpose of industrialization through rapid accumulation. For instance, the developmental strategy of the Great Leap Forward was typical spiritualism in the sense that Mao did not rely on material incentives, but on spiritual rewards to boost people's morale in production. This practice, which stresses the "ultimate interests of the people" rather than the "imminent interests of the people" continued even after Mao died. Wang's idea of humanism of course also appealed to many people who were persecuted during the previous political movements.

While the government was happy when people had certain negative feelings toward the Cultural Revolution, it did not want people to go too far, because that would undermine the legitimacy of the party. If humanism were taken as one of the main theories of Marx, historical materialism as it was would sooner or later be challenged. The party had very good reason to become concerned with this development, because it was historical materialsm that promises the ultimate success of communism and consequently the infallibility of its agent, the party, through which communism is realized.

This was shown dramatically when the party, after many misgivings, finally approved the slogan of humanism, which had been largely advocated by Wang, but at the same time expelled Wang from the party.[27] By doing so, the party hoped to give its own explanation of humanism. This irony reminds us of the similar case of Su Shaozhi, when his concept of "elementary stage socialism" was accepted by the party, but Su himself was purged as a price for it. We are also reminded of the fact that Yan Jiaqi's clear non-Marxist stand did not prevent him from coming to the center of power by joining Zhao Ziyang's brain trust. The non-academic nature of the debate on Marxist humanism was also revealed by the fact that Wang Ruoshui reportedly linked Marxist humanism to some farfetched issues such as *rencai*, or talented people, who are needed in reform. Wang said, "I believe that humanism should be connected with reform. That is to say how to realize the modernization of people. The most important for reform is the issue of talented people. Premier Zhao also said this."[28] As mentioned earlier, the conflicts between the regime and these so-called "dissidents" are more of a confrontation in real world politics, than a battle in terms of theories.[29]

Whether humans are ends or means is another aspect of the debate about humanism. Hu held that humans are both ends and means, while Wang, arguing in line with humanism, insisted that humans are only ends. Hu argued that not only the people, but the party, sometimes could be means to achieve the ultimate happiness of the people. The political implication of Hu Qiaomu's idea was that given the fact that China has significantly become more modernized and the Chinese people as a whole have become better off materially, the sacrifices, including the deaths of millions of lives in the early 1960s, were worthwhile. Furthermore, the current restrictions on the people's freedom may also be viewed as worthwhile sacrifices for the ultimate good of the people in the long term. The message is clear: although the party did make mistakes, on the whole it has managed well; the people cannot ask too much at present, especially in terms of liberty. They have to continue to entrust their lives to the party, which knows what is good for the people in the long run. Wang, however, viewed it in a different way. Wang wanted happiness for the people, especially freedom, now!

Alienation

Refuting the allegation of Hu Qiaomu that the Young Marx was immature in treating the concept of alienation as a basic category in *The Manuscripts*, Wang argued that since alienation belongs to the category of dialectics and is thus universal, it exists not only in capitalist society, but also in socialist society.[30] According to Wang, Mao also believed that alienation was universal.[31] While Wang's analysis of alienation in a philosophical sense is very exhaustive, his metaphor is quite simple:

> Take a mother for example. She loved and pampered her son, took a great deal of pains to bring him up and educate him. But when the son grew up, he became an unfilial good for nothing. He not only refused to listen to his mother, but bullied and tyrannized over her and even maltreated her. The son was no longer taking her as his mother, but regarded her as an outsider or even an enemy. The mother also realized that her son was no longer her son, but had become an alien element in the family.[32]

Echoing Zhou Yang, Wang believed that there are three kinds of alienation in China: ideological alienation, which is in the form of the personality cult; political alienation, which is the phenomenon that the officials who are supposed to be the servants of the people have become their masters; economic alienation, which refers to some unsuccessful economic projects that instead of bringing about benefits to the people have inflicted damage upon them.[33] These forms of alienation, of course, have very little to do with Marx. Apparently, the ideological alienation was targeted at Mao's personality cult, and the economic alienation could also be attributable to Mao, thus the current leadership was not offended. Although Wang fired the first shot against Mao within the party after the Cultural Revolution,[34] his political alienation sounded very much like the rationale of the Cultural Revolution. He argued that the alienated form of the "people's democratic dictatorship" emerged when communist cadres became the masters of the people, instead of public servants.[35]

Few people have denied that under capitalism there is such a phenomenon in which: 1) people are not free because they are subject to the whimsical market forces; 2) some people get more than others, sometimes not through their own labor. If this phenomenon is recognized, it really does not matter much what you call it, for instance, alienation. The existence of this phenomenon has not only been insisted on by Marxists, but also by many mainstream Western theorists. L. von Mises' view on this is that labor is hard and every entrepreneur is a speculator. One has to take risks in doing business. He praised the division of labor, which is the main source of alienation in Marxist discussions.[36] The liberal theorist Daniel Bell said that the theory of alienation "is a fresh, and even fruitful, way of making a criticism of contemporary society."[37]

However, people have disagreed with each other on two other things: 1) Is there anything wrong with this phenomenon? 2) What is the connection between this phenomenon and Karl Marx? The first question is easy to deal with. A Marxist scholar would argue that the capitalist market is the main source of alienation, while von Mises would say that the market is "a democracy in which every penny gives a right to cast a ballot."[38] Equality versus liberty is a value laden question, and consequently there would never be consensus. The second question is contentious but not for the value concerned. Bell insisted that the concept of alienation, though valid, did not belong to Marx. Many others, especially some Western Marxists, disagreed with Bell.

We do find that Marx talked about alienation on the religious, political and economic levels. In feudal society, people created God. Then they depended on God, disregarding the fact that God was actually created by them. The state and church organized religious activities. In a capitalist society, however, civil society and the state became discontinuous. Religion became people's own thing. People tended to believe that they could talk directly to God.

Marx's political alienation largely refers to the role that state plays. Monarchy is the completed expression of the alienation. That means the monarch, created by people, was supposed to represent the people. But it was not the case. The republic is the negation of alienation within alienation. That means the republic, with parliaments and so on, negates the monarchy, and supposedly is run by the people. This is untrue because: 1) although the people are sovereign, they have no power over the conditions of their lives; 2) the bureaucracy is a closed circle.[39]

Marx's economic alienation refers to the phenomenon brought about by the capitalist relations of production. Similar to the case of humanism, the Marxist theory of alienation cannot be discussed without *The Manu-scripts*:

> The activity of production—laboring—is itself alienating under a regime of commodity production. It is not intrinsically "the satisfaction of a need; it is merely a means to satisfy needs external to it. Its alien character emerges clearly in the fact that as soon as no physical or other compulsion exists, labor is shunned like the plague. . . .As a result, therefore man (the worker) only feels himself freely active in his animal functions— eating, drinking. . . in his human functions he no longer feels himself to be anything but an animal. What is animal becomes human and what is human becomes animal.[40]

Generalized markets and mass production are unique phenomena in human history, according to Marx. They appeared at a certain stage of human development. In feudal society, a self-sufficient economy was the dominant form of economy, because at that time the work unit was families. The tools they used were primitive too. With the emergence of the industrial revolution, the situation changed. The main purpose for production had changed from producing for satisfying one's own needs to producing for the purpose of exchange. In order to survive, everybody has to act in accordance with the laws of markets.

Instead of being masters of the markets created by people, according to Marx, people have become the slaves of them. Not only the workers are alienated, but the capitalists are also. People, who have feelings, emotion and so on, have become an abstract being, which can be valued by how much money they can make. With the fetishism of commodities, the relations between humans have also become an abstract one, a seller or a buyer. People were no longer generic social beings. Unlike some thinkers, who considered this alienation as natural, Marx believed that this phenomenon only existed at a certain stage of human development. As it was born, it would die. Marx was not happy with alienation, because he believed it de-humanized mankind. In addition, because of the fact that both workers and capitalists had to enter the relations determined by the markets, surplus value appeared. Workers are, accordingly, exploited.[41] Apparently Marx's alienation on the three levels of religion, politics and economics has very little to do with alienation as defined by Wang Ruoshui.

Probably because of this unclear relationship between Marx's aliena-tion and his own, Wang might have realized that by treating the concept of alienation in this way, he was probably being "metaphysical" in that he rigidly applied the law of the negation of negation (*fouding zhi fouding guiliu*) in dialectics.[42] Nevertheless, Wang saw the positive aspect of being metaphysical. Citing Engels' *Anti-Duhring*, Wang says that as a way of thinking, even metaphysics could be useful.[43] Regardless of the Engels' connection,[44] Wang's move carried extremely important political connotation, because, in the Chinese context, both the dichotomy of materialism/idealism and the dichotomy of dialectics/metaphysics could serve as the touchstone of revolutionary and counterrevolutionary.

Application of Humanistic Philosophy

It has been found that the relations between Wang's theories of humanism and alienation and Marx are ambiguous. Now, we want to find out how his theories relate to the various political alternatives that China has chosen in the past, or may want to choose in the future. This situation is demonstrated clearly in Wang's positions on the four forms of democracy that China has experienced, or is likely to follow: the Confucian democracy of rule for the people, the Maoist Big Democracy of the Cultural Revolution, the Stalinist democracy of the people's democratic dictatorship, and, as a possible choice for China's near future, Western liberal democracy. Although he believes that in all these democracies, alienation is part of life and humans are not free, Wang favors some and condemns the others. He justifies his position by interpreting Marxism in an intriguing way.

Wang first condemned the Confucian "rule for the people." He said if "rule for the people" is democracy, then a feudal emperor also can do it.[45] Wang criticizes Li Zehou's seeming compliment of China's Confucian tradition,

> The central notions of Confucianism are "*li*" (ritual) and "*ren*" (benevolence). Li Zehou says that "*li*" is a tribal political system based on blood connections and hierarchy which are exterior modes. Confucius's conversion of "*li*" to "*ren*" is to turn the exterior norms into man's inner demands. The rigid, forced norms are turned into man's conscious idea. "As a result, man's social and interactive nature is stressed: the order, unity, helping each other, cooperation among the somebodies and the nobodies, old and young in the tribes." He feels that "*ren*" emphasizes the initiatives and independence of the individuals and is the awakening of human self consciousness. This would enable man to realize his position in the universe, his value and the meaning of life. This is a great contribution by Confucius to the Chinese people. Li's view point is not persuasive.[46]

Although he may have shared with Marx in condemning autocracy,[47] Wang seemed to have misinterpreted Li's view on this, because Li made it explicit that the respect of one's elders and filial piety in modern society should no longer be based on economic and political dependence as was the case in feudal society, but on a voluntary basis.[48]

In addition, Confucianism may not be as anti-human as Wang believed. For instance, recent studies by Tu Wei-ming have found that some elements which were attributed to Confucianism may be misleading. The notion of inequality in Confucianism is well known. But Tu interprets the Confucian texts in different ways. Tu points out that Confucianism also believes that "wife is an equal of the husband" (*qizhe qiye*). Tu goes on to say that Mencius's famous saying that "those who use their mind rule, those who use their hands are ruled" can be interpreted differently. It could mean division of labor.[49]

In condemning the Stalinist system, which was established in China in the early 1950s, Wang Ruoshui argued that this power structure leads to the over-concentration of power in the hands of some individuals, the arbitrary rule of some people, and a personality cult.[50] Wang argued, "It's true that Marx spoke of the proletarian dictatorship. But this meant only that the proletariat would have a complete hold on power, not that it would behave in a dictatorial manner. In fact, there should not necessarily be only one party to represent the proletariat in power."[51] This Stalinist democracy and the Confucian rule for the people are actually what Wang term political alienation.

On the "Big Democracy" of the Cultural Revolution, Wang believed that the ten-year disaster was a result of Mao's personality cult.[52] Wang held that the important origins of this error are to be found in his feudal small farm mentality, monarchical mentality and autocratic style of governing.[53] The root of the ten-year disaster is what Wang terms the ideological alienation.

How can China's political system be rebuilt that not only can ensure humanistic values but also be free from various forms of alienation? In other words, what is China's democracy in the future as envisioned by Wang? First, Wang argued that democracy is a state system (*guojia zhidu*). He said:

> Democracy is nothing more than that people have the rights to elect, criticize and exercise surveillance over the government and to manage the country. There are many demonstrations and press criticism of the government in such democratic countries as Britain, France, and the United States. But the political situation in these countries is stable.[54]

How, then, do we interpret the above seemingly casual remarks made by Wang who alleged that the United States, Britain and France are democracies? Is it fair to assume from these sporadic statements that the Western liberal democracy is what is envisioned by Wang as China's future democracy? I think there are good reasons to believe so, because Wang has used Marx's remarks to justify stage theory.

Citing remarks by Marx from his preface to *Critique of Political Economy*, Wang stated that the further back we trace humans into history, the less freedom of the people we would find. Originally, humans belonged to families and tribes. Then it was the various kinds of communes. Only with the emergence of civil society from the 16th century did independent individuals begin to exist. The era in which these individuals exist is the era of capitalism.[55] Wang continued to argue that China now is in the transitional period from pre-capitalist society to capitalist society. Therefore, it is the time for *"Keli fuji"* (to restrain the old ethics and restore one's own individuality) not *"Keji fuli"* (to restrain oneself in order to restore the virtues of the Zhou Dynasty).[56]

Is the political system as envisioned by Wang free from alienation? No. However, Wang argued that although commodity production and the state socialism of China both produce alienation, the Chinese should prefer the former at present. Why is the alienation of commodity production any better than the alienation of state socialism? According to Wang, China is now at a stage of transition from pre-capitalist to capitalist society. Therefore, the alienation of commodity production "is the price we have to pay for social progress."[57] Is socialism the next stage of history? In the foreseeable future, Wang argued, it is impossible to eliminate commodity production and private ownership.[58] Therefore, socialism has comfortably been postponed into an indefinite remote future.

How is Wang's argument related to Marxism? Here, apparently Wang resorted to the economic determinist Marxist conception of history to justify China's current capitalist deveropment. This is a departure from his better known "The Philosophy of A Table" epistemology which is a departure from orthodox Marxist philosphy.

CHAPTER 7

Confucianist Humanism: Li Zehou

Life and Experience

Intellectually, Li shares views with Confucius on some crucial issues, although he has never advocated a total revival of Confucianism. These include the Confucian ontological starting point of focusing on people, especially the notion of "*ren*" (benevolence), which, could mean mutual love. In terms of methodology and epistemology, he believes that direct perception through the senses, a feature of the Chinese cognitive tradition, is useful in getting truth. Li believes beauty leads to truth (*yi mei qi zhen*). He thus rejects both positivism and the post-modernist emphasis on discursive knowledge. Caught in the dichotomy of personal choice as insisted on, for example by Sartre, and collective freedom, he endorses the latter. His notion of benevolence lies in beauty (*yi mei chu shan*) holds that whether free choice and free will are worthwhile for human pursuit depends on to what extent they suit "*shan*" (benevolence), that is, human's concrete existence and development as a whole. Ironically, although he has always tried to avoid real world politics with the exception of his brief involvement during the 1989 Beijing Spring, Li's ideas have been considered by Lin Min as having "become the philosophical premises underlying Deng's modernization programme."[1]

Li Zehou was born in Hankou, Hubei Province, in 1930.[2] He lost his post-office clerk father when he was very young and, before he reached adulthood, his beloved mother died too. In addition to this hard personal life, Li was also immersed in the social turbulence of the mid-forties when he was a teenager. At that time, China was torn by the Anti-Japanese War and the Civil War. The people lived in an abyss of misery. This had a profound impact on his personality, which he describes as melancholy, and on his aesthetics-philosophy career. Li's heros were then, not surprisingly, Lu Xun who saw the world with cold anger and Bing Xin (Xie Bingxin) who saw the world with pure love and innocence. However, Marxism influenced him the most, according to his own accounts.

Li became a student of philosophy at the Beijing University in 1950. Incidentally, all of the three main figures studied in this book who have a humanistic approach were Beijing University philosophy students. This situation parallels the fact that all of the three main figures in this study who start from a scientific position were students of either of natural sciences—such as Hu Qiaomu in physics and Jin Guantao in chemistry, or a discipline in social science which is known for its scientific accuracy, such as Su Shaozhi in economics. This phenomenon confirms Li's own observation: one's research method is closely related with his or her personality and experience in the past.

After college, Li became a researcher at the Institute of Philosophy and Social Sciences, Chinese Academy of Sciences. During the Cultural Revolution, Li, like many other intellectuals, spent much time doing manual labor. According to his own accounts, he probably spent more time doing manual labor than any other person in his work unit. This may have been due perhaps to the jealousy of his colleagues; at age 28, Li had published his book on Kang Youwei and Liang Qichao with one of China's best publishing houses, Shanghai renmin chubanshe. He also had many other good publications.

Intellectually, Li is considered to be moderate in advocating Chinese tradition. Contemporary Chinese intellectuals can be divided into three groups regarding their attitudes towards the Chinese cultural tradition: 1) those who advocate the restoration of Confucianism (*ruxue fuxing*); 2) those who are for the idea that in order to inherit the Chinese tradition, one has to criticize it first (*pipan de jicheng*); 3) those who favor the notion of Western ideas as the essence, Chinese ideas as function (*xi ti zhong yong*).[3] Li belongs to the third group.

The first group is generally referred to as the New Confucianism group. In a narrow sense, this group refers to those who attended the conference Contemporary New Confucianism (*dangdai xinrujia*) sponsored by *China Herald* (*Zhongguo luntan*) in Taibei in 1982. Key figures included Xiong Shili, Liang Shuming, Tang Junyi, Xu Fuguan, and Mo Zongsan. Although they did not attend the conference, Fang Dongmei, Qian Mu and Feng Youlan also belong to this group.[4] Apparently, the core members of this group are overseas Chinese scholars, especially those who are based in Hong Kong and Taiwan. Although Feng Youlan and Liang Shuming are from mainland China, their influence is mainly overseas. Feng was not active during the post-Mao period, probably due to his advanced age, or to his support of the Gang of Four during the Maoist era, or to both. Most of Liang's books were banned during Maoist period, thanks to his confrontation with the party Chairman in 1953. Some of his books were still banned after Mao died. Consequently, the views of this group are not taken to be a main intellectual trend on mainland China.

The second attitude is endorsed by the majority of Chinese intellectuals, as represented by the March Towards the Future group discussed in Chapter Five and the Culture: China and the World group which will be discussed in the next chapter.

Li Zehou is closer to the third group, the Chinese Academy of Culture. This group differs from the New Confucianism group in some important ways: 1) To study Confucius and Confucianism is not equal to advocating Confucianism as a school of thought. Confucianism is a way of knowing Chineseness which has both its positive and negative aspects. 2) National character has to be understood in a historical sense, not in an abstract sense. 3) Confucianism is not just a way of self cultivation as maintained by Liang, but a philosophy of human relationships with the self at the center. 4) "*Zhong ti xi yong,*" which means "Chinese learning as the substance or essence, Western learning for functions" should be replaced by "*xi ti zhong yong*" which means the integration of modernity from the West and the Chinese reality, which includes Confucianism. 5) China's current enlightenment should be in the tradition of the May Fourth Movement as demonstrated in the ideas of Chen Duxiu, Lu Xun and Hu Shi.[5]

Although he was not actively involved in politics during both the Maoist era and the post-Mao era, Li was not a pure scholar who does scholarship for its own sake. As a demonstration of his concern for current affairs of the country, Li says: "I would neither write the kind of books that could have been written 50 years ago, nor would I write the kind of books that could be written 50 years in the future."[6] His works are often hastily done without being based on solid academic grounds. His research areas are very broad, including not only Chinese intellectual history, aesthetics, but also Western intellectual history.

People As the Philosophical Starting Point

For Li Zehou, the "instrumental-social" aspect of ontology is more essential than the "cultural-psychological" one in understanding the world.[6] Li's position may or may not be taken on the ground of the orthodox Marxist notion that social being is more important than social consciousness. For instance, he criticized *Anti-Dühring* by Engels for its frameworking Marxism into a sort of metaphysic and doctrine.[8] This is a standard position by Western Marxists in separating Marx from Engels and in regarding *Anti-Dühring* as the main effort in creating the so-called Marxist philosophy of dialectical materialism. We don't know for sure whether this is a change of mind on behalf of Li regarding orthodox Marxism, because as late as 1978 he still remained with the orthodox Marxist notion that "political orientation is rooted in economics."[9]

Nevertheless, Li seems to have focused on the cultural-psychological aspect in his concrete studies, instead of the more essential instrumental-social aspect of ontology. He says that this is because these two aspects are closely connected. In addition, psychological and cultural problems could be more damaging to people than political and economic ones under certain circumstances. Such is the case in many industrialized countries in the West.[10] Here, Li is apparently referring to such social problems as drugs, prostitution, etc. It may also be that the selection of one's method is connected with one's personality and experience. In a discussion of methodology, he notes that researchers should choose their own methods in accordance with not only the studied object, but also one's own situation, including his personality, etc. [11]

Li's attitude in this regard may look strange in the eyes of a Western intellectual who is used to the individualistic notion that one has to believe that his or her own research is the most important on earth. They may wonder if the cultural-psychological aspect of society is not as important as the instrumental-social one, as Li believes, why does he still focus on it? The common explanation that Li is still very much influenced by Marxism may not be a plausible one, as we mentioned just now that Li questioned the orthodox Marxist philosophy. A Westerner may also find perplexing another aspect of Li's attitude: Although Li's general tone about the Chinese cultural tradition is positive, as we will find later, he always denies the charge that he is advocating the revitalization of Confucianism and in dealing with concrete social problems, he sometimes departs from his philosophical starting point.

There are three dimensions in what Li calls "subjectivity human structure" (*zhutixing renxing jiegou*), a notion similar to philosophy in general terms: 1) the structure of human intellect; 2) the structure of human will; 3) the structure of aesthetics. Li analyzes these structures in terms of aesthetics. Therefore, the structure of human intellect becomes "beauty leads to truth" (*yi mei qi zhen*); the structure of human will becomes the notion that "benevolence lies in beauty" (*yi mei chu shan*); the structure of aesthetics becomes "aesthetic feelings" (*shen mei kuai gan*).[12] We focus on the first two structures, because they are the most relevant to our discussion.

The Structure of Human Intellect

What Li calls the structure of human intellect is apparently epistemology and methodology in Western philosophical terms. Li believes that methodology has to be eclectic, because no single method alone can lead to truth. For instance, Li was one of the first to support Jin Guantao's experiment in applying systems theory to the study of history, although he takes a humanistic philosophical position in a general sense. In the study of aesthetics, Li also encourages a more positivistic approach. However, he does not believe that this positivistic approach would solve all the problems. For instance, systems theory lacks a historical dimension. In this respect, modern hermeneutics is a better method.[13]

Nevertheless, Li gives more emphasis on the Chinese way of thinking, especially when he talks about philosophy in a general sense. This position is very conspicuous in the current Chinese context where iconoclasm is more popular. For Li, the Chinese way of thinking can be described as practical rationality (*shi yong li xing*). This practical rationality is not materialism. Most of China's ancient great thinkers such as Confucius, Mencius and Lao Tze, were not materialists. Their methodology was a kind of dialectics which is different from the term in the Western sense. Western dialectics is a dialectics of concepts, while the Chinese dialectics is a dialectics of action. The Chinese dialectics, which is mainly used in warfare, has three features: 1) Practical rationality which is against voluntarism or the supernatural; 2) Pros and cons have to be weighed in terms of the notion that one is divided into two; 3) Thinking has to be conducted in terms of action and implementation [of theories].[14]

We realize that in terms of methodology, empiricism rather than Hegelian dialectics is the mainstream in the Western way of thinking. Therefore, a more essential contrast is between Western empiricism and the Chinese way of thinking. It is not between Western dialectics and Chinese dialectics. This more essential contrast is demonstrated in Li's following remarks:

in the Chinese tradition, the mainstream thinking is characterized
by understanding through the senses so as to reach a state of the
unity of nature and man. . .Western empiricism. . .has produced
such thinkers as Hume and Popper. However, these thinkers lack
a sort of human thrust as possessed by Hegel and Heidegger who
thus have a better grasp of the sense of human existence. . . . Real
creative thinking is obtained neither from inductions, nor from
deductions of some common laws. It is a kind of free imagination
and mastery directly through the senses. This kind of thinking
can be found in Zhuang Zi and *zen*. They rely on neither logic,
nor language.[15]

Li's observation of this Chinese epistemology is generally acknowledged. This kind of thinking is even reflected in literature. In the most
famous Chinese novel, *The Dream of the Red Mansion (Hong lou meng)*,
truth becomes fiction when the fiction is true; real becomes not-real where
the unreal is real.

In this comparison, Li seems to regard the Chinese way of thinking
as more essential. He shares with Thomas Kuhn in believing that there
may be a connection between artistic expression and truth. Kuhn points
out the interesting phenomenon that many good scientists in the early
years of their career could not decide whether to become musicians or
scientists. Kuhn says that the things embodied in aesthetics and arts could
be the keys to scientific discoveries.[16] It isn't that the problem is one of
deciding whether to be a musician or a scientist. It is rather that aesthetic
criteria do enter into theory-choice. Thus matters of simplicity always
enter. Or more generally, it is an error to bifurcate the scientific and the
aesthetic—as empiricist versions of science always do. Li believes that:
beauty may lead to truth. He says:

In science, the best laws are often the most beautiful. Scientists
often say "How beautiful this law is!" A well known scientist
says that if he has to choose between two kinds of theories, one
is more beautiful, the other is more in accordance with experiments, he would rather choose the former. This is not a joke.
It is a matter of methodology. . . .How wonderful would that
be if the Chinese traditionar notion of the unity between man
and nature is transformed by Marxist philosophy of practice, to
eliminate the mystical and negative aspects, and is applied to
aesthetics![17]

Li reinforces his argument by saying that Zhuang Zi's way of thinking
is not untrue, because contemporary writers often share the experience

described by Zhuang Zi when truth may come in the form of a flash of thought. The structure of arts may be consistent with the structure of life. The Confucian imagination may not be untrue.[18] During the 1923 debate on science, although he believes that neither of the two sides, those who advocated "science" and those who advocated "metaphysics," had any novel philosophical notions, Li regarded the "metaphysicians" as more profound.[19] In addition, he rejects the post-modernist notion that language is the key to understanding the world.[20]

However, Li is not sure about the exact nature of the so called "free perception through the senses" which is the essence of the notion "beauty leads to truth."[21] In other words, if the Chinese way of thinking can be called scientific, since it could lead to truth in one way or another, Li does not know what this science is. This reminds us of the remark made by Liu Qingfeng when she says that nowadays, nobody knows what science is.

Although he is very specific about the good aspects of the Chinese way of thinking, Li is not that specific about its demerits. He mentions in passing that the Chinese way of thinking has been a hindrance in the country's modernization drive. Li says, echoing Liu Qingfeng, that the factors that have caused the backwardness of the development of science and technology in modern times include the Chinese way of thinking, narrow empiricism. The reader is left with a sense of dissatisfaction because of Li's generality on this important issue.

The Structure of Human Will

The so-called structure of human will, which is also what Li calls benevolence lies in beauty (*yi mei chu shan*) is similar to ontology in the Western terms. Although he starts from people philosophically, Li has tried to distinguish himself from those who advocated Marxist humanism. He does not believe that the starting point of Marxism is man, as Wang Ruoshui maintains. Although he recognizes the usefulness of Marxist humanist discussions in terms of social effect, Li refuses to endorse Marxist humanism as a sound theory. Nevertheless, Li maintains that those who attacked Marxist humanism, as Hu Qiaomu did, were bad not only in terms of theory, but also in terms of social effect.[23]

Li says that whether free choice and free will are worthwhile for human pursuit depends on to what extent they suit "*shan*" (benevolence), human's concrete existence and development as a whole.[24] This *shan* is similar to the word *ren*, which appears more than any other word in the book *Lun yu* (*The Analects*). *Ren* (humane-ness, benevolence, kindness) lies at the very core of Confucius's thought.[25] Although Li realizes the ambiguous nature of the Confucian concept *ren*, which could either mean "mutual love" (*ren zhe ai ren*), or "to restore the rituals and ethics of the Zhou Dynasty" (*keji fuli*), he seems to stress the former definition. Li believes that Confucianism centers on mutual human love. This could be revealed by the Chinese character *ren*, which is two people. According to Li, *ren* is world outlook.[26]

Li says that in *ren* "there is not only democratic character, but also humanistic character."[27] Li's identification of some elements in the Chinese tradition as "humanistic" has been consistent. He put forward this view-point as early as 1958 when he published his first book.[28] Li also cites Mencius as saying, " '*ren*' means humans" (*ren zhe, ren ye*).[29] Specifically, humane-ness (*ren*) means that "because you wish to be edified yourself, edify others; because you desire your goals to be met, let others' goals be met."[30] "Do not visit on others what you do not wish for yourself."[31]

In the Chinese tradition, Li says that human's supreme state of spirituality is in the form of aesthetics. Chinese politics is the politics of ethics. Beauty (*mei*) and benevolence (*shan* or *ren*) are not separated.[32] This is not far from the argument that Chinese humanism is a religion of the good and the beautiful.[33] Li argues that it is precisely because of this aesthetic state, free choice and ethics can be realized in disregard of one's interests and even lives.[34] On Chinese humanism, Li says:

> Chinese humanism can be traced to Confucius and Mencius and thus is different from Western humanism which is a product of the Renaissance. In an attempt to free man from the yoke of the church in the Middle Ages, Western humanism starts from the individuals and stresses the independence and freedom of man. Chinese humanism in contrast emphasizes mutual love and cooperation, helping each other.[35]

Apparently, Li emphasizes some aspects of Confucianism in disregard of the others, because there is no consensus regarding the nature of human beings in the Confucian tradition. For instance, Xun Kuang, an important figure in Confucianism is very pessimistic about human nature. Xun believes that "Man is evil in nature. The goodness in behavior is just a disguise," thus law should be enforced.[36] Tu Wei-ming also rejects the notion that in Confucianism altruism is the basis on which human relations should be conducted. It is a holistic view point that regards human relations as centering on the self. These human relations are the philosophical basis for collective unity.[37]

In practice, we also find this kind of ambiguity in China's tradition. On the one hand, there is certainly much truth in the humanistic aspect of the Chinese tradition. For instance, Westerners have always been amazed by the efforts taken by the people under the leadership of the emperors to sustain a better living of themselves. Two American political scientists have noted:

> Perhaps the most impressive example of tyrannical regime that succeeded in creating sustained social and economic progress comes not from Europe, but from China. . . . Particularly note-worthy, in the eyes of many Western observers, was the vast network of dikes, irrigation ditches, and waterways that criss-crossed the immense Chinese realm. This hydraulic system repre-sented a signal achievement, exceeding in scale and scope any public-works construction that governments in pre-modern Europe, even at the height of the Roman Empire, had undertaken. What kind of a civilization could build public works on such a stupendous scale?[38]

However, the other side of the picture is not that impressive. The inside stories of ancient China's courts, as the famous *Twenty-Four Histories (er shi si shi)* records, may well reveal that the ruthlessness of power struggles can hardly support the notion that people are good in nature. The *Twenty-Four Histories* has exerted such a tremendous influence on China's politics that the late Mao was said to have spent more time on it than he did on other books.[39]

The paradoxical elements in China's tradition can also be seen in the notion of equality, since no democratic theories can be discussed without it. On the one hand, man and women were not equal in feudal China. A typical wife in feudal China did not have her name. She was identified by putting together the surnames of her husband and that of her father. The famous classic *The Romance of Three Kingdoms (san guo yan yi)* shows the status of women in ancient Chinese society. One day, Liu Bei, who later became the lord of Shu, had a friend visit him. Lacking good food to entertain his friend, Liu killed one of his wives to make a good meal out of her flesh to feed his friend. On the other hand, however, the existence of inequality may not be attributed to Confucius. As mentioned previously, the inequality between husband and wife may not be attributed to Confucius, because Confucianism also believes *qi zhe qi ye*, which means the wife is the equal of the husband.

Another aspect of Chinese humanism, according to Li, is mutual love and cooperation among people. In the Western Enlightenment tradition, Li says, what distinguishes man from animals is that man has reasoning power; in the Confucian tradition, what distinguishes man from animals is that they are able to form groups and consequently ethics becomes the distinction between man and animals.[40] Li's point is in accordance with the views of Xun Kuang:

> Water and fire have either but no vitality; the grass and the trees have vitality but no capacity for knowledge; the fowl in the air and the beast of the field have the capacity for knowledge but no moral principle; Man, on the other hand, has either, vitality, the capacity for knowledge, and also moral principle, that is why Man is, of all things under the sun, the most valuable. . . . [Man] hath no brawn to match the oxen, or the swiftness of feet to match the horses; yet, the oxen and horse are used in the service of Man. Why? Because man has the capacity to [act and think as a] group, while the animals do not have the capacity to do so.[41]

For Li, this social character of human nature by no means negates individuality. He seems to disagree with the common perception that although the Chinese traditional humanism emphasizes the social aspect of people, it has the deficiency of neglecting the natural aspect which gives rise to individualism. That is, although Chinese traditional humanism did help to contribute to the welfare of the people from time to time, man's individuality was not stressed. Li points out that what Lu Xun called "the backbone of China" has to do with Confucius.[42] Li therefore disagrees with the common perception that Confucian official-scholars had no integrity because, with their minds being poisoned by the Confucian classics and their tendency for bureaucratic careerism, they had no guts to stand for justice. Li argues that the fact that those who devoted their lives to the salvation of the country is precisely because of the good influence of Confucianism.

Application of Humanistic Philosophy

How to treat China's tradition and Western civilization in the modern and contemporary contexts is largely a political question, and quite often, it is reflected in the century-long debate about the *ti* and *yong*. The character *ti* in Chinese can be translated into essence or fundamental principles, while the character of *yong* can be translated into function or mundane matters. China's modernization process in the past 150 years has been characterized mainly by the debate on whether to learn from the West both *ti* and *yong*, or focusing on *yong* marginalizing *ti*, or vice versa, or reject both of them. That is, should there be both Western learning of fundamental principles and mundane affairs, or neither, or one but not the other?

In the late nineteenth century, when the Qing Dynasty was faced with constant foreign invasions, some members of the ruling elites were still totally against modernization. Wo-jen, the Grand Secretary of the Qing Dynasty maintained, "Only people of loyalty and sincerity can help us to subdue foreigners and only people with propriety and righteousness can help us to strengthen ourselves."[43] Those who held the opposite views promoted reform in not only military and industrial areas but also in political systems and ideas. For instance, Yen Fu emphasized social equality, freedom of thought and speech. He called for equality between the emperor and his subjects, father and son, husband and wife and men and women. These radicals were not as influential as the third group headed by Zhang Zhidong, a governor. Zhang theorized the practice of defending China's traditional order through learning foreign technology and invented the policy of *zhong ti xi yong*, or Chinese learning for essence and foreign learning for functions.

What happened after the collapse of the Qing Dynasty in 1911 was a bit different. There were few cries for total rejection of modernization. Nobody was against learning foreign science and technology any longer. The criticisms of traditional Chinese culture became more open and disputes about how to become modernized gained momentum. A central figure in the push for wholesale westernization was Hu Shi, who was not only known for his iconoclastic stand but also for his embrace of science.[44]

The faction which had promoted Chinese learning for substance, western learning for functions also found its counterpart in this period, though in a slightly different manner. The central idea of this group was contained in a widely circulated manifesto, *Reconstruction of Civilization On a Chinese Base*, issued on January 10, 1935 by ten distinguished professors, including Sa Meng-wu, T'ao Hsi-sheng and Ho Ping-sheng. These professors maintained that China is China; it has its own uniqueness. It is useless either to praise or criticize the traditional values. To adopt western civilization is necessary, but the adoption should be based on the needs of present-day China. Because of this, the Chinese first regarded the term modernization as only referring to technology. The term modernization, or *xian dai hua* in Chinese, was first introduced in the 1930s. An article entitled "Problems of China's Modernization" carried by *Ta Kung Pao* in 1936, points out that modernization mainly refers to science, technology and industrial advances.[45]

Li Zehou summarizes his views on the Chinese modernization as *xi ti zhong yong*, which, although sounds like the opposite of Zhang

Zhidong's *zhong ti xi yong*, has special meanings. The notion of *xi ti zhong yong* was first put forward by Chinese historian Li Shu. Li gives special meanings to this notion. Li's *ti* does not mean Chinese learning for fundamental principles. Nor does his *yong* mean Western learning for mundane affairs. According to Li, he adopted this usage because everybody in China knows Zhang's *zhong ti xi yong* and that by reversing the order of the phrase, he wants to be different.

For Li, *ti* refers to modernity in general which not only includes social existence, modern productive modes and life mode, but also ontological consciousness which includes modern understandings of science and technology, politics, economics and culture. This modernity comes from the West. *Yong* refers to adaptation of these modern things. Adaptation means that some of the modern things suit China's needs, and some do not. Even as regards those modern things that fit China, one still has to consider how to implement them under China's conditions.[46]

Li's argument is a departure from those New Confucianists, who want to see a revival of Confucianism in modern times. This is confirmed by Li's stand that although contemporary Chinese enlightenment should be in the May Fourth Movement, the iconoclasm which was demonstrated during the movement has to be criticized:

> Nevertheless, can the iconoclasm and total Westernization in the May Fourth solve the problem [of China]? It is true that we have to continue the May Fourth tradition. But we cannot repeat what we did during the May Fourth Movement; our intellectual level has to surpass it. This is also true in terms of our attitudes towards the tradition. We should not repeat what we did during the May Fourth Movement: to simply throw our tradition away. We should creatively transform tradition.[47]

However, one finds it difficult to relate his interpretation of *ti* and *yong* to his earlier discussions about Chinese traditional philosophy. As we have seen, Li was more sympathetic with China's cultural tradition than with that of the West. In addition, he refuses to share the belief that China's problems are rooted in the country's tradition.[48] But this interpretation about *ti* and *yong* does not seem to carry the same tone. Therefore, Li's application of his humanistic philosophy has to be understood in a concrete manner, that is, to understand his positions on specific issues.

On the one hand, Li criticizes the phenomenon of alienation, which goes hand-in-hand with the material wealth in the West. But he is not specific as to what has caused this alienation, capitalist relations of production, as Marx claimed, or something else. For Li, *ren* could help solve the problem of alienation in the West. Nevertheless, Li also insists that Confucian ethic-purism which is based on the notion that man is good in nature is no longer suitable for modern society.[51]

Although in 1986 he claimed that Marxism was good, he made it explicit in 1993 that he did not believe in the realization of international communism. In addition, Li seems to suggest that the European Community may be a better future of the world than communism.[52] Is this the reason that Li's notion of *xi ti zhong yong* was criticized by the party paper *Renmin ribao* after the 1989 Tiananmen crackdown?[53]

Li has refrained himself from criticizing the economic and political systems of the West. On the contrary, he shares similarities with Su Shaozhi in believing that China has suffered from an insufficient development of capitalism, not only in the sphere of economics, but also in the spheres of politics and culture.[54] This situation was caused by the fact that in modern Chinese history, the issue of the salvation of China has constantly been viewed as more important than enlightenment, the other issue of the May Fourth Movement (*jiuwang yadao qimeng*).[55] This is as much as to say that the introduction of Marxism which later became the dominant ideology of the country was not equal to enlightenment and the Chinese people have been living in darkness since the founding of the People's Republic. Li's position in this regard is more than enough to make the ruler to regard him as dangerous.

Even on the intellectual level, ambiguity has been detected. On the one hand, Li insists that "real creative thinking is obtained neither from inductions, nor from deductions of some 'common laws,' "[56] as was presented previously. On the other hand, he believes that only on the basis of incorporating and introducing the strict logical analysis and deduction of the West, can we creatively transform our traditional way of thinking.[57] Although these two positions may not be in contradiction, the shift of emphasis is obvious. Not surprisingly, Li made the first remark when talking about philosophy in general. He made the second remark when he was commenting on how to do things in contemporary China.

Li does not view himself as in line with the Western critical humanists. In fact, Li's hostility to Western Marxism, especially the Frankfurt School, is of more than usual significance. His view, in brief, is that Western Marxism is characterized by the same voluntarism and ethical purism which was a feature of the extreme leftism of the Cultural Revolution. Li says, "The failure of Mao Zedong in his later years may illustrate some of the problems embodied in the thinking of Western Marxism."[58]

Li envisions the future of the world in very general terms. For Li, the nineteenth century was a century when philosophy focused on overall human existence; the twentieth century is a century when philosophy focused on language; the twenty-first century will be one when increasing attention will be focused on genetic engineering, education, psychology and physiology.[59]

In fact, being too general in style has been characteristic of Li's writings. One of the most significant omissions is that Li does not tell us systematically which aspects of the Chinese tradition, especially what he calls the "democratic character and humanist character"[60] as embodied in Confucianism, fit China in modern times. In other words, it is not clear how in a concrete sense would Li want to realize his *yi mei chu shan*, or benevolence lies in beauty, in China's real situation. As claimed by Li himself, these shortcomings in his writings may be due to his scholarly style. That is to say, Li sees that every approach has its limitations, including his own. Any researcher chooses the method not only because it may suit the studied subject, but also his or her personality. We remember that although Li believes that social existence is more important than social consciousness, he focuses on the latter.

However, Li's ignoring some specific but vitally important points in his study may have been caused not only by his personal idiosyncrasies, but also by other factors. This is because Li is not the only one who overlooks questions of how to institutionalize now what he believes to be the good aspects of Confucianism. It may be called "a common disease."[61] It is always easier to identify some good things in China's past, especially in view of the fact that China has such a long history. It is also not hard to say that we could use some of these things in modern times. Even Mao Zedong acknowledged the usefulness of *gu wei jin yong*, or we should creatively adapt our ancient tradition for today's use. It is difficult, however, to lay out how to institutionalize these good things in modern times. This is partly because the humanistic aspects in Confucianism have historically been closely related to the authoritarian aspects.

The problem of being a proponent of the Chinese cultural tradition is that it has enormous political value that can be exploited by politicians of one kind or another. The authoritarian aspect of the Chinese tradition can be used to argue for power monopoly. As heirs to the May Fourth tradition, the Chinese intellectual community, and to a lesser degree, the Chinese people, have in general adopted a negative view of the Chinese cultural-political tradition. The tragedy of the Chinese tradition is that it is both loved and hated for the wrong reasons. That is why it has been suggested that thoughtful scholars should be cautious about advocating a renewal of traditional Chinese culture given the current situation in China.[62]

Some people indeed have made attempts to apply in a concrete way China's authoritarian-humanistic tradition to the country's current reality.

He Xin, born in 1949 and who became one of the most vocal spokesmen for the conservatives after the 1989 crackdown, was one of them. Echoing Hu Qiaomu, He Xin believes that the people are not wise enough to know their own interests.[63] For the non-intellectuals and the majority of the masses, what they care more are daily life and security, according to He Xin. The standard used by these people to judge the government is not whether there is the American-style freedom and democracy, but social security, employment, opportunities for existence and development.[64]

For He, the starting point to reform the current Chinese political system should be China's ancient democratic tradition, that is, rule for the people. He writes:

> The mechanisms for democracy existed in China's tradition. Before Qin (221 BC), clan democracy and aristocratic democracy were once practiced. In the dynastic periods afterwards, some special systems, aimed at restraining the absolute monarchical power, such as separation of power between the monarchy and the ministers and extending the participation to the common people, were practiced from time to time. For instance, the *chanrang* system, practiced before recorded history, in which the monarchs passed power to another man of merits and prestige without considering his birth, was an attempt to peacefully transfer the monarchical power. In some dynasties, the monarchs were even figureheads, while the ministers were really in charge. Although different from that of the West, China's ancient political and legal systems had a democratic tradition.[65]

He's advocating of the *chanrang* system is on shaky ground. Practiced before China had recorded history, this story was passed to later generations by word of mouth. Yao, Shun, Yu, three of China's earliest monarchs were involved in this system. At Yao's retirement from the throne, he passed the crown to Shu, who was prestigious among the people for his service. When Shu retired, he passed it to Yu, who won his respect from the people by controlling disastrous floods. However, when Yu retired, he passed the crown to his son, whose merits were not clear, thus the *chanrang* system stopped. If this system can be called democratic, what if the monarch refused to pass the power to a good successor, but gave the post to his son, as Yu actually did?

He's argument for the dynastic separation of power is also open to dispute. It is true that sometimes, especially when the emperor was weak or young, the power was in the hands of other people, such as eunuches or other members of the royal family. But as argued convincingly by Jin Guantao, the periods when the emperor was not in charge were often the darkest periods in China's history. They were also likely to be the time when the dynasties were ready to collapse.[66] Even if He was right in saying that when the emperor was not in charge, the ministers took the reign, it does not lead to people's rule. That was a situation in which a tiny minority of people competed for power.

CHAPTER 8

Critical Humanism: Gan Yang

Life and Experience

It is important to point out that the term critical humanism is used in a broad sense for the purpose of analytical convenience. Compared with other intellectuals in this study, Gan Yang in particular does not like "ism."[1] Critical refers to the kind of attitude which is critical of the mainstream Western philosophy, while humanism refers to the philosophical starting point other than the scientific one. Gan Yang and the Culture: China and the World group have drawn strength not only from the post-modernists such as M. Foucault, but also from the so called Neo-Marxists, such as Herbert Marcuse (1898–), Erich Fromm (1900–) and, disputably, J.-P. Sartre and J. Habermas. These Neo-Marxists are not included in our discussion about Marxist humanism in chapter six, largely because Wang Ruoshui and Zhou Yang did not draw intellectual support from these people but directly from the works of Marx. Intellectually, Gan does not believe that truth is obtainable, although through analyzing language we can increase our knowledge about ourselves. Politically, Gan does not believe that total human freedom is obtainable, although freedom is his central concern.

Born in Hangzhou in 1952, Gan Yang is not only the youngest intellectual in this study, but also the only one largely trained after the Cultural Revolution. He was tempered in real life by doing manual labor in Heilongjiang for eight years during the Cultural Revolution. Incidentally, among the six intellectual trends examined in this study, the critical humanist one is the newest. Most members of this group are new graduates from Beijing University and CASS. As Gan says, most intellectual ideas during the 1980s were in the process of taking shape, and consequently these ideas were not systematic theories. This situation may be more so with Gan's group than with other groups. In addition, Gan and his group are among the most conscious in detaching themselves from real world politics among those under study.

Gan went to college after the Cultural Revolution and got his masters in philosophy from Beijing University in 1985. He was one of those students who were selected purely on ground of merit, not on revolutionary basis. In the first few years immediately after the restoration of the old entrance examination system, which was based on merit, quite often, one student was chosen among dozens of candidates. Restoration of the old system, which had been executed before 1966, negated Maoist policy during the Cultural Revolution when college students were chosen on the basis of their revolutionary performance. In a way, the post-Cultural Revolution system, relied more on merit than the pre-Cultural Revolution one, in the sense that while the earlier one still left some room for those students who, at the recommendation of the work units, were exempt from exams, the later one admitted only those who passed the exams. There were no more recommendations from the work units.

Gan has played important roles in Chinese academic circles after college. From 1986, he was the editor of "Treasure-house of Modern Western Scholarship" (*"xiandai xifang xueshu wenku"*), "Treasure-house of New Knowledge" (*"xinzhi wenku"*), "A Collection of Research on Humanities" (*"renwen yanjiu congshu"*), and the Culture: China and the World series. The series and the book *Contemporary Chinese Cultural Consciousness* (*zhongguo dangdai wenhua yishi*) Gan edited are among his major achievements. It should be noted that although this group claims to embrace anti-political politics as will be discussed later, most of these projects were sponsored by the government.

Most of the board members of Culture: China and the World are the newly trained intellectuals who got their degrees after the Cultural Revolution. The academic interest of these people is by and large in the areas of the humanities and philosophy. The series carries an elitist tone by targeting mainly those who are well trained instead of the general public. Among the three sub-series, the first, Modern Scholarship, is mainly to serve academics in research institutes. This elitist tendency is even reflected in their life-style. As a demonstration of their love for freedom, and perhaps, for their modern-elite taste, they often have parties to which they invite actors and actresses to perform for them. Some of them even showed their modern life-style by swimming in reservoirs, naked.

Politically, this group emphasizes professionalism and independence of scholarship. In other words, it advocates depoliticized politics. This attitude reminds us of what Vaclav Havel says:

> I favor "anti-political politics," that is, politics not as the technology of power and manipulation, of cybernetic rule over humans or as the art of the useful, but politics as one of the ways of seeking and achieving meaningful lives, of protecting them and serving them. I favor politics as practical morality, as service to the truth, as essentially human and humanly measured care for our fellow-humans. It is, I presume, an approach which, in this world, is extremely impractical and difficult to apply in daily life. Still, I know no better alternative.[2]

Gan Yang is also the editor of the book *Contemporary Chinese Cultural Consciousness*. The significance of this book can be seen in the fact that two publishing houses based in Hong Kong and Taiwan published this book simultaneously in 1989. Gan wrote a long introduction and a summary for the book which is divided into two volumes. The first volume is devoted to discussions of Chinese issues, especially China's cultural tradition, while the second volume is largely a collection of articles that comment on the works of Western philosophers.

The theme of the book can be seen from the titles of the two volumes in which the book is divided. In the Hong Kong edition, the respective titles are "Rebellion" (*"fanpan"*) and "Puzzled" (*"kunhuo"*). In the Taiwan edition, however, the respective titles are "Rebellion" and "Searching for Ways" (*"xunlu"*). The change of the title for the second volume may carry significant political implications. The Hong Kong edition was published in May 1989, before the Tiananmen incident, while the Taiwan edition was published in October 1989, after the incident. Apparently, the Taiwan edition is more explicit in saying that China's way out lies in the works of the people discussed in the second volume: Max Weber (1864–1920); Daniel Bell; Lev Shestov (1866–1938); Walter Benjamin (1892–1940); Theodor Adorno (1903–1969); H. Marcuse; E. Fromm; M. Heidegger; M. Foucault.

Clearly, most authors in the second volume have adopted an intellectual position other than the mainstream Western philosophy. For those whose positions are not very clear, some aspects of their thought are emphasized in the volume while others are down played. For instance, Weber's thought has been resorted to by both the mainstream and the non-mainstream. Gabriel Almond uses four terms to characterize diversity in political science: hard, soft, left, and right. He uses hard and soft, largely scientific categories, to describe whether the methodology is quantitative or holistic. He uses left and right to clarify political ideologies. "Soft Right," in Almond's terms, refers to those who follow Max Weber.[3] Actually, the ideas of Marx and Weber have been perceived by Ronald H. Chilcote as constituting a dichotomy in political science from which the leftists and the rightists draw strength.[4] Nevertheless, in the volume edited by Gan, Chinese scholar Su Guoxun focuses on the tension between the Weber's formal rationality and substantive rationality. The tone is clearly different from those adopted by Almond and Chilcote in the sense that Weber is perceived as taking both a supportive and a critical position towards the Western industrial society.[5]

Comparatively speaking, Gan has written less than most other Chinese intellectuals discussed in this study. Besides the book he edited, some of his articles also have a couple of versions. For instance "From the Critique of Rationality to the Critique of Culture" was published both in the book that Gan edited and in *Dushu* (*Book Reading*), one of the most respected journals for intellectuals based in Beijing. Not only has Gan written considerably less than other intellectuals, but the majority of his works are in the form of critiques of the works of Western scholars. For instance "From the Critique of Rationality to the Critique of Culture" and "Man, Symbols and Culture" are largely a critique of Ernst Cassirer's (1874–1945) works. "The Enemy of Freedom" is an introduction of Isaiah Berlin's (1909–) ideas. Perhaps in defense of his own economical way of writing, Gan says ironically that although Berlin has written much less than many Chinese intellectuals, who publish at least one book a year, Berlin's works are far more valuable. Scholarship is not counted in terms of volumes.[6]

On the issues of rationality, human freedom and Chinese tradition, Gan Yang has written the following three articles correspondingly: "From the Critique of Rationality to the Critique of Culture;" "The Concept of Freedom;" "Confucianism and Modernity." The first two issues deal with the philosophical starting points, while the third one deals with the issue of how this philosophy can be applied in China's situation.

Gan agrees with those critical humanist philosophers in maintaining that logical rationality as endorsed by Kant and other Enlightenment philosophers should be replaced by the linguistic prelogic approach. Liberty is the ultimate goal of Gan Yang, although he differs from the Western philosophers regarding the means by which this liberty can be reached. Gan also argues that tradition should not be viewed as a fixed entity in the past, but as something that is continuously taking shape. He thus refutes some contemporary Confucianist scholars who want to see a revival of Confucianism. This position of Gan departs from the often nostalgic vision of the past by people like Marcuse, as perceived by many people. Gan argues that the core of contemporary Chinese culture should be the spirit of scientific rationality, which is not only different from positivism but also from the practical rationality as embodied in ancient Chinese culture.

People As the Philosophical Starting Point

Logical Rationality Versus Linguistic Prelogic Approach

Although Kant was the forerunner of the modern Western humanistic tradition, the twentieth-century philosophers who started in Kant's tracks have deviated from him. In Kant's terms, rationality largely refers to the principles embodied in mathematics and classic physics. The various critical humanist thinkers with whom Gan agrees insist that the starting point of research should be language, not logical rationality. The critique of the pure rationality of Kant should be replaced by a critique of language. The attempts made by Heidegger, Gadamer, Habermas, Cassirer, and Ricoeur are all aimed at replacing logical rationality in the scientific tradition with a prelogic linguistic approach in the humanistic tradition. Habermas criticizes logical rationality which is fixed on cognitive-instrumental aspects. He also says:

> Linguistic communication that aims at mutual understanding— and not merely at reciprocal influence—satisfies the presupposition for rational utterances or for the rationality of speaking and acting subjects. We have also seen why the rationality inherent in speech can become empirically effective to the extent that communicative acts take over the steering of social interactions and fulfill functions of social reproduction of maintaining social lifeworld.[7]

Gan Yang has taken a position in line with this critical humanist position. Instead of discussing "logical" and "illogical" matters in positivistic terms, Gan feels that attention should be paid to "prelogic" and mythology.[8] He says:

> The mainstream Western philosophy has consistently studied logical thinking by assuming that it is the most basic and preliminary form of thinking. The Western cultural tradition has also

been oriented in accordance with this assumption. . . . [P]hiloso-
phy [in the West] is largely an "epistemological" study based on
natural science. . . . [I believe] that human knowledge and culture
are not based on logical concepts and logical thinking, but on
metaphorical thinking which is based on prelogical concepts and
expressions.[9]

Gan believes that Cassirer's interpretations of the universe are similar
to China's Taoist tradition in the sense that both are against positivism.
Cassirer is one of the Neo-Kantians.[10] But the critical humanist interpretation is different from that of Taoism in that while the latter believes in
self reflection, a method that borders on mysticism, the former, with the
belief that the key to understand the universe is language, intends to
demystify language. Language mystifies our understanding of the world.
Consequently, in order to comprehend the world, we have to understand
language, Gan concludes. Nevertheless, Gan does not believe that truth
is obtainable. "Who can find the truth? Nobody, except God," he said.[11]

Comparing the Chinese language and the European languages, Gan
argues that the illogical Chinese language may have an advantage with
which people can understand the world. He says that before the encounter
with the Western culture, Chinese culture had been one without logic and
grammar, although this does not mean that the Chinese have never used
logic in thinking. However, the basic characteristic of the development
of Chinese traditional culture is that it does not stress the logical function
of language. In the last hundred years or so, this feature of the Chinese
language has been treated as a weakness. Nevertheless, it is precisely this
weakness that has brought the prelogicalness into full play. Not surprisingly, Gan says, some European scholars have regarded the grammar and
logic in their own language as a weakness.[12]

Positive Liberty Versus Negative Liberty

Gan Yang's viewpoint concerning human freedom is closely connected
with his evaluation of the tradition of Western humanism. Before going
to his views concerning human freedom, we may want to trace briefly
the development of modern humanism in the West. Generally speaking,
modern Western humanism is actually a rediscovery of nature, using nature
to interpret human beings, which is the naturalization of human beings.
The medieval supernaturalism is nothing but the alienation of rationalism.
Without realizing the social nature of human beings, this kind of humanism

can lead to the recognition of individuality and the value of individuals, but it also can lead to the opposition between science and value.

Kant is not only relevant in discussions about the starting point of philosophy, he is also often resorted to when people discuss the crucial issue of human freedom, because these two issues are closely related to each other. Kant explicitly introduced the anthropological question, what is man?, into philosophy. Soren Kierkegaard (1813–1855) ridiculed philosophers like Hegel (1770–1831) who generated grandiose systems to answer all questions—except one: What does it mean to be an existing individual person? Friedrich Nietzsche (1844–1900), celebrated the freedom of the self-surmounting person who rose above the mediocrity and conformity of the masses in order to create meaning and values and to live dangerously and joyfully. Marx protested vigorously against the reification or "thingfication" of persons in bourgeois capitalist society—a society that was stifling the free, conscious activity that distinguishes the human being from the rest of nature.[13] Later on, Sartre also contributed much to the discussion of humanism with his existentialism. The critique of humanism by critical humanist philosophers was often directed against Kant, and against the ideals of the Enlightenment that he built into our understanding of what philosophy is.

There are five dimensions of the concept of Western humanism, most of which are derived from Kant: 1) The human existence is ascribed as a "universal essence." In other words, people are the center of the world, not in the physical sense, but in the philosophical sense. 2) People are autonomous and free. 3) People are transcendental in the sense that human mind is instrumental in constructing the world we experience. 4) There is also belief in scientific progress. Science progresses and knowledge grows in a cumulative fashion. 5) The last, which is also probably the most important notion of humanism, is belief in the social-historical progress of people.

However, critical humanist theorists disagree with these views. Heidegger and Derrida criticize the so-called universal essence viewpoint as metaphysical. Heidegger does not consider his rejection of the Sartre type humanism as anti-humanistic or inhumane. On the contrary, Heidegger is trying to avoid the subjectivism and idealism he thinks make traditional humanism itself inhumane. On the problem of autonomy, Heidegger, Derrida and Foucault criticize it as not being social and historical. On the issue of transcendence, the critical humanists want to project a total philosophical revolution, where either affirming or denying subjectivity would no longer have a point. Foucault and Derrida are also against Kant's beliefs regarding scientific progress and social-historical progress.[14]

Gan is less optimistic than Kant about the European philosopher's judgement of the universe and man. He has taken a position closer to the critical humanists. Gan believes that man can never be totally free, although human freedom is his central concern. This position is similar to many post-modernists who would respond to the question—What does freedom mean?—by saying that the question was unfruitful and misleading. They would insist that the inquirer might more profitably inquire how many ways and in what ways man used the word free.

Following Berlin, Gan distinguishes positive liberty from negative liberty, with the former referring to the sort of liberty that the nineteenth-century authors of Romanticism endorsed, and the latter referring to liberty of citizens (*gongmin ziyou*). Again, following Berlin, Gan believes that positive liberty often lends a hand to autocracy, because the romantic self realization as advocated by these authors of Romanticism is supposed to go beyond what humans are. All forms of persecution are conducted in the name of helping people realize this transcendence,[15] Gan argues. Commenting on the works of Berlin and Weber, Gan says:

> The premise as well as the disappointing aspect of pluralism in value is that it does not promise the possibility of a system in which all kinds of values can be realized. What it stresses is that values are in fact always in conflict with one another. As a result, the realization of one value would inevitably harm some other values.[16]

For this reason, Gan advises Chinese intellectuals to free themselves from the Confucian scholars' habit of the heart, their eagerness to get involved in real world politics. In the view of Gan, the country would be better off without too many attempts by the intellectuals for national salvation. If one does not want to save the world but to save himself or herself—not intending to liberate the world but to liberate oneself—he or she would contribute to the emancipation of the world and mankind, he argues. The two slogans raised during the May Fourth Movement, democracy and science, are not to the point, according to Gan. Without "individual freedom," how can one talk about democracy and science?[17] He says:

> I believe that the biggest lesson for the Chinese intellectuals in the last century is that they have always put society, nation and the people above everything else. They have never dared to regard "the freedom of individuals" as the first principle. In their view, individual freedom is a private matter. . . . In my opinion, this

kind of attitude is the seed for their eventual loss of autonomy. Because if their remarks are always made for the others [society, nation and the people], they would be speechless once others do not need their service. . . .The loss of autonomy of Chinese intellectuals is not due to their irresponsibility to society, but the opposite.[18]

Attacking Li Zehou, Gan says that the utopian nature of the May Fourth Movement went against human emancipation. As was discussed previously, Li believes that there were two interacting themes of the May Fourth Movement: enlightenment and national salvation. The first one was later overwhelmed by the former. Gan attacks Li by saying that the movement was a means to transform society. It is not real freedom.[19]

Application of Humanistic Philosophy

Modernity versus Tradition

A critic says that although Gan's main study areas are Gadamer and Ricoeur, his point of departure is closer to Habermas in the sense that Gan is critical of not only the Chinese cultural tradition, but also the imported scientism.[20] This judgement may partly be approved by Gan himself, because the critic's article is included later in the book that Gan edited. But given his advice to Chinese intellectuals about not getting involved in politics, Gan may not share with Habermas's high sense of moral purpose in the same way.[21] In addition, the contents of Gan's humanism may be different from Habermas. Gan says:

Ethic oriented culture (traditional culture) inevitably has a human touch, knowledge oriented culture inevitably cuts back on the human touch. . . . Because of this, modern man inevitably has a sense of loss in heart. In other words, regarding the traditional culture, we have to be both negative, critical, and positive, nostalgic; towards modern society, we not only have a feeling of expectation, longing, but also a deep sense of doubt and insecurity. . . .We have to fight on two frontiers: not only be critical about traditional culture, but also critical about modern society.[22]

Gan believes that this tension should be the focus of Chinese intellectuals' attention, not the methodological approach of systems theory,

cybernetics and information theory.[23] This is an indirect attack against
the Jin Guantao group. However, in the above paragraph, Gan is not very
specific about ethic oriented and knowledge oriented cultures, although
the later one most likely refers to Western modern society. But does ethic
oriented culture, which is supposed to have a "human touch," refer to
Chinese traditional culture, or to the Western traditional culture? This is
crucial, because the two cultural traditions are drastically different.

There is certainly a "human touch" in the Chinese tradition, as was
discussed previously. Those Western philosophers from whom Gan has
borrowed ideas have also noted the difference between the Chinese cultural tradition and that of the West. Weber says that according to Confucianism, "Human nature was disposed to the ethically good," and man
is "in principle adequate for fulfilling the moral law."[24] "Human nature
tends toward goodness, just as water tends to flow downward," as stated
in one of the nine classic texts of Confucianism, the *Meng Tze*.[25] Therefore,
for Confucianism, the corresponding individual ideal was the elaboration
of the self as a universal and harmoniously balanced personality, in this
sense a microcosm.[26] Instead of seeking meaning in conquering the world,
Confucianism turns to man himself for the meaning of life. As Weber recalls
in connection with Confucianism:

> The right path to salvation consisted in adjustment to the eternal
> and supra-divine orders of the world, Tao, and hence to the re-
> quirements of social life, which followed from cosmic harmony.[27]

There may not be a human touch of such kind in the Western tradition. Weber notes that puritanism believes that men were held to be sinful
by nature. "Men are equally wicked and fail ethically; the world is a vessel
of sin; and there can be no difference in creatural wickedness in the face
of lord."[28] Consequently, there is great tension between man and the world
in the Western tradition. For Puritanism, man is "in a state of tension with
the irrationalities of the world," but Confucianism "reduced tension with
the world to an absolute minimum."[29]

Gan also uses Gadamer's theory to refute those who advocate a revival
of Confucianism. He cites Gadamer as saying that tradition is not some
fixed thing that we have inherited, but something that we have produced
and are constantly producing. This is because we not only understand
the development of tradition but also are involved in this development.
We therefore define tradition.[30] This viewpoint is also in line with Habermas'
position. Habermas says,

> The cultural reproduction of the lifeworld ensures that newly
> arising situation is connected up with existing conditions in the

world in the semantic dimension: it secures a continuity of tradition and coherence of knowledge sufficient for daily practice. Continuity and coherence are measured by the rationality of the knowledge accepted.[31]

Using this theory, Gan criticizes those attempts made by some modern Confucianist scholars for their utopian vision of the revival of China's Confucian tradition. He says that although Confucianism and Taoism are and will be the components of Chinese culture at present and in the future, they cannot become the central value of China's culture. They have to be the marginal and subordinate elements.[32]

Gan's critical position towards the Chinese traditional culture is different from some of the critical humanist philosophers from whom he has borrowed ideas in the sense that the Westerners often view the past with a more nostalgic feelings than Gan. According to a Chinese scholar, Marcuse is such an example.[33] This is striking in view of the fact that the Western cultural tradition may have less of a human touch than the Chinese tradition.

Gan realizes that with the replacement of traditional society by a commercial one, capitalist relations of production would inevitably lead to a loss of holiness. Thus, people, especially the more sensitive intellectuals, would feel a kind of rootlessness and meaninglessness. Commodity fetishism and alienation and the popularization of mass culture make intellectuals feel strongly the degradation of spiritual life and the collapse of values in modern society.[34] This is consistent with the position taken by the critical humanists in the West. For instance, Habermas believes that even the advance of science and technology is linked to political oppression. Habermas believes that "[t]he domination of nature has remained linked to the domination of Man."[35] He argues that in an age when science and technology reign supreme and the life of the individual is increasingly fragmented, science and technology can only help us to evaluate the consistency of our goals, they cannot help us determine which goals are intrinsically worthwhile or even morally obligatory.[36]

Gan also appears to be more positive about the Western political system than those critical humanist thinkers. He believes that such things as liberty, democracy and rule of law are positive, and have been established smoothly in commercial society. In a traditional culture such as feudal China, people were not equal before the law, if there was law at all. The friends or relatives of the royal families and powerful people were often, if not always, exempt from the law. But, "in a rational lifeworld, principles of legal order and morality tied less to concrete forms of life."[37] Everybody is equal before the judicial procedure, at least in theory.

Gan seems to agree with Weber who argued that the Chinese cultural tradition which is not based on logical rationality, but linguistic rationality may not be good for modernity. Weber said, "in the magic garden of heterodox (Taoism) a rational economy and technology of modern occidental character was simply out of the question."[38] The Chinese cultural tradition is incompatible with Baconism. Bacon argues that people should contemplate things as they are, without superstition or imposture, error or confusion. His concern with methods by which scientific evidence could be tested gave a powerful impetus to the development of science in the seventeenth century, and indeed to the modernization process in the West.

China's Future

Gan agrees with the view that the prolonged recession in the West since the 1960s is not accidental. It is a result of the vulnerable mechanism of the Western development model: big enterprise; mass production, big market, all based on the separation between laborers and the means of production, the separation between enterprises and community, and the separation between economic activities and society. This is the so-called First Industrial Divide. In recent decades, the West has been seeking new alternatives which may be based largely on the integration between labors and the means of production, the integration between enterprises and community and that between economic activities and society. This may be called "the Second Industrial Divide."[39]

Gan argues that China does not have to follow the steps of the Westerners by going through the First Industrial Divide and then to the second one. Actually, he says, the robust economy of China's countryside during the reform era was not brought about by the separations as mentioned. For instance, the main purpose of China's village-town enterprises was not to make profits as was the case with the Western enterprises, but to provide jobs to local people and to increase their welfare as a whole. China's reform has not seen massive migration of the peasants to big cities as happened everywhere else in the world. Indeed, Gan argues that China may go directly to the Second Industrial Divide.[40]

Then, what is the role that the Chinese scholarship should play to help China move in that direction? We have seen ambiguities in Gan's positions. In general terms, Gan favors what he calls the spirit of scientific rationality. He makes it clear that this "scientific rationality" refers to neither the positivistic spirit as embodied in the mainstream Western thinking, nor the "practical rationality" as embodied in Confucianism.[41] He has not been specific about this scientific rationality.

But when commenting on how can Chinese scholarship help China's modernization drive, Gan criticized the situation in China where the subjects of philosophy, intellectual history and humanities are given more emphasis while social sciences are on the margin. Gan argues that in the next century, social sciences should take the lead in the Chinese scholarship.[42] This is clearly different from the position that Gan took on another occasion when he insisted that China should pay more attention to the twentieth-century European continental scholarship, which stresses philosophy and humanities, rather than social sciences as emphasized by the Anglo-American scholarship in this century.[43] Gan's emphasis on social sciences is also a departure from the Western critical humanists who have never liked the disciplinary boundaries and positivist domination in Western social sciences in the first place.

Furthermore, Gan does not seem very concerned about the profound theoretical confusion in American social sciences in the last two decades. He sees this theoretical crisis in a positive light by calling it "an integration between the social sciences and humanities."[44] With people's understanding towards science becoming more sophisticated in the last few decades, some basic philosophical assumptions, especially the over-emphasis on quantitative methods in American social sciences, have been undermined.[45] This is because, as Gan himself is aware of, the establishment of the Western social sciences was directly linked to the development of Western societies.[46]

We have seen that on a philosophical level, Gan favors the European-continental style prelogic linguistic approach; on a concrete level, that is, in his analysis of contemporary Chinese society, he puts more emphasis on the Anglo-American social sciences, predominantly characterized by logic rationality. This dichotomy reminds us of the case with Li Zehou. On the philosophical level, Li insists that "real creative thinking is obtained neither from inductions, nor from deductions of some 'common laws,' "[47] which are characteristics of Anglo-American social sciences. When dealing with concrete social problems, such as, how to transform the Chinese society, Li believes that "only on the basis of incorporating and introducing the strict logical analysis and deduction of the West, can we creatively transform our traditional way of thinking."[48]

The dichotomy between the philosophical approach and real world politics can also be seen from Gan's advocating the Anglo-American style, piece-by-piece evolution characterized by the British Glorious Revolution and the American Revolution in contrast to the European continental total social transformation characterized by the French Revolution. Gan argues that China should follow the steps of the British and the Americans in changing society.[49]

Therefore, it seems difficult to separate scholarship from politics as Gan has always believed: "scholarship is scholarship; literature is literature; doing favors for neither the ruler nor the ruled; social forces in every sphere should try to obtain independence from political power. . . ."[50] What we have seen is: scholarship is soley scholarship when only the abstract philosophical issues are concerned; scholarship becomes not pure scholarship when it deals with social reality. It seems that it is awfully hard for Chinese intellectuals, with the exception perhaps of the few who have no understanding of the times, such as Hu Qiaomu, to see a different alternative for China's development. It is harder for them to find a feasible way to help intellectually in China's endeavor.

PART IV

Conclusion

CHAPTER 9

The New Thinking and
the Chinese Political Culture

I n this book I have examined the Marxist scientism of historical materialism, (chapter three), the Chinese-style scientism of technological determinism (chapter four), the empirical scientism of systems theory (chapter five), Marxist humanism (chapter six), the updated version of Confucianism (chapter seven), and critical humanism (chapter eight). From these discussions some important conclusions have been reached.

First, although most of these intellectuals put forward their theories in the name of Marxism, their theories are only ambiguously connected with Marx, and quite often, no necessary connections have existed in between. This is significant in that with the exception of perhaps Gan Yang, all the other five intellectuals, at least at some point in their careers, claimed that their theories were created in line with Marxism. Even the so-called Habermasian Gan could also be called a Marxist, because Habermas is considered by many in the West a reformed Marxist, in spite of his own denial.

We have found, however, that Hu Qiaomu's Marxist scientism of historical materialism is by and large a product of the international communist movement during which Marx's ideas were altered in order to suit historical contingencies. Su Shaozhi's technological determinism is a combination of some parts of orthodox Marxism, empirical scientism and, above all, China's tradition in emphasizing technology to suit political needs, to the neglect of developing comprehensive scientific theories. Jin Guantao's empirical scientism was originally created in the name of historical materialism that he later dropped.

Wang Ruoshui's analysis of alienation was created with the assumption that it belongs to the category of dialectics. Consequently, it does not belong exclusively to Marx, because dialectics was first created by Hegel. Although endorsing Marxism on a general level, a position which became unclear in recent years, Li Zehou has never linked systematically his theories with those of Marx. Gan Yang does not want to identify himself as a Marxist.

Second, although three of them have created their theories in the name of science, an ambiguity has also existed between their theories and science. The failure of the world communist movements has thrown Hu Qiaomu's Marxist scientism into the garbage can. Su Shaozhi's scientific socialism is not scientific, because it is not a coherent theory. The scientistic nature of Jin Guantao's theory is revealed by the fact that once it is used in explaining Chinese history, it becomes inadequate.

Third, although generally the three versions of humanism are less politicized, their ideas have drifted far from the intellectual roots where they have drawn strength. Wang Ruoshui's humanism actually stands in opposition to Marx's intellectual enterprise in the sense that Marx's alienation theory is a critique of capitalism, while Wang's alienation theory is a critique of state socialism that forgives capitalist alienation. Wang's rationale is that capitalist alienation is the price we have to pay in order to get rid of the alienation of state socialism for social progress. This argument is not characteristically humanistic. Although he has more sympathy with China's intellectual tradition, Li Zehou has different preferences when it comes to solving China's current problems. In addition, his political platform is vague and he has refrained from criticizing comprehensively the Western political and economic system. Although Gan Yang is perhaps the most conscious about the situation where scholarship is used for political purpose, his humanistic approach drifted from its original roots. Although he shares much with the Western critical humanists philosophically, he differs from them in being less nostalgic towards the past and being more sympathetic towards the positivism-dominated social sciences when it comes to the current Chinese social transformation.

These intellectuals should be viewed as trying to fill in the intellectual vacuum left by the Cultural Revolution. In this chapter, we further discuss this fill-in mentality by relating it to some other important intellectual-political phenomena in China's modern history such as iconoclasm, democracy, and post-Mao mass political culture. We will find that the Chinese endorsement of scientism is closely connected not only with the holistic-monistic and utopian Chinese cultural tradition as was discussed in chapter two, but also with historical contingencies throughout the last century and half. In addition, the peculiar nature of Chinese mass political culture in the post-Mao period has also lent a hand to the booming of scientism during the period. The various versions of humanism lack these qualities and thus were not as influential as scientism in remolding political consciousness.

Scientism inherits the Chinese intellectual-political tradition of being holistic and monistic. All aspects of social consciousness are regarded as an inseparable whole where there is only one legitimate source of truth. This situation was clearly demonstrated in the following intellectual-political phenomena in China's modern history: 1) the emergence of scientism in Chinese modern and contemporary history has always been accompanied by iconoclasm; 2) as inseparable parts of the May Fourth tradition, Mr. Science has always been more acceptable to the Chinese people than Mr. Democracy.

China's current enthusiasm for science, which sometimes becomes scientism, has its counterpart in the late nineteenth century and early twentieth century. The first wave of China's appreciation of science began in China following its defeat by the British in the 1840 Opium War. This war proved to the Chinese intellectuals that modern Western weaponry was superior to Chinese swords and spears. In the 1860s, the Chinese enthusiasm was characterized by an appreciation of Western technology, which was demonstrated by the fact that China imported large amounts of modern weaponry. Using Western technology, it also built many modern plants to make advanced guns and munitions.

The second stage of Chinese enthusiasm for sicence came following another humiliating defeat suffered by the Chinese in 1895. Although the Chinese Beiyang Fleet, modeled after the Western navy, was larger than the Japanese fleet, it was destroyed in Bohai Bay by the Japanese. The Chinese navy's impotency, which was connected with the corruption of the Qing Dynasty, came to a full exposure. Consequently, the Chinese intellectuals came to a new awareness: Modern technology alone cannot save China. Modernization cannot be accomplished without scientific changes in the political system. Intellectuals like Kang Youwei, Liang Qichao, and Tan Sitong began to lobby Emperor Guangxu to reform.

The third stage, which led directly to all around attacks on Confucianism and new worship of science, was characterized by a realization that political systems cannot be changed without a change in people's consciousness. This new awareness was largely the result of the failure of the Hundred Days Reform in 1898, when reformers who were supported by Emperor Guangxu tried to reform the Qing dynastic system by adopting some measures derived from Western countries and Japan. Although the Empress Dowager and conservatives succeeded in suppressing the reformers, the trend for enlightenment continued. The collapse of the Qing Dynasty in 1911 paved the road for a new period of enlightenment, which was characterized by iconoclasm and scientism.

Ironically, the development of scientism after Mao paralleled the case of the late nineteenth and early twentieth centuries in going through three stages: 1) Recent scientism began with a new worship of modern technology, approximately from 1977 before Deng came to power to the early 1980s. 2) Chinese bureaucracy proved to be ill prepared to handle modern science and technology. Accordingly, it was reported widely in the media that large amounts of imported products did not suit China. This led to a new awareness, beginning in the early 1980s, that China cannot become modernized without changing its political system along scientific lines. 3) But, finally, political reform met with great difficulty, a situation that led directly to a realization that the political system cannot be changed without a change of consciousness. This was shown by the increasing concern with the Chinese cultural tradition since 1984.

Therefore, the overwhelming Chinese acceptance of science as a new ideology has been mixed with all-round attacks on the Chinese tradition. In a sense, iconoclasm, whether against the Confucian tradition or the Maoist tradition, and scientism go hand-in-hand. This parallel between iconoclasm and an embrace of scientism has raised a question: Is there a logical link between the two? Commenting on China's recent surge of pragmatism, which is closely related to scientism, Lucian W. Pye says that any version of pragmatism, especially a version that can command the adherence of both a ruling circle and a national population, must inescapably reflect a set of basic predispositions, a kind of latent, unarticulated ideology.[1] Pye's remark has been echoed by some Chinese thinkers who believe that iconoclasm has been a distinct phenomenon not only in China's intellectual history but also in the world.[2] So, perhaps, has been scientism.[3] There may be indeed a logical link between iconoclasm and scientism. The two seemingly opposite notions of iconoclasm and scientism are linked by a holistic and monistic understanding of the universe, which is characteristic of Chinese intellectual and political orientation. Iconoclasm is the precondition for the surge of scientism, while scientism is a major by-product of iconoclasm.

This situation is also demonstrated by the samples chosen to study scientism and iconoclasm. The two books on the two issues are *Scientism in Chinese Thought: 1900–1950*, first published in 1965 by D. W. Y. Kwok, and *Crisis in Chinese Consciousness*, published in 1979 by Yu-sheng Lin. As samples of study, Kwok focuses on Chen Duxiu (Ch'en Tu-hsiu), Hu Shi (Hu Shih) and Wu Zhihui (Wu Chih-hui), while Lin studies exclusively Chen Duxiu, Hu Shi, and Lu Xun in their respective endeavors. The intimate relationship between the two phenomena can be seen by the fact that Lu Xun and Wu Zhihui are the only two people who do not overlap in their studies. Comparing the current surge of scientism with the one in the 1920s, similarities as well as differences have been found. This leads to the conclusion that the current surge is more politicized, less intellectual than the previous one. The most important similarity between the two is that accompanying the rise of scientism, there has been iconoclasm, a notion impling a comprehensive anti-tradition attitude.

The other phenomenon that reveals the intimate relationship between the Chinese holistic-monistic cultural tradition and the modern endorsement of scientism was that as two slogans of the 1919 May Fourth movement were Mr. Democracy (*de xiansheng*) and Mr. Science (*sai xiansheng*), the fate of Mr. Science has been wonderful. Generally speaking, the Chinese have approved science almost unanimously in the last century. The Chinese obsession with science was disrupted only twice in the last century, both occurring during the Mao era: one was the Great Leap Forward; the other was the Cultural Revolution.[4] This has only confirmed the observation made by Hu Shi seventy years ago. Hu remarked:

> During the last thirty years or so there is a name which has acquired an incomparable position of respect in China; no one, whether informed or ignorant, conservative or progressive, dares openly slight or jeer at it. The name is Science. The worth of this almost nationwide worship is another question. But we can at least say that ever since the beginning of reformist tendencies (1890s) in China, there is not a single person who calls himself a modern man and yet dares openly to belittle Science.[5]

The fact that Mr. Science has been accepted without much reservation is striking in the light of the fact that the Chinese acceptance of Mr. Democracy has not been that easy. Most of the time, modifiers have to be added to it. Thus we have the people's democratic dictatorship and the Three Principles of the People (*san min zhuyi*) which are livelihood of the people, nationalism and democracy. Sometimes democracy is treated as a form of decentralization and is put at the other end of the spectrum as opposed to centralization.[6] Thus we have the party rhetoric: we not only have to have democracy, but also centralization and vice versa.

While science sounds positively neutral, and thus everyone is likely to endorse it, this is not true of democracy. There have been too many forms of democracy, a situation that calls for modifiers attached to it all the time. Historically, democracy does not share the good reputation that science does. For instance, in Aristotle's time, democracy meant rule by the mob, or the poor, or the masses. That's probably why until about the 1840s, democracy was generally considered a bad thing.[7] In the last century and half, most people have agreed to endorse democracy on an abstract level. However, they cannot agree on the real meaning of democracy. The situation in China is no less perplexing. It has its own forms of democracy.

The Chinese firstly had "*Min Ben*," or "rule for the people." As we discussed in the chapter dealing with Li Zehou, the essence of *Min Ben* is to rule benevolently, but not necessarily to ask for the consent from the ruled. As Mencius put it, "The people are most important, society comes second, the ruler comes last."[8] However, there is the other side of the coin for the idea of rule for the people. It could degenerate into merely a means for the rulers to rule, a strategy. The notion of this rule for the people still has admirers today. For instance, some official party documents issued in recent years claim that rule for the people is democracy. The documents, in an attempt to "improve the work style of the party so that the country can become more 'democratic,' " encouraged the cadres to "listen to the masses," "let the masses talk," "to get to know the happiness and sufferings of the masses."[9]

The second form of democracy that the Chinese have had is what is called the Stalinist Democracy or the People's Democratic Dictatorship (*renmin minzhu zhuanzheng*). The Chinese system was established following the model of the Soviet Union in the early 1950s. Together with Confucian legacies, it has run through much of PRC's history, except the period of the Cultural Revolution, as the predominant form of government. Two aspects coexist in this system: For the people, it is democratic; for the enemies, it is dictatorship.[10] This system was based on the Marxist-Leninist notion that Western style democracy carries little meaning for the people. This is because capitalist alienation has deprived people of any real choice in their lives.[11]

The third form of democracy that the Chinese have witnessed is the Maoist Democracy: Big Democracy (*da minzhu*), which was in full force during the Cultural Revolution, although the Hundred Flowers Movement of 1957 could be seen as big democracy on a limited scale. In the ten-year disaster, especially in the first three years, bureaucracy was largely smashed, respect for law was eliminated (even lip service), and the people actively and also blindly participated in the country's political process. This turbulent period, especially from 1966 to 1969, is probably closer to the realization of the original meaning of democracy: rule by the mob.

Fourthly, there is the Western-style constitutional democracy, which many contemporary Chinese intellectuals have viewed as suitable for China. For these people, democracy has taken on the meaning of rule by the people. Here, rule by the people largely refers to the conventional Western interpretations of democracy, which implies a form of government whose characteristics include universal suffrage, elections, party politics, freedom of speech, separation of powers and sovereignty of law.

Finally, as a matter of a future goal, the Chinese have envisioned communist democracy. Communist democracy, which is different both from the system which Lenin created in Russia and the Chinese system under Mao, refers to a system that not only has realized "political emancipation," as is the case in the United States and Britain, but also "human emancipation," a situation in which capitalist alienation has been eliminated and people really are able to control their lives.[12] Although the Soviet Union under Stalin and China under Mao to a large extent eliminated capitalist alienation, new problems were created and consequently the people did not rule, as the concept of democracy promised.

In view of the fact that the battle over the real meaning of democracy has far from being settled and there were so many forms of democracy, some scholars held in 1970 that, almost all of the existing systems in the world can be considered "different approaches to democratic government."[13] Of course, this is not to say that under these democracies, the people actually rule. Given their habit of heart for unanimity, the Chinese people have found it easier to accept Mr. Science than Mr. Democracy which could mean too many different things.

Although we have realized that the triumph of scientism over humanism during the post-Mao era is connected with China's holistic-monistic cultural tradition, this has not adequately answered the questions, because some species of humanism have intellectual, socioeconomic and political origins in China's past too. For instance, the Chinese cultural tradition is noted for its strong emphasis on humanistic values. Why does contemporary intellectual Chinese thought, which has a strong scientistic flavor, have to inherit the monistic-holistic Chinese tradition, but not the humanistic one? The many inhuman acts of the Cultural Revolution also called for a more humanistic response. Why is contemporary Chinese thought not as sensitive to the inhuman aspects of the Cultural Revolution as to the voluntarist aspects?

It seems that historical contingencies have played a part in the transformation of political consciousness during various periods of Chinese modern history. They may have contributed to the failure of humanism as the main ideology to reshape Chinese consciousness. In the case of the 1923 debate between science and metaphysics, Marxist humanism was not part of the debate that engaged dialectical materialism. The various species of Neo-Marxism had not been introduced into China. During the post-Mao period, the gradual loss of influence of Marxist humanism after the mid-1980s has been the result of government repression and in accordance with the gradual erosion of Marxism in general.

With its rule for the people tradition, Chinese culture is perhaps more closely linked with humanitarian concerns than with the neutral science. Consequently, in the late nineteenth century and early twentieth century, it was easily viewed as responsible for the humiliations China suffered in the last two centuries, because its door was forced open mainly by the products of science: guns; munitions; ships; etc. As a negation of the Maoist regime, which was a combination of elements of China's feudal tradition and Stalinism, the new political culture during the post-Mao era found it hard to totally endorse Confucianism. This is so in spite of the fact that the regime may try to use the authoritarian elements of the Chinese tradition to legitimize its one-party rule and some individual intellectuals may take advantage of the relaxed political atmosphere to revitalize Confucianism. Confucian humanism, although perhaps still deep in most Chinese people's hearts, is unlikely to surge as a major voice among academic circles because the May Fourth iconoclastic tradition has continued to this day.

The various schools of Western humanism have never had a strong voice in China. In spite of the fact that Chiang Kai-shek and Chen Lifu held political power and advocated Henri Bergson's (1859–1941) vitalism as well as some versions of Confucianism in the 1923 debate, the various versions of scientism triumphed. During the post-Mao period, critical humanism has not been as influential as scientism, partly because it does not even try to appeal to the general population. More importantly, how can a pre-modern society like China endorse post-modernism?

The situation where intellectual debates are always heavily influenced by real world events, especially political events, has become worse in China in the last century. This is demonstrated in the fact that when one compares the 1923 debate over science to the transformation of Chinese consciousness during the post-Mao era, the latter is more politicized.

First, while those who upheld scientism in the early 1920s sincerely believed the omnipotent power of science, those who upheld similar lines in the 1980s did not. For instance, by the early 1920s, the mechanical and monistic vision of Newtonian physics had already been challenged by Albert Einstein's theories of Grand Relativity and Special Relativity. However, in the fields of social sciences, the impact of Einstein's theories had not been felt by most people. That is why people like Chen Duxiu, Hu Shi, and Wu Zhihui may have really believed the omnipotent power of science in the Newtonian sense. Things in the 1980s were different. For most Chinese social scientists, science is not omnipotent. People are unlikely to endorse scientism on an abstract level. However, many people still endorse it when it comes to concrete studies.

The second difference is that while the battle line in the 1923 debate was drawn between scientism and humanism, the line in the 1980s was less clear. Real world politics played a more important role in the post-Mao era. So there was no real academic debate during this era. For instance, Wang Ruoshui and the humanist school, although seemingly embracing something other than scientism, do not target some of those who embrace scientism such as Jin Guantao and Su Shaozhi. Instead of attacking Hu Qiaomu's historical materialism, they target a political object, that is, political alienation; the servants of the people have become the masters. Although his focus is on the less essential aspect of ontology, the cultural-psychological one, Li Zehou encourages Jin's experiment of adopting systems theory in the study of Chinese history. Concentrating on the issue of developing productive forces, Su Shaozhi attacks none of the three species of humanism. Although not happy with the fact that there was too much irrationalism, Jin Guantao has never attacked any humanistic philosophers. Most people often disagree on the question of whether the CCP is able to carry out a Westernization.[14]

The third difference, which is related to the second one and is also part of the politicization of intellectual pursuits, is that most people who have adopted a scientific stand are more or less connected with the regime. Hu Qiaomu was a party theorist; Su Shaozhi played an important role within the regime; Jin's theory was widely believed to have been endorsed by Zhao Ziyang. Along the line of humanism, the situation is different. Wang's Marxist humanism was not liked by the regime from the very beginning. The critical humanist scholars such as Gan Yang are noted for their anti political politics. This position not surprisingly has alienated them from the authorities. The more accomplished Confucianist scholars such as Tang Yijie and Liang Shuming are far from establishment intellectuals. Such was not the case in the 1920s where we have found that Wu Zhihui, though associated institutionally with Kuomintang, advocated anarchism. Needless to say, Chiang Kai-shek and Chen Lifu, who advocated Bergson's vitalism and some versions of Confucianism, were among the ruling elites.

The peculiar nature of Chinese political culture during the post-Mao era also lends a hand to the emergence of scientism. This political culture was formed not only by China's tradition, but also the failure of the Cultural Revolution and the many socioeconomic and political problems caused by the reform. In academic terms, "political culture" may be interpreted as the attitudinal and behavioral matrix within which the political system is located.[15] Its dimensions can also be described as, not exclusively, consciousness, spontaneity and ideology. The booming of scientism during this period can be attributed to 1) the fragmented nature of Chinese political culture, 2) the low level of political tolerance, which is a legacy of the Chinese holistic-monistic tradition favoring unanimity, 3) political apathy, and 4) that the three species of scientism have been able to remold political culture on three levels: idealistic; operational; tolerated.

A fragmented political culture is one whose population lacks broad agreement upon the way political life should be conducted. The population separates into groups isolated from one another by contradictory and incompatible orientations toward political life. This may involve different sets of political identifications, irreconcilable differences about what rules of the game should prevail in civic life, different regime orientations or other conflicts. Quite often, extreme distrust exists between opposing groups.[16]

Chinese political culture during the post-Mao period can be described as fragmented. China's situation during the post-Mao era, especially in the late 1980s, reminds people of the description offered by the French philosopher Alexis de Tocqueville about a declining civilization:

> the old customs of a people are changed, public morality is destroyed, religious belief shaken, and the spell of tradition broken . . . the country then assumes a dim and dubious shape in the eyes of its citizens; they no longer behold it in the soil they inhabit in the usages of their forefathers; nor in religion, which they doubt, nor in the laws, which do not originate in their own authority; nor in the legislator, whom they fear and despise. The country is lost to their senses . . . and they retire into a narrow and unenlightened selfishness.[17]

Social dislocations caused by the Cultural Revolution and the subsequent reform have caused much suffering to people. This is most clearly demonstrated in the mentality of the so called lost generation, the generation to which Gan Yang and Jin Guantao belong. These middle-aged people, who used to be Mao's Red Guards, "have suffered more than any other generation," as commented by *Remin ribao*.[18] In response to Mao's call, many of these people spent their golden youth in the country-side to be educated by the poor and lower-middle peasants. They had no formal education, because all of the schools were closed. When Deng came back to power, he decided to use educated people. The former Red Guards were too old to go to school. In their mid-forties, many of these individuals lacked career opportunities. This is doubly so for those without good connections or special skills. Most of them did not want to marry while staying in the countryside. When Deng let them go back home to cities, many found that their best age to find a suitable spouse had already passed. To make the situation worse, the government made a change in marriage laws so that people can get married younger. This further reduced the former Red Guards' chances.

To dramatize the suffering of these people caused by the Cultural Revolution, *Remin ribao* carried a short story that told a tale happening at a high school in China during the Cultural Revolution. A deserted newly-born baby was found in a toilet. The Red Guards suspected that this bourgeois act was conducted by Li, an eighteen-year old girl, who had early discovered to have flirted with a boy, Yuan. Both of them were also Red Guards. The girl was being investigated. The boy, knowing nothing about sex and child birth, thought that the baby was indeed his, because he had kissed the girl twice. In an attempt to relieve his girl friend of the responsibility, he confessed to the party secretary that the baby was his, and the girl was innocent. Upon hearing the news about the confession, the girl cut her belly open with a pair of scissors to show that the baby was not theirs. Two months later, she was released from the hospital, with a certificate from the doctor, which shows that she was still a virgin. The newspaper commented while carrying the story:

> It was during these ages that the once heroic Red Guards, the now middle-aged people who have endured more hardship than any other generations, had spent their youth. Is it because of the distorted ages that produced the distorted personalities, or vice versa?[19]

Youths have lost hope for their country. Dissident magazine, *Zhongguo zhichun* (*China Spring*) conducted a survey in 1984, that showed only about 40 percent of Chinese students studying in the United States wanted to stay. In 1988, 93 percent of them wanted to stay.[20] It is revealing if we consider the fact that in the late 1930s and 1940s, many Chinese intellectuals and students risked their lives to go to Yenan, the communist guerrilla base, to join the revolution, first against the Japanese and then against the Kuomintang. They gave up their comfort abroad or in big cities of China. In 1919, when the roughly 3,000 Chinese students studying in Japan learned that the Chinese *Beiyang* government had let the defeated Germany transfer its benefits in Shandong to Japan instead of letting China restore its rights, they immediately went back to China collectively to protest. In spite of a weak war lord government, a divided and foreign-occupied country, people at that time had hope. It is even more revealing if we recall that at the beginning of the Cultural Revolution, millions of Red Guards voluntarily gave up their comfort in the cities to go to the countryside to be educated by the peasants.

The sufferings caused by the Cultural Revolution have been mixed with that caused by reform. From the mid-1980s on, many money-losing enterprises were closed or only partially in operation because the government no longer subsidized them. Workers, who were in Mao's time the leading class, are being sent home with 70-percent of pay. Even for the peddlers, who are supposed to be among those who had benefited the most from the reform, life has not been easy. They have to rack their brains to evade taxes, otherwise not much money can be made. They must also bribe tax officials, otherwise their business will be threatened.

These sufferings have seriously influenced the mental health of the Chinese people. A survey found that "in China, there are now about 10 million seriously mentally ill people. The number is on the rise. Fifty to sixty-percent of the mental illness is caused by social factors, rather than psychological ones."[21] Another survey found that "China's mentally disturbed people are more numerous in proportion than many other countries. A sample survey conducted by the Chaoyang Hospital in Beijing shows that 73 percent of the mental illness is connected with social factors."[22]

The disastrous Cultural Revolution and the subsequent problems unleased by the reform, such as corruption, brought the reputation of Marxism into an all-time low. According to an officially endorsed survey conducted in 1988, more than 60-percent of the college students from 47 Chinese universities did not believe that communism was the future of the world.[23] At the various preparatory meetings for the Sixth Session of the 11th National Party Congress in 1982, there were serious talks among the document drafters that Mao and Lenin should not be given too much credit in the congress resolution. It was due to Deng Xiaoping's intervention, which may very well have been out of political motivations, that these anti-Mao and anti-Lenin attempts failed.[24] Another survey conducted by CASS in 1988 shows that the majority of a provincial city's people's deputies whose selections are largely under control of the party did not believe that Marxism was the only ideology that could lead the Chinese people to happiness. In addition, twice as many of them do not believe that China is more democratic than Western countries.[25]

In spite of the 1989 Tiananmen incident, the reform faction, which has been the mainstream of the Chinese ruling elite, has largely stuck to the reformist line. Given the bitter experiences of the past, it seems that those who favor central planning have been gradually losing ground. According to a senior adviser of the Chinese government on economic policies, there are currently three schools of thought in economics in China. The first school, mainly those who are based in the State Council's Planning Commission, believes that China's current economic problems are due to the reform, thus more planning should be called for. The second are those who favor marketization and, to various degrees, privatization. Most of these people are mainly based in some universities and research institutions. The third school, those who favor a gradual movement towards more market mechanism without committing themselves to any fixed models are mainly based in CASS. According to this adviser, the government has adopted the viewpoint of the third school.[26]

However, Marxism has not been replaced by another established ideology, either Confucianism or liberalism. Both of the elements of the altruistic communist culture and that of the traditional Chinese culture could be found in the 1950s, and even early 1960s. But a study conducted in Shanghai in 1988 shows that out of the 18 core values of Chinese tradition, only about half of them are still considered valid by the respondents.[27] However, only about 20 percent of the respondents of a survey conducted in Beijing in 1987 favor drastic social changes in the direction of liberalism.[28] We have good reason to believe that in other parts of the country, especially in the countryside, a smaller percent of the population would be in favor of drastic change in the direction of liberty.

Another aspect of the Chinese political culture is its intolerance for diverse opinions. This is clearly a legacy of the Chinese holistic-monistic tradition that favors unanimity. This aspect of Chinese political culture has always drawn attention from Western Sinologists.[29] A recent study reveals that the Chinese are indeed among the least tolerant among many nations in the world. Fewer than one-fifth of the Chinese respondents were willing to allow sympathizers of a deviant viewpoint to express their views in a meeting as compared to two-fifths to three-quarters of the populations in countries like Australia, Germany, Great Britain, and the United States in the 1960s.[30]

Elements of utopianism as embodied in the Chinese tradition can also be found in the political culture during the period. After the fall of the Gang of Four, the Chinese government led by Hua Guofeng immediately announced its ambitious construction plan: to build X number of Daqing Old Fields and Y number of Dazhai Counties across the country. This plan was later dropped, because it had no scientific base at all. The 14th National Party Congress held in 1992 inherited this utopianism. It announced that in 10 years, China should reach the level of moderately rich (*xiaokang*); in another 20 years, at the 100 anniversary of the party, China should have accomplished the establishment of a mature system; in another 30 years, i.e., at the 100 anniversary of the founding of the People's Republic, the socialist modernization has to be accomplished.[31] These slogans were announced because the people whose mentality has been influenced by utopianism need them. Science promises to solve all problems, not only social and economic problems, but also political problems. On a theoretical level, to observe objective law promises the inevitable success of communism, as insisted by Hu Qiaomu; to develop productive forces promises to improve the standard of living of the people, as claimed by Su Shaozhi; and systems theory promises to better understand history, as claimed by Jin Guantao.

In spite of the fact that the Chinese people seem to be living in a sort of value confusion, their political tolerance is low, and they want a quick fix economically, they do not desire drastic change of social structure in any direction. In other words, there is a certain amount of political indifference among the general population. It was found that some 72 percent of Chinese citizens stated that both national and local governments had no effect on their daily lives.[32] In addition, it was shown that in their "expectation of equal treatment," the Chinese citizens in 1990 were not very different from Germans, Italians and Mexicans in 1963, despite China's reputation for corruption and government abuse.[33]

Under this situation, a seemingly neutral thing such as science would be an ideal candidate to be used to unite the people. A fragmented political culture implies that different values, with none being dominant, are in big conflict with each other. A fragmented political culture, which still has a habit for unanimity, needs a neutral idea that everyone can agree on. Scientism suits this need. People want to find the truth. Utopianism and political indifference among the general population also call for such a neutral thing as science to be an ideology.

Not only has scientism reflected the Chinese political culture in general which can be described as fragmented, low in political tolerance, indifferent in political participation and utopian, but also its three versions have been able to remold Chinese political culture on three levels: idealistic; operational; tolerated.[34] The fact that the post-Mao surge of scientism is largely a psychological response to some symptoms as demonstrated during the Cultural Revolution, but not a rational treatment of disease is directly connected with Chinese political culture both in a horizontal level and sequential level.

By horizontal, I mean that the three species of scientism have played instrumental roles in remolding Chinese political culture on three levels in that the communist ultimate goal is satisfied (idealistic), the utilitarian policies of the current regime are justified (operational) and the growing need of the people for pluralism is also met (tolerated). By sequential, I mean to say that historical materialism was most acceptable in the late 1970s and early 1980s when voluntarism had to be corrected. Hu's insistence on observing objective laws in opposition to voluntarism was very well received, especially in the late 1970s. It was closely connected with the debate on seeking truth from facts, which helped break with the Maoist past and paved the path for reform. Su's technological determinism has been getting more useful since the mid 1980s for its depoliticized nature. Jin's empirical scientism is getting popular because people's desire for pluralism has been growing especially since the mid and late 1980s.

However, at any given stage, different aspects of political culture exist. For instance, Jin's pluralist approach had influence in the first stage while Hu's historical materialism still has followers today, no matter how small in number they are. In view of this situation, we may say that the three species of scientism as represented by Hu, Su and Jin, have been used to remold different versions of Chinese political culture. Roughly speaking, they have responded respectively to what I term the idealistic, operational and tolerated versions of political culture in China's reality. The idealistic version refers to the realization of communism; the operational version refers to the depoliticized approach of concentrating on developing productive forces; the tolerated version refers to various kinds of pluralism.

To conclude, the Chinese intellectuals have struggled to fill an intellectual vacuum created by the failure of the Cultural Revolution, the subsequent gradual loss of influence of Marxism as a whole, and to re-vision a polity for China. Were they successful in this intellectual endeavor? I have shown that some of their theories are not consistent and comprehensive and some are still in the process of taking shape. Were they successful in the political endeavor of remolding Chinese political culture during the period? What happened in the Beijing Spring of 1989 showed that the gap between the ruling elites and the masses was huge. Science as a political symbol has failed to remold the Chinese political culture in the last decade and it is unclear what else can the Chinese use to do so in the future. What has happened to those establishment intellectuals under study who tried hard to remold the Chinese political culture during the period? With the exception of Hu Qiaomu, who died after Tiananmen, either happily or bitterly, all have gone abroad: Jin Guantao and Liu Qingfeng are now doing research in Hong Kong; Su Shaozhi, Wang Ruoshui, Li Zehou and Gan Yang are teaching, doing research or working on Ph.D in the United States. Are they in the right place? Only time can tell.

Notes

Notes to Introduction

1. The first issue was confiscated by authorities, apparently for some "problematical" essays in the issue. See Kalpana Misra, "Rethinking Marxism in Post-Mao China: The Erosion of Official Ideology, 1978–1984," doctoral dissertation in political science, The University of Michigan, 1992.
2. Xu Liangying, *Science and Socialist Construction In China* (New York: M.E. Sharpe, Inc., 1982), p. 211.
3. Hong Yung Lee, *From Revolutionary Cadres to Party Technocrats in Socialist China* (Berkeley, CA: University of California Press, 1991), p. 268. Also Li Cheng and Lynn White, "The Thirteenth Central Committee of the Chinese Communist Party: From Mobilizers to Managers," *Asian Survey*, Vol. XXVIII, No. 4, April 1988.
4. Harry Harding, *China's Second Revolution* (Washington D.C.: The Brookings Institution, 1987), p. 155.
5. *Mingbao yuekan* (Hong Kong), September 1987, pp. 19–20.
6. Su Shaozhi, Woguo shehuizhuyi jingjiyanjiu zhongde ruogan wenti; (Certain Issues in the Study of China's Socialist Economy) (Shanghai: Shanghai renmin chubanshe, 1980), pp. 71–84.
7. This information was released by *Xinhua*. It was carried in *Zhongyang ribao* (Taiwan), August 8, 1992, p. 4.
8. Ding Xue-liang, "Xin makesizhuyi dui zhongguodalu de yingxiang" ("Neo-Marxism's Influence Over China"), *Minzhu Zhongguo*, February, 1991, pp. 38–49.
9. Ibid., pp. 38–49.
10. See Wang Ruoshui, "Wo de shenbian" ("My Self Defense"), *Mingbao yuekan* (Hong Kong), September 1989, p. 88.

11. Michel Bonnin and Yves Chevrier "The Intellectual and the State: Social Dynamics of Intellectual Autonomy During the Post-Mao Era," *The China Quarterly*, No. 127, September 1991, p. 57. Also see Zou Yizhi, "Jin Guantao fufu yinxiang" ("Impression of Jin Guantao and His Wife Liu Qingfeng"), *Mingbao yuekan* (Hong Kong), September, 1987, p. 19.

12. W. L. Chong, "Su Xiaokang on His Film 'River Elegy,'" *China Information*, Vol. IV. No. 3 (Winter 1989–1990), p. 52.

13. See Manfred Henningsen's article, "Democracy or the Promise of 'Civil Society,'" in *Linking Present Decisions to Long-Range Visions: Selection of Papers from the XI World Conference of the World Futures Studies Federation* (WFSF), edited by Mika Mannermaa (Budapest: Research Institute for Social Studies, 1992), p. 203.

14. Zou Yizhi, "Jin Guantao fufu yinxiang," *Mingbao yuekan*, September 1987, p. 19.

15. The information concerning the three major editorial boards is obtained from Su Wei's article "Bashiniandai Beijing zhishijie de wenhua quanzi" ("Cultural Circles Among Beijing Intellectuals in the 1980s"), *Zhongguo zhichun*, January, 1992. Also see Chen Lai, "Sixiang chulu de sandongxiang" ("Three Trends in Intellectual Thought"), *Dangdai* (Taiwan), 21 ed., January, 1988. Another source is Bonnin and Chevrier, "The Intellectual and the State: Social Dynamics of Intellectual Autonomy During the Post-Mao Era," *The China Quarterly*, No. 127, September 1991, p. 57.

16. See Tu Wei-ming, "Cultural China: The Periphery as the Center," *Daedalus*, Vol. 120, No. 2, Spring 1991.

Notes to Chapter 1

1. D. W. Y. Kwok, *Scientism in Chinese Thought (1900–1950)* (New York: Biblo and Tannen, 1971), p. 21.

2. This situation is particularly true in some disciplines in social sciences such as political science and sociology. See, for instance, Michael Hass, *Polity and Society: Philosophical Underpinnings of Social Science Paradigms*, (New York, Westport, CT, London: Praeger, 1992), Gabriel A. Almond, *A Discipline Divided: Schools and Sects in Political Science* (Newbury Park, CA: Sage Publications, 1990), and Howard J. Wiarda ed., *New Directions in Comparative Politics* (Boulder, CO: Westview, 1985).

3. Liu Qingfeng, *Rang kexue de guangmang zhaoliang ziji* (*Let the Light of Science Shine Over Ourselves*) (Chengdu: Sichuan renmin chubanshe, 1984), p. 2.

4. Thomas S. Kuhn, *The Essential Tension: Selected Studies in Scientific Tradition and Change* (Chicago: The University of Chicago Press, 1977), p. 148.
5. Ibid., pp. 40–41.
6. Thomas S. Kuhn, *The Structure of Scientific Revolutions* (Chicago: The University of Chicago Press, 1962), pp. 2–4.
7. Bill Brugger and David Kelly, *Chinese Marxism During the Post-Mao Era*, (Stanford, CA: Stanford University Press, 1990), p. 78.
8. Peter Manicas, *A History and Philosophy of Social Sciences* (Oxford: Basil Blackwell, 1987), p. 249.
9. Thomas Kuhn, The *Essential Tension: Selected Studies in Scientific Tradition and Change*, p. 137.
10. Peter Manicas, *A History and Philosophy of Social Sciences*, p. 262.
11. Ibid., p. 9, p. 249, p. 10.
12. See David Harvey, *The Condition of Post-Modernity* (Oxford: Basil Blackwell, 1989), "Part I". Also Alex Callinicos, *Against Post-Modernism: A Realist Critique* (New York: St. Martins Press, 1990).
13. James R. Townsend, "Politics in China," in Gabriel A. Almond and G. Bingham Powell, Jr., *Comparative Politics Today: A World View* (Boston: Little, Brown and Company, 1984), p. 385.
14. Actually, researchers from other disciplines are able to describe exactly the same situation without referring to these political science jargons of "Maoist political culture" and "bureaucratic political culture." See, for instance, Merle Goldman, *China's Intellectuals: Advice and Dissent* (Cambridge: Harvard University Press, 1981).
15. Andrew J. Nathan, "Is Chinese Culture Distinctive ?—A Review Article," *The Journal of Asian Studies*, Vol. 52, No. 4, November 1993, pp. 923–936. Also Andrew J. Nathan and Tianjian Shi, "Cultural Requisites for Democracy in China: Some Findings from a Survey," *Daedalus*, Vol. 122, No. 2, Spring 1993, pp. 95–123.
16. Tom Sorell, *Scientism: Philosophy and the Infatuation with Science* (London: Routledge, 1991), p. x and p. 4.
17. R.G. Owen, *Scientism, Man, and Religion* (Philadelphia: The Westminster Press, 1952), p. 20. Cited in Kwok, *Scientism in Chinese Thought*, p. 20.
18. Kwok has identified two main species of scientism in China during the first half of the twentieth century: 1) "materialistic scientism," which is subdivided into "dialectical materialism" and "philosophical materialism," 2) "empirical scientism." See Kwok, *Scientism in Chinese Thought*.
19. Tom Sorell, *Scientism: Philosophy and the Infatuation with Science*.
20. Ibid., p. 127 and pp. 176–177.

21. Hohn Wellmuth S.J., *The Nature and Origins of Scientism* (Milwaukee: Marquette University Press, 1944), pp. 3–5.

22. "Metaphysics" can be an attempt to characterize existence or reality as a whole, instead of, as in the various natural sciences, particular parts or aspects thereof. Materialism and idealism are examples of metaphysics in this sense. See, *A Dictionary of Philosophy* (New York: The Macmillan Press Ltd., 1984), pp. 229–230.

23. According to this interpretation, dialectics departs from metaphysics in two ways: 1) dialectics emphasizes change, while metaphysics down plays change; 2) dialectics emphasizes totality, while metaphysics stresses parts. See Xing Bisi et al. eds., *Makesizhuyi sixiang baoku* (*Treasure-House of Marxist Thought*) (Haikou: Nanhai chubangongsi, 1990), pp. 72–80.

24. Michael Haas, *Polity and Society: Philosophical Underpinnings of Social Science Paradigms.*

25. The Chinese term *xuan xue* can refer to different things. *Xuan xue* can be translated either into "metaphysics," as Kwok does, or "mystical," as Jo-Shui Chen does. See Kwok, *Scientism in Chinese Thought*, and Jo-Shui Chen, "Review of the book, *Li Ao: Buddhist, Taoist, or Neo-Confucian?*" by T. H. Barett, *The Journal of Asian Studies*, Vol. 52, No. 4, November 1993, p. 975.

26. See D. W. Y. Kwok, *Scientism in Chinese Thought*, p. 24.

27. See, Liu Qingfeng, "Ershishiji zhongguo kexuezhuyi de liangcixingqi," (The Two Surges of Chinese Scientism in the Twentieth Century) *Ershiyi shiji* (Hong Kong), April, 1991.

28. Derek Sayer, *Marx's Method* (New Jersey: Humanities Press, 1979).

29. Maurice Mandelbaum, *History, Man, & Reason: A study in Nineteenth-Century Thought* (Baltimore and London: The Johns Hopkins Press, 1971), p. 27. Also Terrell Carver, *Engels* (Oxford: Oxford University Press, 1981).

30. This linkage should be viewed in a flexible way. It is just a tendency. For instance, Wu Zhihui, an anarchist, believes in materialistic scientism too.

31. Tom Sorell, *Scientism: Philosophy and the Infatuation with Science*, p. 35 and p. 37.

32. Su Shaozhi, "A Decade of Crises at the Institute of Marxism-Leninism-Mao Zedong Thought," *The China Quarterly*, June 1993, pp. 335–351.

33. Liu Qingfeng, *Rang kexue de guangmang zhaoliang ziji*, pp. 165–205.

34. See Charles O. Hucker, *China's Imperial Past: An Introduction to Chinese History and Culture* (Stanford, CA.: Stanford University Press, 1975), p. 69.

35. Richard Baum, *Scientism and Bureaucratism in Chinese Thought: Cultural Limits of the "Four Modernizations"* (Sweden: University of Lund, 1981), pp. 15–16.
36. R. R. Palmer and Joel Colton, *A History of the Modern World* (New York: Alfred A. Knopf, 1971), pp. 335–336.
37. David Hoy, "Jacques Derrida" in Quention Skinner ed., *The Return of Grand Theory in the Human Science* (Cambridge: Cambridge University Press, 1985), pp. 46–47.
38. Xu Chongwen, *Yong makesizhuyi pingxi xifang sichao* (*To Analyze Western Intellectual Thought with Marxism*) (Chongqing: Chongqing chubanshe, 1990), pp. 346–407.
39. Some members of this group, such as Habermas and Adorno may not be considered as belonging to Neo-Marxism, because they openly criticize the main ideas of Marxism.
40. Xu Chongwen, *Xifang makesizhuyi luncong* (*A Collection of Articles on Western Marxism*) (Chongqing: Chongqing chubanshe, 1989), p. 20.
41. Lin Min, "The Search for Modernity: Chinese Intellectual Discourse and Society, 1978-88—the Case of Li Zehou," *The China Quarterly*, December 1992, pp. 969–998.
42. C. P. Snow, *The Two Cultures and the Scientific Revolution* (New York: Cambridge University Press 1961), pp. 1–22.
43. Plato, *The Republic* (New York: Basic Books, 1968).
44. Aristotle, *The Politics* (New York: Oxford University Press, 1962).
45. John Locke, *Second Treatise on Civil Government* (New York: New American Library, 1965).
46. Jean-Jacques Rousseau, *The Social Contract and Discourse on Inequality* (New York: Washington Square Press, 1967).
47. Max Weber, *The Theory of Social and Economic Organization* (New York: Oxford University Press, 1974), pp. 87–157.
48. Yang Guorong, "Wang Guowei de neizai jinzhang: kexuezhuyi yu renbenzhuyi de duizhi," (The tension within Wang Guowei: the confrontation between scientism and humanism) *Ershiyi shiji* (Hong Kong), 11th edition, June 1992, p. 36.
49. Ibid., pp. 34–41.
50. Ronald H. Chilcote, *Theories of Comparative Politics: The Search for a Paradigm* (Boulder, Colorado: Westview Press, 1981), pp. 112.
51. Peter Moody, Jr. *Opposition and Dissent in Contemporary China* (Stanford, CA: Hoover Institution Press, 1977), p. 114 and pp. 167–184.
52. Merle Goldman, *China's Intellectuals: Advice and Dissent*, p. 1.
53. Ibid., pp. 2–8.
54. Carol L. Hamrin and Timothy Cheek, eds. *China's Establishment Intellectuals* (Armonk, NY: M.E. Sharpe, 1986), p. 4.

55. Carol Hamrin and Timothy Cheek, eds. *China's Establishment Intellectuals,* pp. 13–15.
56. Peter Moody, Jr., *Opposition and Dissent in Contemporary China,* pp. 167–84.
57. David Kelly in Merle Goldman, with Timothy Cheek and Carol L. Hamrin eds., *China's Intellectuals and the State: In Search of a New Relationship* (Cambridge, MA: Council on East Asian Studies, Harvard University, 1987), p. 163.
58. Goldman and Cheek further divided these intellectual leaders into: 1) ideologists; 2) academics and professionals; 3) critical intellectuals. (Goldman and Cheek in Goldman, et al, eds., *China's Intellectuals and the State: In Search of a New Relationship,* 1987), pp. 1–7) Apparently, the basis on which these distinctions were made is neither tradition nor social functions.
59. James J. Williams, "Fang Lizhi's Expanding Universe," *The China Quarterly,* September, 1990, p. 82.
60. David Bachman and Dali Yang, [trans. and ed.] *Yan Jiaqi and China's Struggle for Democracy* (Armonk, NY: M.E. Sharpe, 1991), p. xiii.
61. Frederick Wakeman, "The Price of Autonomy: Intellectuals in Ming and Ching Politics," *Daedalus,* 1972, Spring, pp. 55–67.
62. Ibid., p. 35.
63. Yu Ying-shih, "Zhongguo zhishifenzi de bianyuan hua" ("The Marginalization of Chinese Intellectuals"), *Ershiyi shiji* (Hong Kong), 6th issue, August, 1991, pp. 18–19.
64. D. Simon in Goldman, with Cheek and Hamrin eds., *China's Intellectuals and the State: In Search of a New Relationship,* p. 156.
65. Lynn White and Li Cheng in Chang King-Yuh ed., *Mainland China After the Thirteenth Party Congress,* (Boulder, CO: Westview Press, 1990), p. 454.
66. R. Wagner in Goldman, with Cheek and Hamrin eds., *China's Intellectuals and the State: In Search of a New Relationship,* p. 219.
67. Cited in Perry Link, *Evening Chats in Beijing: Probing China's Predicament,* (New York, London: W. W. Norton & Company, 1992), p. 24.
68. Yan made the remarks in a conversation with me in Honolulu in June 1993.
69. Su wrote this in a letter to me dated December 1991.
70. Zhou Zezong, "Preface" to *Zhongguo de jiliang (China's Backbone)* in Lu Keng and Liang Qindong eds., (Hong Kong: Baixing wenhuashiye youxiangongsi, 1990), p. iii.
71. Wei Zhengdong, "Wenhua zhongguo de xiang zheng" ("Symbol of Cultural China") in Lu Keng and Liang Qindong eds., *Zhongguo de jiliang,* p. 39.

Notes to Chapter 2

1. Tu Wei-ming, *Rujia ziwo yishi de fansi* (*Self Reflection on the Sense of Self Awareness of Confucianism*) (Taibei: Lianjing chubanshiye gongsi, 1990), p. 69.
2. Hu Shih (Hu Shi), *The Development of the Logical Method in Ancient China* (New York: Paragon Book Reprint Corp., 1963).
3. Charles O. Hucker, *China's Imperial Past: An Introduction to Chinese History and Culture* (Stanford, CA. Stanford University Press, 1975), p. 70.
4. Frederic L. Bender ed., *Karl Marx: The Essential Writings* (New York: Harper Torchbooks, 1972), pp. 164–229.
5. Karl A. Wittfogel, *Oriental Despotism: A Comparative Study of Total Power* (New York: Vintage Books, 1981).
6. Benjamin Schwartz, "Introduction," Yu-sheng Lin, *The Crisis of Chinese Consciousness* (Madison: The University of Wisconsin Press, 1979), p. ix.
7. Charles O. Hucker, *China's Imperial Past: An Introduction to Chinese History and Culture*, pp. 70–71.
8. Tu Wei-ming, *Rujia ziwo yishi de fansi*, p. 166.
9. Interpreted by Kang Youwei in Yao Peng et al. eds., *Zhongguo sixiang baoku* (*Treasure House of Chinese Thought*) (Beijing: Zhongguo guangbo chubanshe, 1990), p. 404.
10. Charles O. Hucker, *China's Imperial Past: In Introduction to Chinese History and Culture*, pp. 22–95.
11. Liao Yuren, "Ruhe jiasu sanminzhuyi quanmian dengshang dalu" ("How to Quicken the Process During Which The Three People's Principles Conquer Mainland China") in Qi Fang, *Heping yanbian zhanlue de chansheng jiqi fazhan* (*The Origin and Development of the Strategy of Peaceful Restoration of Capitalism*) (Beijing: Dongfang chubanshe, 1990), p. 197.
12. Mao Zedong, "Du Bo Gu yi *Bianzhengfa weiwulun yu lishi weiwulun* yishu de pizhu," ("Read *Dialectical Materialism and Historical Materialism* translated by Bo Gu") in *Mao Zedong zhexue pizhuji* (*A Collection of Mao Zedong's Comments on Philosophy Works*), in *Makesi zhuyi sixiang baoku* (*Treasure House of Marxism*), Xing Bisi, et al. eds., (Haikou: Hainan chubangongsi, 1990), p. 125.
13. Feng Xianzhi, "Mao Zedong du malie zhuzuo" ("Mao Zedong read works by Marx, Engles, Lenin and Stalin"), *Xinhua wenzhai* (Beijing), February, 1991, p. 202.
14. It has also been found that Mao quotes more than five times as much from Confucian classics than he does from the works of Marx and

Engels. See Lucian Pye, *Mao Tse-tung—The Man in the Leader* (New York: Basic Books, Inc. Publishers, 1976), p. 240.

15. Feng Xianzhi "Mao Zedong du malie zhuzuo," p. 202.

16. *The Manuscripts* were written from March to August of 1844. They were intended to be part of a grand project about political economy and other social, political and judicial issues. Marx later gave up the project, because it covered too wide of an area. Parts of *The Manuscripts* were first published in 1927 in the Soviet Union. See Xu Xing, *Chinese Politics in Reform* (Hong Kong: Pioneer Publishers, 1986), pp. 185–186.

17. Bill Brugger and David Kelly, *Chinese Marxism During the Post-Mao Era*, p. 122.

18. Ibid., p. 83. and p. 122.

19. See Quan Yanchi, *Lingxiu lei* (*The Tears of the Leader*) (Beijing: Zhonggongzhongyang dangxiao chubanshe, 1990), p. 52.

20. Ibid., pp. 62–65.

21. Tianjinshi Geming Weiyuanhui, *Wuchanjieji wenhuadageming zhongyao wenxian xuanbian* (*A Selection of Important Works of the Cultural Revolution*) (Tianjin: Tianjin renmin chubanshe, 1969), p. 42.

22. This was put forward by Mao on January 28, 1958. See Quan Yanchi, *Zouxia shentan de Mao Zedong* (*Mao Zedong, Who Steps Down from the Shrine of God*) (Beijing: Zhongwai wenhua chubangongsi, 1989), p. 51.

23. Stephen Uhalley, Jr. *A History of the Chinese Communist Party*, (Stanford: CA Hoover Institution Press, 1988), p. 147.

24. Mark Selden, *The Political Economy of Chinese Socialism* (Armonk, New York: M. E. Sharpe, 1988), p. 15.

25. Li made the remarks at the East West Center on June 14, 1991.

26. Yao Xianguo, *Liangji fenhua: fuyin haishi zainan* (*Polarization of Wealth: Fortune or Disaster*) (Beijing: Xueyuan chubanshe, 1989), p. 2.

27. Suzanne Ogden, *China's Unresolved Issues* (Englewood Cliffs, New Jersey: Prentice Hall, 1989), p. 274.

28. Hu Jian, *Dongdang de xiaofei jiegou* (*The Fluctuating Consumption Structure*) (Beijing: Xueyuan chubanshe, 1989), pp. 11–15.

29. Ibid., pp. 13.

30. Mark Selden, *The Political Economy of Chinese Socialism*, pp. 15–17.

31. "1990 World Population Data Sheet," Population Reference Bureau, Inc., Washington, D.C. Quoted in Tu Wei-ming "Cultural China: The Periphery as the Center," p. 5.

32. Cited in Manfred Henningsen "Democracy or the Promise of 'Civil Society,' " in *Linking Present Decisions to Long-Range Visions, I.* published in April 1992 by Erzsebet Gidai, Research Institute for Social Studies, p. 192.

Notes to Chapter 3

1. See Hu Qiaomu, "Dangqian sixiang zhanxianshang de ruogan wenti" ("On Some Issues in the Current Ideological Front"), *Hong Qi*, (Beijing) 23rd Vol. 1981, p. 10 and Hu Qiaomu, "Guanyu rendaozhuyi he yihua wenti" ("On Humanism and the Issue of Alienation"), *Renmin ribao*, January, 27, 1984, p. 5.
2. Wolfgang Bartke, *Who's Who in the PRC* (Oxford: K.G. Saur, 1987), p. 156.
3. See Quan Yanchi, *Ling xiu lei*, p. 83.
4. See Ai Zhu, "Kan Hu Qiaomu shizenyang chumai Deng Xiaoping" ("See How Hu Betrayed Deng Xiaoping"), *Mingbao yuekan* (Hong Kong), April 1984, p. 19.
5. See Bill Brugger and David Kelly, *Chinese Marxism in the Post-Mao Era*, p. 122.
6. The so-called "liberal intellectuals" refer to those intellectuals who had an orientation of "promoting professional autonomy, and improving the prevailing system by expressing a variety of viewpoints within a broad ideological framework." Merle Goldman, *China's Intellectuals: Advise and Dissent*, p. 2.
7. Merle Goldman, *China's Intellectuals: Advise and Dissent*, p. 147.
8. Ibid., pp. 32–33.
9. Wolfgang Bartke, *Who's Who in the PRC*, p. 156.
10. See Ai zhu, "Kan Hu Qiaomu shizenyang chumai Deng Xiaoping," p. 19.
11. See Maurice Meisner, "The Chinese Rediscovery of Karl Marx," *Bulletin of Concerned Asian Scholars*, Vol. 17, No. 3, July-September, 1985.
12. Hu Qiaomu, *Zhongguo gongchandang zenyang fazhanle makesizhuyi—wei jinian jiandang qishi zhounian zuo* (*How has the CCP Developed Marxism—in Celebration of the 70th Anniversary of the Party* (Beijing: Renmin chubanshe, 1991), pp. 4–5.
13. Hu Qiaomu, "Guanyu rendaozhuyi he yihua wenti," pp. 4–5.
14. Second International (1889–1914) was an international organization of the workers movement at that time. With Engels, Kautsky and Plekhanov on one side and Bernstein on the other, theoretical battles were fought over the issues of: 1) stage theory; 2) polarization of wealth between the workers and capitalists; 3) base/superstructure dichotomy. The less economic reductionist Bernstein lost the battle within the Second International. Therefore, Second International Marxism generally refers to the economic reductionist interpretation of Marx. China's "orthodox Marxism" is by and large in this tradition.

15. Feng Xianzhi, "Mao Zedong du malie zhuzuo," p. 202.
16. Ibid., p. 204.
17. Hu Qiaomu, "Guanyu rendaozhuyi he yihua wenti" p. 2.
18. Ibid., p. 2.
19. Cited in Derek Sayer, *Marx's Method*, p. 112.
20. Cited in Peter Manicas, *A History and Philosophy of Social Sciences*, p. 101.
21. Ibid., p. 101.
22. Hu Qiaomu, "Guanyu rendaozhuyi he yihua wenti," p. 5.
23. See Daniel Bell, "The 'Rediscovery' of Alienation," in *Marx's Socialism*, ed. by Shlomo Avineri (New York: Lieber-Atherton, Inc., 1972), pp. 59–79.
24. Derek Sayer, *The Violence of Abstraction: The Analytic Foundations of Historical Materialism*, (Oxford and New York: Basil Blackwell, 1987), p. ix.
25. "Makesi maigupiao," (Marx buys stocks) *Shenzhou Xueren* (*China's Scholars Abroad*), February 1993, p. 47. (No author)
26. Hu Qiaomu, "Guanyu rendaozhuyi he yihua wenti."
27. Ibid., p. 2.
28. Ibid., p. 5.
29. Quoted by Frederic L. Bender ed., *Karl Marx: The Essential Writings* (Boulder, CO: Westview, 1986), p. 163.
30. Quoted in Philip Corrigan, Harvie Ramsay and Derek Sayer, *Socialist Construction and Marxist Theory* (New York: Monthly Review Press, 1978), p. 19.
31. Ibid., p. 28.
32. Quoted by Alan Hunt, *Marxism and Democracy*, (London: Lawrence and Wishart, 1980), p. 23.
33. Hu Qiaomu, "Guanyu gongchan zhuyi sixiang de shijian," ("On the practice of communist ideology"), *Renmin ribao*, September 24, 1982, p. 1.
34. Hu Qiaomu, "Dangqian sixiang zhanxianshang de ruogan wenti," p. 12.
35. Hu Qiaomu, "Guanyu rendaozhuyi he yihua wenti," p. 5.
36. Hu Qiaomu, "Dangqian sixiang zhanxianshang de ruogan wenti," p. 12.
37. Hu Qiaomu, "Zhongguo gongchandang zenyang fazhanle makesizhuyi," pp. 36–37.
38. Hu Qiaomu, "Dangqian sixiang zhanxianshang de ruogan wenti," p. 12.
39. Hu Qiaomu, "Zhongguo gongchandang zenyang fazhanle makesizhuyi," p. 26.
40. Ibid., pp. 26–27.

Notes to Chapter 4

1. Maurice Meisner, "The Chinese Rediscovery of Karl Marx," p. 3.
2. Ding Xue-liang, "The Disparity Between Idealistic and Instrumental Chinese Reformers," *Asian Survey*. Vol. 18, No. 11, November 1988, pp. 1121–1126. Also see Gordon Chang's comments on Su Shaozhi's remarks on Marxism in China, *Bulletin of Concerned Asian Scholars*, Vol. 20, No. 1, 1988. p. 27.
3. Andrew J. Nathan, *China's Crisis: Dilemmas of Reform and Prospects for Democracy* (New York: Columbia University Press, 1990), p. 180.
4. Bill Brugger and David Kelly, *Chinese Marxism in the Post-Mao Era*, pp. 5–6.
5. Ibid., p. 34. Chen Zhangjin, "Su Shaozhi jiqi zhengzhi gaige linian" ("Su Shaozhi and His Political Reform Beliefs"), *Zhongguodalu wenti yanjiu* (Taiwan), Vol. 30, Ed. 7, January 1988, pp. 52–53. According to Su Shaozhi himself, "Zhao's speech (at the 13th National Party Congress) centered on the 'primary-stage of socialism,' the concept originally developed by Su Shaozhi and Feng Lanrui." See, Su Shaozhi, "A Decade of Crises at the Institute of Marxism-Leninism-Mao Zedong Thought, 1979–89," *The China Quarterly*, No. 134, June 1993, p. 350.
6. Chen Zhangjin, "Su Shaozhi jiqi zhengzhi gaige linian," pp. 52–53.
7. Su Shaozhi, *Woguo shehuizhuyi jingjiyanjiu zhongde ruoganwenti* (*Certain Issues in the Study of China's Socialist Economy*) (Shanghai: Shanghai renmin chubanshe, 1980), p. 30.
8. Ibid., p. 64.
9. Chen Zhangjin, "Su Shaozhi jiqi zhengzhi gaige linian," p. 53.
10. Ibid., pp. 52–53.
11. See Huang Jin, "Zhao Ziyang xiatai diyun" ("An Analysis of the Fall of Zhao Ziyang,") *Mingbao yuekan* (Hong Kong), April 1990, pp. 39–40.
12. Su Shaozhi, "A Decade of Crises at the Institute of Marxism-Leninism-Mao Zedong Thought, 1979–89," p. 348.
13. The account by Bill Brugger and David Kelly that "Su's expulsion from the Communist Party in August 1987 was part of the price Zhao [Ziyang] was forced to pay to have the elementary-stage of socialism theory adopted as policy in October" is not accurate. See, Bill Brugger and David Kelly, *Chinese Marxism in the Post-Mao Era*, p. 34. Su did not lose party membership. Zhao was said to have remarked that the theorist's "articles had played a good role in reform and opening up." See Su Shaozhi, "A Decade of Crises at the Institute of Marxism-Leninism-Mao Zedong Thought, 1979–89," p. 348.

14. According to Yan Jiaqi, his own appointment was approved by Deng Xiaoping. If that's the case, and given the high status of the committee, Su's appointment may also have been approved by Deng. This is based on Yan's speech in Honolulu, Hawaii, March 3, 1990 organized by the Center for Chinese Studies, University of Hawaii at Manoa.

15. Su Shaozhi, *Democratization and Reform* (Nottingham: Spokesman, 1988), p. 113.

16. Su Shaozhi, *Marxism in China* (Nottingham: Spokesman, 1988), p. 18.

17. Su Shaozhi, *Democratization and Reform*, p. 68.

18. Lucio Colletti, *From Rousseau to Lenin: Studies in Ideology and Society* (New York: Monthly Review Press, 1972), pp. 68–69.

19. See F.A. Hayek, *Law, Legislation and Liberty* (Chicago: University of Chicago Press, 1979), pp. 12–30.

20. Cited in Su Shaozhi, *Democratization and Reform*, p. 88.

21. Karl Marx, *A Contribution to the Critique of Political Economy* (1859). Cited in "Responses to Hua Shiping's 'All Roads Lead to Democracy.'" *Bulletin of Concerned Asian Scholars*, Vol. 24, No. 1, January–March, 1992, p. 56.

22. Quoted in Lucio Colletti, *From Rousseau to Lenin: Studies in Ideology and Society*, p. 64.

23. Ibid., p. 64.

24. Su Shaozhi, *Democratization and Reform*, pp. 90–93.

25. Ibid., pp. 90–92.

26. Bernstein argues that the development of productive forces would bring about a social structure not like a smooth-sided pyramid with the capitalist class at the apex, but a stepped pyramid in which blocks of decreasing width were superimposed upon each other. See Eduard Bernstein, *Evolutionary Socialism* (New York: Scribner's, 1961), pp. 28–94.

27. Kerr argues that industrialization rationality will bring about an increasingly unified world in terms of social division of labor, patterns of consumption, and modes of cooperation. This is in disregard of the different political, economic and cultural backgrounds of the countries involved. Industrialization also makes the management more professionally oriented, decentralized instead of dictatorial, and constitutional instead of personal. In addition, it is the managers who play a decisive role in developing the industrial work force, not only in recruiting workers but also in getting them to be committed to industrial employment with the demands it makes on them. See Clark Kerr, *Industrialism and Industrial Man: The Problems of Labor and Management in Economic Growth* (New York: Oxford University Press, 1964), chapters 6 and 7, part II. The ideological nature of

convergence theory has been pointed out by scholars in the field. See, for instance, Deane Neubauer, "Convergence Theory Revisited," *Occasional Papers in Political Science*, University of Hawaii, January 1990, Vol. 3, No. 3, pp. 77–92.

28. Chen Xianda, *Makesizhuyi jibenyuanli jiaocheng (A Textbook of Basic Theories in Marxism)* (Beijing: Zhongguo renmindaxue chubanshe, 1988), p. 97.

29. Su Shaozhi, *Woguo shehuizhuyi jingjiyanjiu zhongde ruoganwenti*, pp. 70–71.

30. Su Shaozhi, *Democratization and Reform*, p. 170. Su made similar remarks else where. See, Su Shaozhi "Rethinking Socialism in the Light of China's Reforms," *China Information*, Vol. VI. No. 1, Summer 1991, p. 13. Also Su Shaozhi, "Su Questions Chinese Marxism," *Messenger*, published by China Times Center for Media and Social Studies, November 15, 1993, p. 8.

31. Su Shaozhi, *Democratization and Reform*, p. 59.

32. Ibid., p. 84.

33. Su Shaozhi, *Woguo shehuizhuyi jingjiyanjiu zhongde ruoganwenti*, p. 83 and p. 71.

34. Kautsky considered "the breakdown of existing society as inevitable, since we know that economic development creates with a natural necessity conditions which force the exploited to strive against private property." Quoted by Lucio Colleti, *From Rousseau to Lenin: Studies in Ideology and Society*, p. 55. For Kautsky, socialism was the inevitable product of capitalist development, because of the economic effects of that development and their political consequences. The economic tendencies of capitalism involve an increasing polarization, the decline of the peasantry and urban petty bourgeoisie, the concentration of capitalist production, and the growth of the organized working class to that it finally encompasses a majority of the population. See Alan Hunt, *Marxism and Democracy* (London: Lawrence and Wishart, 1980), p. 23.

35. This was quoted by Su Shaozhi, in "A Symposium on Marxism in China Today," p. 32.

36. Jiang Zemin, "Zhongguo zouxiang ershiyi shiji" ("China Marches Towards the Twenty-First Century"), *Renmin ribao*, May 18, 1991, p. 1.

37. See Suzanne Ogden's *China's Unresolved Issues*. In the last sentence of the book, Ogden remarked, "'Socialism with Chinese characteristics' (i.e., Dengist socialism) now means anything that helps China modernize." p. 353.

38. Su Shaozhi, *Democratization and Reform*, p. 175.

39. Ibid., pp. 162–163.

40. Ibid., p. 158.
41. *Bai xing* (Hong Kong), September, 1, 1991, p. 22.
42. Su Shaozhi, *Woguo shehuizhuyi jingjiyanjiu zhongde ruoganwenti*, pp. 84–85.
43. See Kalpana Misra's dissertation, "Rethinking Marxism in Post-Mao China: The Erosion of Official Ideology, 1978–84." p. 176.
44. This was based on *Papers of the Center for Modern China*, published by the Center for Modern China based in Princeton. Back cover.
45. Su Shaozhi, *Woguo shehuizhuyi jingjiyanjiu zhongde ruoganwenti*, p. 74.
46. Ibid., pp. 60–80.
47. Ibid., p. 63.
48. Ibid., p. 81.
49. Su said that he had to refuse the request from some to write a book on China's political economy. He said, "I was, however, hard to put to it when you asked me to contribute. This is because, in my opinion, as both the subjective and objective conditions are not ripe for writing a book on political economy (socialist part), it is hardly possible to begin to talk about system. For this reason, I am at the moment a "liquidationist" in the study of the systems of political economy. See Su Shaozhi, *Democratization and Reform*, p. 106.
50. Su Shaozhi, *Democratization and Reform*, p. 110.
51. Su Shaozhi "A Symposium on Marxism in China Today," in *Bulletin of Concerned Asian Scholars*, Vol. 20, No. 1, 1988, p. 14.
52. Su Shaozhi, "Jianchi kexue shehuizhuyi daolu" ("Stick to the Road of Scientific Socialism"), *Dushu*, (Beijing) May, 1979, p. 4.
53. Su Shaozhi, *Democratization and Reform*, p. 94.
54. Su Shaozhi, *Marxism in China*, pp. 13–52.
55. T. Bottomore et al., *A Dictionary of Marxist Thought* (Cambridge: Harvard University Press, 1983), p. 44.
56. Alan Hunt, *Marxism and Democracy*, p. 52.
57. Su Shaozhi, *Marxism in China*, p. 37.
58. Su Shaozhi, *Democratization and Reform*, p. 141.
59. According to orthodox Marxism, although superstructure is determined by the base, the former does have impact on the latter. Sometimes, the latter can be decisive. However, "in the last instance," using Engels' rhetoric, superstructure is determined by the base. See T. Bottomore et al., *A Dictionary of Marxist Thought* (Cambridge: Harvard University Press, 1983), p. 44. Also see Alan Hunt, *Marxism and Democracy*, p. 52.

Notes to Chapter 5

1. See Jin Guantao, "Wo shi zenyang pandeng sixiang jietide" ("How Do I Climb up the Ladder of Thought?"), *Mingbao yuekan* (Hong Kong), March 1988, pp. 54–55. Also see Chen Zhangjin "Jin Guantao yu zhongguo wenhua chulu de tantao" ("Jin Guantao's Exploration of the Way Out for Chinese Culture"), *Zhongguo dalu yanjiu* (Taiwan), August, 1988, Vol. 31, 5th Ed., pp. 78–79.

2. Jin Guantao, "Wo shi zenyang pandeng sixiang jietide", p. 60.

3. Ibid., p. 61.

4. Jin Guantao, *Ren de zhexue* (*The Philosophy of Man*) (Taibei: Shangwu yinshuguan, 1988), pp. 3–17.

5. Bill Brugger and David Kelly, *Chinese Marxism in the Post-Mao Era*, p. 73.

6. Jin Guantao, *Zhengti de zhexue* (*Philosophy of the Whole*), (Chengdu, Sichuan: Renmin chubanshe, 1987), pp. 6–11.

7. Jin Guantao, "Wo shi zenyang pandeng sixiang jietide," p. 57.

8. He Zhama, "Jin Guantao weishenmo yao fouding shizaide keguanxing" ("Why Does Jin Guantao Want to Negate the Objectivity of Being?"), *Xinhua wenzhai* (Beijing), January 1990, pp. 26–28.

9. Jin Guantao and Liu Qingfeng, "Tantao zirankexue he shehuikexue tongyi de fangfalun" ("Explore a Method Which Unites Natural Sciences and Social Sciences"), in *Wenti he fangfa ji* (*A Collection on Issues and Methods*) (Shanghai: Shanghai renmin chubanshe, 1986), pp. 392–98.

10. Jin Guantao and Liu Qingfeng, "Tantao zirankexue he shehuikexue tongyi de fangfalun." pp. 392–393.

11. Their views concerning scientific norms are not as rigid as they look here. See Liu Qingfeng, *Reng kexue de guangmang zhaoliang ziji*, p. 2.

12. Jin Guantao and Liu Qingfeng, *Xingsheng yu weiji—lun zhongguo fengjian shehui de chaowending jiegou* (*The Cycle of Growth and Decline—on the Ultrastable Structure of Chinese Society*) (Changsha: Hunan renmin chubanshe, 1984), p. 9. Also see Karl Marx, *The Economic & Philosophic Manuscripts of 1844* (New York: International Publishers, 1964), pp. 142–43.

13. See, Derek Sayer, *Marx's Method*, pp. 110–134.

14. Jin Guantao, *Zhengti de zhexue*, pp. 105–107.

15. Ibid., pp. 108–110.

16. Jin Guantao, "Wo shi zenyang pandeng sixiang jietide", p. 59.

17. Ibid., p. 54.

18. The book is in the name of Jin Guantao and his wife Liu Qingfeng. Given the fact that the 1992 edition of the book makes it explicit that the theoretical basis of this book is *Zhengti de zhexue*, we may say that Jin has played a bigger role. Therefore, although discussions in this section are concerned with both Jin and Liu, the reader should realize that Jin is the chief author and the theories discussed in this section should be viewed in accordance with Jin's position in philosophy as was discussed previously.

19. Jin Guantao and Liu Qingfeng, *Xingsheng yu weiji* (1984), pp. 4–8.

20. Jin Guantao, *Zhengti de zhexue*, p. 264.

21. Jin Guantao and Liu Qingfeng, *Xingsheng yu weiji—lun zhongguo fengjian shehui de chaowending jiegou* (*The Cycle of Growth and Decline—On the Ultrastable Structure of Chinese Society*) (Hong Kong: The Chinese University Press, 1992), pp. 96–104.

22. These three theories of cybernetics, information theory and systems theory cannot be separated. For the convenience of presentation, in the following, I will just use the more common "systems theory" to represent them all.

23. Jin Guantao and Liu Qingfeng, *Xingsheng yu weiji*, (1984) pp. 8–10.

24. Jin Guantao and Liu Qingfeng, *Xingsheng yu weiji* (1992), p. 310.

25. Robert Lilienfeld, "Systems Theory as an Ideology," *Social Research*, Winter, 1975, pp. 637–674.

26. Jin Guantao and Liu Qingfeng, *Xingsheng yu weiji*, (1984) p. 10.

27. Robert Lilienfeld, "Systems Theory as an Ideology," p. 657.

28. Jin Guantao, "Wo shi zenyang pandeng sixiang jietide", pp. 56–57.

29. Jin Guantao and Liu Qingfeng, *Xingsheng yu weiji*, (1992), pp. 277–300.

30. Liu Qingfeng, "Da Huan Xuewen" ("In response to Huan Xuewen"), *Ershiyi shiji* (Hong Kong), October, 1991, 7th Ed., pp. 147–149.

31. Jin Guantao, *Zhengti de zhexue*, pp. 108–109.

32. Robert Lilienfeld, "Systems Theory as an Ideology," p. 673.

33. He Zhama, "Jin Guantao wei shen mo yao fouding shizai de keguanxing" pp. 26–28.

34. Jin Guantao and Liu Qingfeng, *Kaifang zhong de bianqian: Zailun zhongguo shehui chaowending jiegou* (*The Transformation of Chinese Society (1840–1956)—The Fate of Its Ultrastable Structure in Modern Times*) (Hong Kong: The Chinese University Press, 1993), pp. 2–3.

35. Chen Zhangjin, "Zouchu zhongguo chuantong wenhua de kunjiu?" ("Going out of the Dilemma of Chinese Cultural Tradition?"), *Zhongguo dalu yanjiu* (Taiwan), Vol. 31. 10th Ed. April, 1989, p. 63.

36. Jin Guantao and Liu Qingfeng, *Kaifang zhong de bianqian*, pp. vii–viii.

37. See Jin Guantao, "Socialism and Tradition: The Formation and Development of Modern Chinese Political Culture," *The Journal of Contemporary China*, No. 3, Summer 1993, pp. 3–17.

38. Yan Jiaqi, *Wo de sixiang zizhuan (My Intellectual Autobiography)* (Hong Kong: Sanlian shudian, 1988), p. 2, p. 39 and pp. 7–10.

39. David Bachman and Dali L. Yang, trans. and eds., *Yan Jiaqi and China's Struggle for Democracy* (Armonk: M.E.Sharpe, Inc., 1991), p. xxvii.

40. Yan Jiaqi, *Wo de sixiang zizhuan*, p. 96–98.

41. David Bachman and Dali L. Yang, *Yan Jiaqi and China's Struggle for Democracy*, p. 34.

42. James Madison says:

> It may be a reflection on human nature, that such devices (as checks and balances) should be necessary to control the abuses of government. But what is government itself, but the greatest of all reflections on human nature? If men were angels, no government would be necessary. If angels were to govern men, neither external nor internal controls on government would be necessary.

Cited in Thomas M. Magstadt and Peter M. Schotten, *Understanding Politics—Ideas, Institutions, and Issues* (New York: St. Martin's Press, 1988), pp. 91–93. L. von Mises also remarks that the study of man is like the study of physics. Ludwig von Mises, *Human Action, A Treatise on Economics* (Hew Haven: Yale University Press, 1963), p. 2.

43. Yan Jiaqi, *Wo de sixiang zizhuan*, p. 96.

44. Yan's speech in Honolulu, March 3, 1990. This meeting was sponsored by the Center for Chinese Studies, University of Hawaii at Manoa on March 3, 1990.

45. Niccolo Machiavelli, *The Prince*, trans. and ed. by Robert M. Adams. (New York: W.W. Norton and Company Inc. 1965), p. 270.

46. Yan Jiaqi, Talk on March 3, 1990 in Honolulu, sponsored by center for Chinese studies, University of Hawaii, U.S.A.

47. Yan Jiaqi, "Ducaizhe de zhixu he shangdi de zhixu," ("The Order of the Autocrat and the Order of God"), *Xinwen ziyou daobao* (Press Freedom Herald) July, 20, 1990. Also Yan, Honolulu speech, 1990.

48. Shiping Hua, "One Servant, Two Masters: The Dilemma of Chinese Establishment Intellectuals," *Modern China*, Vol. 20, No. 1, Jan. 1994, p. 105.

49. Yan Jiaqi, *Wo de sixiang zizhuan*, p. 96, p. 54.
50. Ibid., pp. 96–98.
51. Hayek argues that capitalism satisfies humans' selfish nature, because in this kind of system, everybody is free to pursue his or her own self interest. The self interest, if handled in a proper way, is good for society, because capitalism forces everybody to provide a good service to others, thus they unintentionally serve the interests of the others. F. A. Hayek, *Law, Legislature and Liberty: A New Statement of the Liberal Principles and Justice and Political Economy* (Chicago: University of Chicago Press, 1973), p. 89.
52. *Zhongyang Ribao* (Taiwan), May 13, 1990, p. 4.
53. David Bachman and Dali L. Yang, *Yan Jiaqi and China's Struggle for Democracy*, pp. 149–150.

Notes to Chapter 6

1. Chen Zhangjin, "Wang Ruoshui yu wutuobang jiushu," ("Wang Ruoshui and the Salvation of Utopia"), *Dangdai zhongguo yanjiu* (Taiwan), Vol. 29, Ed. 5, November 1986, p. 63.
2. Timothy Cheek, "Habits of the Heart: Intellectual Assumptions Reflected by Mainland Chinese Reformers from Teng T'o to Fang Li-chih," *Issues and Studies*, Vol. 24, No. 3, March 1988. PP. 49–51.
3. Ding Xue-liang, "The Disparity Between Idealistic and Instrumental Chinese Reformers," pp. 1121–1126. Also see Gordon Chang's comments on Su Shaozhi's remarks on Marxism in China, *Bulletin of Concerned Asian Scholars*, Vol. 20, No. 1, 1988. p. 27.
4. Andrew J. Nathan, *China's Crisis: Dilemmas of Reform and Prospects for Democracy*, p. 180.
5. Bill Brugger and David Kelly, *Chinese Marxism in the Post-Mao Era*, pp. 5–6.
6. The author used to be an editor with *Xinhua*.
7. Wang Ruoshui, *Zai zhexue zhanxianshang* (*On the Frontier of Philosophy* (Beijing: Renmin chubanshe, 1980), pp. 3–6.
8. Ibid., p. 58.
9. Ibid., pp. 420–427.
10. Ibid., p. 427.
11. See Wang Ruoshui, *Wei rendao zhuyi bianhu* (*In Defense of Humanism* (Beijing: Sanlianshudian, 1986), p. 33.
12. See Wang Ruoshui, "Wo de shenbian" ("My Self Defense"), *Mingbao yuekan* (Hong Kong), September 1989, p. 88.

13. Wang Ruoshui "Wo de shenbian," p. 88.
14. Wang Ruoshui, "Cong pizuo daoxiang fanyou" ("From Criticizing Leftism to Attacking Rightism"), *Mingbao yuekan* (Hong Kong), March 1989, p. 5.
15. Ibid., p. 11.
16. Wang Ruoshui, "Comments by Wang Ruoshui" [on Shiping Hua's article "All Roads Lead to Democracy"], *Bulletin of Concerned Asian Scholars*, Vol. 24, No. 1, January–March, 1992, p. 57.
17. Wang Ruoshui, *Wei rendao zhuyi bianhu*, p. 203.
18. Wang Ruoshui, "Ren, rende benzhi, rende jiefang" ("Man, Man's Nature and Man's Emancipation"), *Shixue Lilun*, February, 1989, p. 14.
19. Wang Ruoshui, *Wei rendao zhuyi bianhu*, p. 92.
20. Ibid., p. 204. Karl Marx and Frederick Engels, *Makesi Engesi Quanji* (*Works of Marx and Engels*) (Beijing: Renmin chubanshe), pp. 163–164.
21. Paul Thomas, *Karl Marx and the Anarchists* (London: Routledge & Kegan Paul Ltd, 1980), p. 168.
22. Wang Ruoshui, *Wei rendao zhuyi bianhu*, p. 200.
23. Wang Ruoshui, "Lun rende benzhi he shehui guanxi," ("On the Nature of Man and Social Relations"), *Xin Qimeng* (Beijing) December 1988, pp. 1–21. See Derek Sayer, *Marx's Method*, p. 112.
24. Wang Ruoshui, *Wei rendao zhuyi bianhu*, p. 262.
25. Ibid., p. 243.
26. Ontology is a division of metaphysics that speculates on what is the basic substance of reality. See Michael Haas, *Polity and Society*, p. 1.
27. See Wang Ruoshui, "Wo de shenbian." P. 90.
28. Lu Keng, "Beijing Hui Wang Ruoshui," ("Meet Wang Ruoshui in Beijing"), *Bai Xing*, September 1, 1985, p. 18.
29. I dealt with this theme in details in my paper entitled "Chinese Dissidents versus Government: A Conflict of Theories or a Battle in Real World Politics." It was presented at The 43rd Annual Convention of the Association of Asian Studies held in New Orleans, U.S.A., in April 1991.
30. Wang Ruoshui, "Shehuizhuyi meiyou yihuama?" ("Is There No Alienation in a Socialist Society?") *Xin Qimeng*, (Beijing) April 1989. pp. 56–58.
31. Wang Ruoshui, *Wei rendao zhuyi bianhu*, p. 202.
32. Wang Ruoshui, "On Estrangement," *Selected Writings on Studies of Marxism*, published by the Institute of Marxism-Leninism-Mao Zedong Thought, Chinese Academy of Social Sciences, (Beijing) May 1981, No. 12, p. 2.

33. Wang Ruoshui, *Wei rendao zhuyi bianhu*, pp. 189–199.
34. Wang Ruoshui "Wenhuadageming de jiaoxun shi gerenchongbai" ("The Lesson We Learned from the Cultural Revolution Was Personality Cult"), *Mingbao yuekan* (Hong Kong), February 1980, pp. 2–15.
35. Wang Ruoshui, *Wei rendao zhuyi bianhu*, pp. 89–98.
36. Ludwig von Mises, *Human Action*, p. 290, p. 144, p. 164.
37. Daniel Bell, "The Rediscovery of Alienation" in *Marx's Socialism*, ed. by Shlomo Avineri (New York: Lieber-Athertaon Inc., 1972), p. 61.
38. Ludwig von Mises, *Human Action*, p. 271.
39. See Paul Thomas, *Karl Marx and the Anarchists*. pp. 56–122.
40. Karl Marx, *The Economic and Philosophic Manuscripts of 1844* (Moscow: Progress Publishers, 1974), p. 66.
41. Cited in Paul Thomas, *Karl Marx and the Anarchists*, p. 61.
42. In Western philosophy, metaphysics can mean many different things. But the main charge against metaphysics by orthodox Marxists is: 1) It does not see the fact that everything changes; 2) It does not see that all things in the universe are related. See, Xing Bisi et al. eds. *Makesi zhuyi sixiang baoku*, pp. 81–85.
43. Wang Ruoshui, "Makesizhuyi he xuepai wenti" ("Marxism and Schools of Thought"), *Dushu*, (Beijing) September, 1986, p. 12.
44. Engels believed that as a way of thinking, metaphysics was useful in the eighteenth century, because it was a century when scientists concentrated on collecting materials. The nineteenth century, however, was a century for scientists to process these materials. Therefore, metaphysics was not as useful as dialectics. Xing Bisi et al. eds. *Makesi zhuyi sixiang baoku*, p. 82.
45. Wang Ruoshui, *Wei rendao zhuyi bianhu*, p. 15.
46. Wang Ruoshui, "Lun rende benzhi he shehui guanxi," p. 17.
47. Marx says: "The only operative principle of the autocratic system is to hold human beings in contempt, such that a human being is not permitted to be a human being." Cited in Li Jinquan, "On the Historical Status of Confucianist Humanistic Thought," *Chinese Studies in Philosophy*, Fall 1991, p. 38.
48. Li Zehou, *Zou wo ziji de lu* (*To Be True To Myself*) (Beijing: Sanlianshudian chubanshe, 1986), p. 278.
49. Tu Wei-ming, *Rujia ziwo yishi de fansi* (*Self Reflection of the Self Consciousness of Confucianism*) (Taibei: Lianjing, 1990), p. 89, p. 77.
50. Wang Ruoshui, *Wei rendao zhuyi bianhu*, p. 65.
51. Cited in Andrew Nathan, *China's Crisis: Dilemmas of Reform and Prospects for Democracy*, p. 7.
52. Wang Ruoshui, "Wenhuadageming de jiaoxun shi gerenchongbai."p. 2.

53. Cited in Yan Jiaqi, *Wo de sixiang zizhuan*, p. 33.
54. Cao Hongliang, "Xinwenziyou—fang Wang Ruoshui" ("Press Freedom—an Interview with Wang Ruoshui"), *Xinwen Xueyuan* (Beijing), January 1989, pp. 2–4.
55. Wang Ruoshui, "Lun rende benzhi he shehui guanxi," pp. 1–14.
56. Ibid., p. 17. Wang made use of the sound of the famous statement by Confucius to express the opposite meaning.
57. Wang, Ruoshui, "Lun rende benzhi he shehui guanxi," pp. 14–21.
58. Ibid., p. 15.

Notes to Chapter 7

1. Lin Min, "The Search for Modernity: Chinese Intellectual Discourse and Society, 1978–88—the Case of Li Zehou," *The China Quarterly*, December 1992, p. 971.
2. Lin Min has confused Li's birth place, Hankou, with his hometown, Changsha. See Ibid., p. 972.
3. See Guo Qiyong, "Kunjingzhong de chensi," ("Self Reflection in the Dilemma"), *Dangdai* (Taiwan), January, 1988, pp. 38–45. "Xi ti zhong yong" as advocated by Li Zehou has unique connotations as will be explored later.
4. Tu Wei-ming, "Jicheng wu-si, fazhan ruxue" ("Developing Confucianism in the May Fourth Tradition"), *Dushu*, (Beijing) June, 1989, p. 114.
5. Li Zehou, *Zou wo ziji de lu*, pp. 223–26.
6. Ibid., p. 201.
7. Ibid., pp. 282–83.
8. Li Zehou, *Zhongguo xiandai sixiang shilun* (*Contemporary Chinese Intellectual History*) (Beijing: Dongfang chubanshe, 1987), pp. 162–63.
9. Li Zehou, *Zhongguo jindai sixiang shilun* (*Modern Chinese Intellectual History*) (Taibei: Fengyun shidai chubangongsi, 1991), p. 478.
10. Li Zehou, *Zou wo ziji de lu*, pp. 282–83.
11. Ibid., pp. 31–32.
12. Ibid., p. 285.
13. Ibid., pp. 31–32.
14. Ibid., p. 209.
15. Ibid., pp. 218–19.
16. Ibid., pp. 288–289.
17. Ibid., pp. 87–88.
18. Li Zehou, *Huaxia meixue* (*Chinese Aesthetics*) (Beijing: Zhongwai chubangongsi, 1989), pp. 114–166.

19. Li Zehou, *Zhongguo xiandai sixiang shilun*, p. 53, p. 59.
20. Li Zehou, *Zou wo ziji de lu*, p. 206.
21. Ibid., pp. 288–89.
22. Li Zehou, *Zhongguo gudai sixiang shilun* (*Ancient Chinese Intellectual History*) (Beijing: Renmin chubanshe, 1985), pp. 34–37.
23. Li Zehou, *Zhongguo xiandai sixiang shilun*, pp. 200–203.
24. Li Zehou, *Zou wo ziji de lu*, p. 292.
25. "*Ren*" also has to be considered in relations with other key notions of Confucianism. "People's innate tendency to feel sympathetic is the base for '*Ren*' (benevolence), people's innate tendency to dislike evilness is the base for '*Yi*' (loyalty), people's innate tendency to be nice to others is the base for "*Li*"(courtesy and etiquette), people's innate tendency to distinguish good from evil is the base for '*Zhi*' (wisdom). Zhongguo zhexueshi bianxiezu, *Zhongguo Zhexueshi* (*A History of Chinese Philosophy*) (Shijiazhuang: Hebei renmin chubanshe, 1980), p. 69.
26. Li Zehou, *Zhongguo gudai sixiang shilun*, p. 201, p. 28, p. 230.
27. Ibid., p. 15.
28. Li Zehou, *Kang Youwei, Tan Sitong sixiang yanjiu* (*On the Thought of Kang Youwei and Tan Sitong*) (Shanghai: Renmin chubanshe, 1958), p. 3.
29. Li Zehou, *Zhongguo gudai sixiang shilun*, p. 16, p. 15, p. 22.
30. *Lun Yu*, the "*Yongye*" section. Cited in Li Jinquan, "On the Historical Status of Confucianist Humanistic Thought," *Chinese Studies in Philosophy*, Fall 1991, p. 35.
31. Lun Yu, chapter "Weilinggon," cited in Li Jinquan "On the Historical Status of Confucianist Humanistic Thought," p. 35.
32. Li Zehou, *Huaxia meixue*, p. 33.
33. Andrew Chih, *Chinese Humanism: A Religion Beyond Religion* (Taipei: Fu Jen Catholic University Press: 1981), pp. 183–240.
34. Li Zehou, *Zou wo ziji de lu*, p. 294.
35. Ibid., p. 208.
36. Xun Kuang, *Fajia zhuzuo xuan* (*Selections of the Legalists*) (Shanghai: Remin chubanshe, 1975), Vol. 1, p. 187.
37. Tu Wei-ming, "Ruxue chuantong jiazhi yu minzhu" ("The Confucian Traditional Values and Democracy"), *Dushu*, (Beijing) April, 1989, p. 92.
38. Thomas M. Magstadt and Peter M. Schotten, *Understanding Politics*, p. 151.
39. Wang Shubai, "Mao Zedong de zhongxi wenhua guan" ("Mao Zedong's Ideas on the Cultures of the West and the East"), *Xinhua Wen Zhai* (Beijing), May 1987, p. 181.
40. Li Zehou, *Huaxia meixue*, p. 48.

41. In Xun Zi, chapter "Wang zhi" (The methods of the monarch), cited in Li Jingquan "On the Historical Status of Confucianist Humanistic Thought," p. 37, p. 36.
42. Li Zehou, *Zhongguo gudai sixiang shilun*, p. 39.
43. Yu-ming Shaw, *Chinese Modernization* (San Francisco: Chinese Materials Center Publications, 1985), p. 56.
44. Hu Shi, *Selected Essays of Hu Shi* (Taipei: Commercial Books, 1983), Vol. 3, p. 23.
45. *Ta Kung Pao*, October 10, 1936.
46. Li Zehou, *Zou wo ziji de lu*, p. 227–232.
47. Ibid., p. 273.
48. Perry Link, *Evening Chats in Beijing*, p. 157.
49. Li Zehou, "Guanyu minzuzhuyi" ("On Nationalism"), *Mingpao yuekan* (Hong Kong), February 1993, pp. 55–56.
50. Li Zehou, *Zhongguo gudai sixiang shilun*, p. 39.
51. Li Zehou, *Zou wo ziji de lu*, p. 278.
52. Li Zehou, "Guanyu minzuzhuyi." pp. 55–56.
53. Lin Min, "The Search for Modernity: Chinese Intellectual Discourse and Society, 1978–88—the Case of Li Zehou," p. 986.
54. Li Zehou, *Zhongguo jindai sixiang shilun*, p. 364.
55. Ibid., p. 369.
56. Li Zehou, *Zou wo ziji de lu*, pp. 218–219.
57. Ibid., p. 279.
58. Li Zehou, *Zhongguo xiandai sixiang shilun*, p. 144. Also Li Zehou, *Zou wo ziji de lu*, pp. 178–80.
59. Li Zehou, *Zou wo ziji de lu*, p. 295.
60. Li Zehou, *Zhongguo gudai sixiang shilun*, p. 15.
61. Tu Wei-ming identifies two problems in the current discussions about Confucianism: 1) People like Liang Shuming do not see problems of Confucianism, just praise it; 2) People just focus on the humanistic aspects of Confucianism. There are no discussions of how to institutionalize social systems in accordance with Confucianism. See, Tu Wei-ming, *Rujia ziwo yishi de fansi*, pp. 214–15.
62. Tu Wei-ming, *Rujia ziwo yishi de fansi*.
63. He Xin, *Dongfang de fuxing: Zhongguo xiandaihua de mingti yu qiantu* (*The Revitalization of the East: the Thesis and Future of China's Modernization*) (Harbin: Heilongjiang jiaoyu chubanshe, 1991), p. 138.
64. Ibid., p. 223.
65. Ibid., p. 91.
66. Jin Guantao and Liu Qingfeng, *Xingsheng yu weiji*, (1984), pp. 100–103.

Notes to Chapter 8

1. Gan Yang, "Zhongguo shehui fazhan yu falu chengxu wenti yantaohui fayan zhaiyao" ("Conversation at the Seminar on Chinese Social Development and Legal Procedure"), *Papers of the Center for Modern China*, Vol. 4, No. 32, August 1993, p. 17. Gan's printed speech was based on recording and has not been verified by the author.

2. Cited in Manfred Henningsen, "Democracy or the Promise of 'Civil Society,' " p. 203.

3. Gabriel Almond, *A Discipline Divided: Schools and Sects in Political Science*. pp. 16–23.

4. Ronald Chilcote, *Theories of Comparative Politics: Search for a Paradigm*. pp. 81–138.

5. Su Guoxun, "Lixinghua jiqi xianzhi" ("Rationality and its Limitations"), in Gan Yang ed., *Zhongguo dangdai wenhua yishi (Contemporary Chinese Consciousness)* (Hong Kong: Joint Publishing, 1989), pp. 283–333.

6. Gan Yang, "Ziyou de diren" ("The Enemy of Freedom"), *Dushu*, (Beijing) June 1989, p. 123.

7. Jürgen Habermas, *Theory of Communicative Action* (Boston: Beacon Press, 1987), Vol. 2, p. 86.

8. Gan Yang, "Cong lixing de pipan dao wenhua de pipan" ("From the Critique of Rationality to the Critique of Culture") in Gan Yang ed., *Zhongguo dangdai wenhua yishi*, pp. 557–580.

9. Ibid., p. 565.

10. Some well known Neo-Kantians include: Ernst Cassirer, (1874–1945), Hermann Cohen (1842–1918), and Paul Natorp (1854–1924). These people started with the Kantian humanistic tradition, but later on drastically revised the Kantian theories.

11. Gan Yang, "Zhongguo shehui fazhan yu falu chengxu wenti yantaohui fayan zhaiyao," p. 18.

12. Gan, "Cong lixing de pipan dao wenhua de pipan," pp. 573–75.

13. Alburey Castell and Donald M. Borchert, *An Introduction of Modern Philosophy* (New York: Macmillan Publishing Co., Inc., 1983), pp. 78–79.

14. See David Hoy, "Jacques Derrida" in Quention Skinner ed., *The Return of Grand Theory in the Human Science* (Cambridge: Cambridge University Press, 1985), pp. 47–49.

15. Gan Yang, "Ziyou de linian: wu-si chuantong zhi queshimian" ("The Concept of Freedom: the Mistake of the May Fourth Movement"), *Dushu*, (Beijing) May, 1989, p. 16.

16. Gan Yang, "Ziyou de diren," p. 125.

17. Gan Yang, "Ziyou de linian: wu-si chuantong zhi queshimian," p. 19.
18. Ibid., pp. 12–13.
19. Ibid., p. 15.
20. Chen Lai, "Sixiang chulu de sandongxiang."
21. According to Ingram, "the most striking feature of Habermas' published works from the past two decades is its sense of moral purpose." See, David Ingram, *Habermas and the Dialectics of Reason* (New Haven: Yale University Press, 1987), p. 1.
22. Gan Yang, "Cong lixing de pipan dao wenhua de pipan," p. iii.
23. Ibid., p. v.
24. Max Weber, *The Religion of China* (New York: the Free Press, 1951), p. 227.
25. Mencius, *Sacred Books of Confucius* ed. and trans. by Chin Chai and Winberg Chai (New York: University Books, 1965), p. 97.
26. Max Weber, *The Religion of China*, p. 228.
27. Ibid., p. 228.
28. Ibid., p. 238.
29. Ibid., p. 227.
30. Gan Yang, "Bashiniandai wenhua taolun zhongde yixie wenti," p. 23. Also see Gan Yang, *Women zai chuangzao chuantong* (*We are Creating Tradition*) (Taipei: Lianjing chubangongsi, 1989).
31. Jürgen Habermas, *Theory of Communicative Action*, Vol. 2, p. 140.
32. Gan Yang, "Bashiniandai wenhua taolun zhongde yixie wenti," p. 29.
33. Zhao Yuesheng, "Chaoyue-fouding-lixing: lun makusi pipan de shehuizhexue" (Transcendence-negation-rationality: On Marcuse's critical social theory) in Gan Yang ed., *Zhongguo dangdai wenhua yishi*, p. 439.
34. Gan Yang, "Cong lixing de pipan dao wenhua de pipan," p. v.
35. Jürgen Habermas, *Toward a Rational Society*, p. 86.
36. David Ingram, *Habermas and the Dialectics of Reason*, p. 1.
37. Jürgen Habermas, *Theory of Communicative Action*, Vol. 2, pp. 145–46.
38. Max Weber, *The Religion of China*, p. 227.
39. Gan Yang, "Xiangtu zhongguo chongjian yu zhongguo wenhua qianjing" ("Reconstruction of China's Countryside and the Prospect of Chinese Culture"), *Ershiyi shiji* (Hong Kong), No. 16, April 1993, p. 6.
40. Ibid., p. 5.
41. Gan Yang, "Bashiniandai wenhua taolun zhongde yixie wenti," pp. 34–35.
42. Gan Yang, "Xiangtu zhongguo chongjian yu zhongguo wenhua qianjing," p. 5.
43. Gan Yang, "Cong lixing de pipan dao wenhua de pipan," p. 557.

44. Gan Yang, "Xiangtu zhongguo chongjian yu zhongguo wenhua qianjing."
45. Economics is, perhaps, an exception. See Michael Haas, *Polity and Society: Philosophical Underpinnings of Social Science Paradigms.* Also Ada W. Finifter, ed. *Political Science: The State of the Discipline II* (Washington, D.C.: American Political Science Association, 1993).
46. See Peter Manicas, *A History and Philosophy of Social Sciences*, pp. 193–240.
47. Li Zehou, *Zou wo ziji de lu*, pp. 218–219.
48. Ibid., p. 279.
49. Gan Yang, "Yangqi 'minzhu yu kexue,' dianding 'ziyou yu zhixu'" (Sublate 'democracy and science,' give 'liberty and order' a try), *Ershiyi shiji* (Hong Kong), 3rd Edition, February, 1991, pp. 8–9.
50. Ibid., pp. 7–10.

Notes to Chapter 9

1. Lucian Pye, "On Chinese Pragmatism in the 1980s," *The China Quarterly*, No. 106, June, 1986, p. 207.
2. Ben Schwartz in Yu-sheng Lin, *Crisis of Chinese Consciousness* (Madison, WI: University of Wisconsin Press, 1979), p. 5. Also Yu-sheng Lin, "Guanyu zhongguo yishi de weiji—da Sun Longji" ("On The Crisis of Chinese Consciousness—In Response to Sun Longji"), *Ershiyi shiji* (Hong Kong), 3rd ed., February, 1991, p. 142.
3. According to Liu Qingfeng, the triumph of the monistic materialistic scientism is a unique Chinese phenomenon. This situation is connected with the traditional Chinese way of thinking, which stresses direct perception through the senses. See "Ershishiji zhongguo kexuezhuyi de liangci xingqi" ("The Two Surges of Chinese Scientism in the Twentieth Century"), *Ershiyi shiji* (Hong Kong), 4th ed. April, 1991.
4. Mao's famous statement down playing the role of science runs as follows, "It is still necessary to have universities; here I refer mainly to colleges of natural science and engineering. However, it is essential to shorten the length of schooling, revolutionize education, put proletarian politics in command. . . ." See Tianjinshi Gemingweiyuanhui, *Wuchanjieji wenhuadageming zhongyao wenxian xuanbian* (*A Selection of Important Works of the Cultural Revolution*) (Tianjin: Tianjin renmin chubanshe, 1969), pp. 775–776.
5. Cited in D. W. Y. Kwok, *Scientism in Chinese Thought*, p. 12.
6. Hu Qiaomu, "Lun rendao zhuyi he yihua wenti." p. 5.

7. See C. B. Macpherson, *The Real World of Democracy* (Oxford: Oxford University Press, 1976), pp. 1–35.

8. Zhongguo zhexue shi bianxiezu, *Zhongguo zhexue shi* (*A History of Chinese Philosophy*) (Shijiazhuang: Hebei renmin chubanshe, 1980), p. 69.

9. Liu Binyan et al., *Ziyou minzhu xiandaihua de husheng* (*Call for Freedom, Democracy and Modernization*) (Taibei: Xinmei chubanshe, 1988), pp. 15–121.

10. Mao Zedong, *Selected Works of Mao Tse-Tung* (New York: International Publishers, 1964), Vol. V, p. 413, p. 417.

11. Lenin said, "never forget that the state even in the most democratic republic, and not only in a monarchy, is simply a machine for the suppression of one class by another." He added, "the more democratic it is, the cruder and more cynical is the rule of capitalism." Quoted by Alan Hunt, *Marxism and Democracy*, p. 32.

12. On the Marxian conception of "alienation," see Paul Thomas, *Karl Marx and the Anarchists*, pp. 61–75. For the incompatibility of capitalism and democracy, see Peter Manicas, *War and Democracy*, pp. 234–236.

13. See Dorothy Pickles, *Democracy* (London: B.T. Batsford Ltd, 1970), pp. 21–22.

14. See Hua Shiping, "All Roads Lead to Democracy," *Bulletin of Concerned Asian Scholars*, January–March, 1992.

15. See Stephen White, "Continuity and Change in Soviet Political Culture," *Comparative Political Studies*, Vol. 11, No. 3, October 1978, p. 381.

16. Walter A. Rosenbaum, *Political Culture* (New York, Praeger Publishers, Inc., 1975), p. 37.

17. Cited in John A. Moore, Jr. and Myron Roberts, *The Pursuit of Happiness: Government and Politics in America* (New York: Macmillan Publishing Company, 1989), p. 8.

18. *Renmin ribao*, February 27, 1989.

19. Ibid.

20. A speech given in University of Hawaii March, 1989 by Wang Bingzhang, founder of *Zhongguo zichun*, a Chinese dissident magazine published in the United States.

21. *Renmin ribao*, March 11, 1989.

22. *Renmin ribao*, April 1, 1989.

23. Liu Xiangyang, "Wenping re" ("Obsession with College Diplomas"), in Xiao Qinfu, *Wuci langchao* (*Five Waves*) (Beijing, Renmindaxue chubanshe, 1989), p. 132.

24. Wen Jize, "Inaugural Address to 1983 Students," Graduate School, CASS, September, 1983. Wen was then President of the Graduate School, CASS. Wang Ruoshui was one of the drafters. He drafted the part of the resolution which deals with Mao. Apparently because of his critical attitudes toward the late party Chairman that his draft was killed. See Wang Ruoshui, "Wenhuadageming de zhongyao jiaoxun shibixu fandui gerenmixin."

25. Hu Jie, "Guanyu yi shi renda daibiao zhengzhi taidu de diaocha" ("An Investigation of the Political Views of the Deputies of a China's Municipal People's Congress," *Mingbao yuekan* (Hong Kong), November, 1988, p. 114.

26. Li Jingwen is Director of the Metrological Economics Institute of CASS. He made the remarks at a talk with some PRC students at the East West Center on June 14, 1991.

27. See Godwin Chu, "Change in China: where have you gone Mao Zedong?" *Ceterviews*, July–August 1989, p. 7.

28. These liberalism-oriented people are identified in the survey as "optimists" and "radicals." One can reasonably speculate that in other parts of the country, the percentage will be even lower. See, Jianhua Zhu, Xinshu Zhao, and Hairong Li, "Public Political Consciousness in China," *Asian Survey*, Vol. XXX, No. 10, October 1990, pp. 992–1006.

29. Lucian W. Pye, *The Spirit of Chinese Politics*, (Cambridge, MA: Harvard University Press, 1992), pp. 67–84.

30. Andrew Nathan and Tianjian Shi, "Cultural Requisites for Democracy in China: Some Findings from a Survey," *Daedalus*, Vol. 122, No. 2, Spring 1993, pp. 95–123.

31. Wang Jin, "Shisida: xin de lichengbei" (The 14th Party Congress: a new mile stone), *Renmin ribao*, October 19, 1992, p. 3.

32. Andrew Nathan and Tianjian Shi, "Cultural Requisites for Democracy in China: Some Findings from a Survey." The situation in cities, especially major ones such as Beijing, may be different. A study conducted in Beijing in 1987 shows that only about 20 percent of the respondents can be identified as apolitical. See Jianhua Zhu, Xinshu Zhao and Hairong Li, "Public Political Consciousness in China."

33. Andrew Nathan and Tianjian Shi, "Cultural Requisites for Democracy in China: Some Findings from a Survey."

34. These terms of "idealistic" "operational" and "tolerated" versions of political culture are revisions of Gabriel A. Almond's theory. Almond held in 1983 that there were three versions of political culture in a communist social reality: 1) the official or ideological political culture that is a mix of exhortation and imputation; 2) the operational political culture or what the regime is prepared to tolerate and believes it has

succeeded in attaining; 3) the real political culture based on evidence such as opinion surveys and other kinds of research or on inferences drawn from the media or official statements. While it is useful to divide different aspects of political culture, Almond's terms do not convey to the readers a clear picture. By identifying these aspects as "official or ideological" "operational" and "real," this approach does not make it explicit that these different aspects are closely related. For instance, the current Chinese political culture on an "operational" level of developing productive forces is by no means "unreal" than the "real" version: the pluralistic orientation. Even the part which is the most detached from the current Chinese mentality, the "official or ideological" version, has appeal to the Chinese people to certain extent by an implication of respecting "objective laws" and of rejecting the Maoist voluntarism. My approach of dividing political culture into "idealistic," "operational" and "tolerated" is an attempt to solve this problem. See Gabriel A. Almond "Communism and Political Culture Theory," *Comparative Politics*, January 1983, pp. 127–138.

Bibliography

A Dictionary of Philosophy (New York: The Macmillan Press Ltd., 1984).

Ai, Zhu, "Kan Hu Qiaomu shizenyang chumai Deng Xiaoping" ("See how Hu Qiaomu betrayed Deng Xiaoping") *Mingbao yuekan* (Hong Kong), April 1984.

Almond, Gabriel A., "Communism and Political Culture Theory," *Comparative Politics*, January 1983.

————. *A Discipline Divided: Schools and Sects in Political Science* (Newbury Park, CA: Sage Publications, 1990).

Aristotle, *The Politics* (New York: Oxford University Press, 1962).

Bachman, David and Dali Yang, [trans. and eds.] *Yan Jiaqi and China's Struggle for Democracy* (Armonk, NY: M.E. Sharpe, 1991).

Bartke, Wolfgang, *Who's Who in the PRC* (Oxford: K.G. Saur, 1987).

Baum, Richard, *Scientism and Bureaucratism in Chinese Thought: Cultural Limits of the "Four Modernizations"* (Sweden: University of Lund, 1981).

Bell, Daniel, "The Rediscovery of Alienation" in *Marx's Socialism*, ed. by Shlomo Avineri (New York: Lieber-Athertaon Inc., 1972).

Bender, Frederic L. ed., *Karl Marx: The Essential Writings* (Boulder, Co.: Westview, 1986).

Bernstein, Eduard, *Evolutionary Socialism* (New York: Scribner's, 1961).

Bottomore, T. et al., *A Dictionary of Marxist Thought* (Cambridge: Harvard University Press, 1983).

Bonnin, Michel and Yves Chevrier "The Intellectual and the State: Social Dynamics of Intellectual Autonomy During the Post-Mao Era," *The China Quarterly*, No. 127, September 1991.

Brugger, Bill, and David Kelly, *Chinese Marxism during the Post-Mao Era*, (Stanford, CA: Stanford University Press, 1990).

Cao, Hongliang, "Xinwenziyou-fang Wang Ruoshui," ("Press Freedom—an Interview with Wang Ruoshui") *Xinwen Xueyuan* (Beijing) January 1989).

Carver, Terrell, *Engels* (Oxford: Oxford University Press, 1981).

Castell, Alburey and Donald M. Borchert, *An Introduction of Modern Philosophy* (New York: Macmillan Publishing Co., Inc., 1983).

Chang, Gordon, comments on Su Shaozhi's remarks on Marxism in China, *Bulletin of Concerned Asian Scholars*, Vol. 20, No. 1, 1988.

Cheek, Timothy, "Habits of the Heart: Intellectual Assumptions Reflected by Mainland Chinese Reformers from Teng T'o to Fang Li-chih," *Issues and Studies*, Vol. 24, No. 3, March 1988.

Chen, Jo-Shui, "Review of the book, *Li Ao: Buddhist, Taoist, or Neo-Confucian?* by T. H. Barett," *The Journal of Asian Studies*, Vol. 52, No. 4, November 1993.

Chen, Lai, "Sixiang chulu de sandongxiang" (Three Trends in Intellectual Thought), *Dangdai* (Taiwan), 21 ed. January, 1988.

Chen, Xianda, *Makesizhuyi jibenyuanli jiaocheng (A Textbook of Basic Theories in Marxism)* (Beijing: Zhongguo renmindaxue chubanshe, 1988).

Chen, Zhangjin, "Wang Ruoshui yu wutuobang jiushu" ("Wang Ruoshui and the Salvation of Utopia"), *Zhongguo dalu yanjiu* (Taiwan), Vol. 29, ed. 5, November 1986.

———. "Su Shaozhi jiqi zhengzhi gaige linian" ("Su Shaozhi and his Political Reform Beliefs"), *Zhongguo dalu yanjiu* (Taiwan), Vol. 30, ed. 7, January 1988.

———. "Jin Guantao yu zhongguo wenhua chulu de tantao" ("Jin Guantao's exploration of the way out for Chinese culture"), *Zhongguo dalu yanjiu* (Taiwan), August, 1988, Vol. 31, 5th ed.

———. "Zouchu zhongguo chuantong wenhua de kunjiu?" ("Going out of the Dilemma of Chinese Cultural Tradition?"), *Zhongguo dalu yanjiu* (Taiwan), Vol. 31. 10th ed. April, 1989.

Chih, Andrew, *Chinese Humanism: A Religion Beyond Religion* (Taipei: (Taibei) Fu Jen Catholic University Press: 1981).

Chilcote, Ronald H., *Theories of Comparative Politics: The Search for a Paradigm* (Boulder, Colorado: Westview Press, 1981).

Chong, W. L., "Su Xiaokang on His Film 'River Elegy,' " *China Information*, Vol. IV. No. 3 (Winter 1989–1990).

Chu, Godwin, "Change in China: where have you gone Mao Zedong?" *Ceterviews*, July–August 1989.

Colletti, Lucio, *From Rousseau to Lenin: Studies in Ideology and Society* (New York: Monthly Review Press, 1972).

Collinicos, Alex, *Against Post-Modernism: A Realist Critique* (New York: St. Martins Press, 1990).

Corrigan, Philip, Harvie Ramsay and Derek Sayer, *Socialist Construction and Marxist Theory* (New York: Monthly Review Press, 1978).

Ding, Xue-liang, "The Disparity Between Idealistic and Instrumental Chinese Reformers," *Asian Survey*. Vol. 18, No. 11, November 1988.

————. "Xin makesizhuyi dui zhongguo dalu de yingxiang" ("Neo-Marxism's Influence over China"), *Minzhu Zhongguo*, February, 1991.

Feng, Xianzhi, "Mao Zedong du malie zhuzuo" ("Mao Zedong Read Works by Marx, Engels, Lenin and Stalin"), *Xinhua wenzhai* (Beijing), February, 1991.

Finifter, Ada W., ed., *Political Science: The State of the Discipline II* (Washington, D.C.: American Political Science Association, 1993).

Gan, Yang, "Ziyou de linian: wu-si chuantong zhi queshimian," ("The Concept of Freedom: the Mistake of the May Fourth Movement"), *Dushu*, (Beijing) May, 1989.

————. "Ziyou de diren" ("The Enemy of Freedom") *Dushu*, June 1989.

————. "Cong lixing de pipan dao wenhua de pipan" ("From the Critique of Rationality to the Critique of Culture") in Gan Yang ed., *Zhongguo dangdai wenhua yishi* (*Contemporary Chinese Cultural Consciousness*) (Hong Kong: Joint Publishing Co., LTD, 1989).

————. *Women zai chuangzao chuantong* (*We are Creating Tradition*) (Taipei: (Taibei) Lianjing chubangongsi, 1989).

————. "Yangqi 'minzhu yu kexue,' dianding 'ziyou yu zhixu" (Sublate 'democracy and science,' give 'liberty and order' a try), *Ershiyi shiji* (Hong Kong) Third Edition, February, 1991.

————. "Xiangtu zhongguo chongjian yu zhongguo wenhua qianjing" ("Reconstruction of China's Countryside and the Prospect of Chinese Culture"), *Ershiyi shiji* (Hong Kong), No. 16, April 1993.

————. "Zhongguo shehui fazhan yu falu chengxu wenti yantaohui fayan zhaiyao" (Conversation at the Seminar on "Chinese Social Development and Legal Procedure"), *Papers of the Center for Modern China*, Vol. 4, No. 32, August 1993.

Goldman, Merle, *China's Intellectuals: Advice and Dissent* (Cambridge: Harvard University Press, 1981).

Guo, Qiyong, "Kunjingzhong de chensi," ("Self Reflection in the Dilemma"), *Dangdai* (Taiwan), January, 1988.

Habermas, Jürgen, *Theory of Communicative Action* (Boston: Beacon Press, 1987), Vol. 2.

Hamrin, Carol L. and Timothy Cheek, eds., *China's Establishment Intellectuals* (Armonk, NY: M.E. Sharpe, 1986).

Harding, Harry, *China's Second Revolution* (Washington, D.C.: The Brookings Institution, 1987)

Harvey, David, *The Condition of Post-Modernity* (Oxford: Basil Blackwell, 1989), Part I.

Hass, Michael, *Polity and Society: Philosophical Underpinnings of Social Science Paradigms* (New York, Westport, CT, London: Praeger, 1992).

Hayek, F. A., *Law, Legislature and Liberty: A New Statement of the Liberal Principles and Justice and Political Economy* (Chicago: University of Chicago Press, 1973).

He, Xin, *Dongfang de fuxing: Zhongguo xiandaihua de mingti yu qiantu* (*The Revitalization of the East: the Thesis and Future of China's Modernization*) (Harbin: Heilongjiang jiaoyu chubanshe, 1991).

He, Zhama, *"Jin Guantao weishenmo yao fouding shizaide keguanxing"* ("Why does Jin Guantao want to negate the objectivity of being?"), *Xinhua wenzhai* (Beijing), January 1990.

Henningsen, Manfred, "Democracy or the Promise of 'Civil Society,' " in *Linking Present Decisions to Long-Range Visions: Selection of Papers from the XI World Conference of the World Futures Studies Federation* (WFSF), edited by Mika Mannermaa (Budapest: Research Institute for Social Studies, 1992).

Hoy, David, "Jacques Derrida" in Quention Skinner ed., *The Return of Grand Theory in the Human Science* (Cambridge: Cambridge University Press, 1985).

Hu, Jian, *Dongdang de xiaofei jiegou* (*The Fluctuating Consumption Structure*) (Beijing: Xueyuan chubanshe, 1989).

Hu, Jie, "Guanyu yi shi renda daibiao zhengzhi taidu de diaocha" ("An Investigation of the Political Views of the Deputies of a China's Municipal People's Congress"), *Mingbao yuekan* (Hong Kong), November, 1988.

Hu, Qiaomu, "Dangqian sixiang zhanxianshang de ruogan wenti" ("On Some Issues in the Current Ideological Front"), *Hong Qi*, (Beijing) 23rd Vol. 1981.

————. "Guanyu gongchan zhuyi sixiang de shijian," ("On the Practice of Communist Ideology"), *Renmin ribao*, September 24, 1982.

————. "Guanyu rendaozhuyi he yihua wenti" ("On Humanism and the Issue of Alienation"), *Renmin ribao*, January, 27, 1984.

————. *Zhongguo gongchandang zenyang fazhanle makesizhuyi—wei jinian jiandang qishi zhounian zuo*, (*How Has the CCP Developed Marxism—in Celebration of the 70th Anniversary of the Party*), (Beijing: Renmin chubanshe, 1991).

Hu, Shih, (Hu Shi) *The Development of the Logical Method in Ancient China* (New York: Paragon Book Reprint Corp., 1963).

————. *Selected Essays of Hu Shi* (Taipei (Taibei): Commercial Books, 1983, Vol. 3.

Hua, Shiping, "Chinese Dissidents versus Government: A Conflict of Theories or a Battle in Real World Politics." It was presented at *The 43rd Annual Convention of the Association of Asian Studies*, held in New Orleans, U.S.A., in April 1991.

————. "All Roads Lead to Democracy," *Bulletin of Concern Asian Scholars*, January–March, 1992.

————. "One Servant, Two Masters: The Dilemma of Chinese Establishment Intellectuals," *Modern China*, Vol. 20, No. 1, January, 1994.

————. "Chinese Scientism and Political Culture," *Asian Thought and Society*, Vol. 19, No. 55, January–April 1994.

Huang, Jin, "Zhao Ziyang xiatai diyun" ("An Analysis of the Fall of Zhao Ziyang"), *Mingbao yuekan* (Hong Kong), April 1990.

Hucker, Charles O., *China's Imperial Past: An Introduction to Chinese History and Culture* (Stanford, CA. Stanford University Press, 1975).

Hunt, Alan, *Marxism and Democracy*, (London: Lawrence and Wishart, 1980).

Ingram, David, *Habermas and the Dialectics of Reason* (New Haven: Yale University Press, 1987).

Jiang, Zemin, "Zhongguo zouxiang ershiyi shiji" ("China Marches Towards the Twenty-First Century"), *Renmin ribao*, May 18, 1991, p. 1.

Jin, Guantao and Liu Qingfeng, *Xingsheng yu weiji—lun zhongguo fengjian shehui de chaowending jiegou (The Cycle of Growth and Decline—On the Ultrastable Structure of Chinese Society* (Changsha: Hunan renmin chubanshe, 1984).

————. (with Liu Qingfeng), "Tantao zirankexue he shehuikexue tongyi de fangfalun" ("Explore a method which unites natural sciences and social sciences"), in *Wenti he fangfa ji* (A Collection on Issues and Methods) (Shanghai: Shanghai renmin chubanshe, 1986).

————. *Zhengti de zhexue (Philosophy of the Whole)*, (Chengdu: Renmin chubanshe, 1987).

————. "Wo shi zenyang pandeng sixiang jietide" ("How Do I climb up the Ladder of Thought?"), *Mingbao yuekan* (Hong Kong), March 1988.

————. *Ren de zhexue (The Philosophy of Man)* (Taibei: Shangwu yinshuguan, 1988).

————. (with Liu Qingfeng), *Xingsheng yu weiji—lun zhongguo fengjian shehui de chaowending jiegou (The Cycle of Growth and Decline—On the Ultrastable Structure of Chinese Society)* (Hong Kong: The Chinese University Press, 1992).

————. (with Liu Qingfeng), *Kaifang zhong de bianqian: Zailun zhongguo shehui chaowending jiegou (The Transformation of*

Chinese Society (1840–1956)—The Fate of Its Ultrastable Structure in Modern Times) (Hong Kong: The Chinese University Press, 1993).

————. "Socialism and Tradition: The Formation and Development of Modern Chinese Political Culture," *The Journal of Contemporary China*, No. 3, Summer 1993.

Kelly, David, in Merle Goldman, with Timothy Cheek and Carol L. Hamrin eds., *China's Intellectuals and the State: In Search of a New Relationship* (Cambridge, MA: Council on East Asian Studies, Harvard University, 1987).

Kerr, Clark, *Industrialism and Industrial Man: The Problems of Labor and Management in Economic Growth* (New York: Oxford University Press, 1964).

Kuhn, Thomas S., *The Structure of Scientific Revolutions* (Chicago: The University of Chicago Press, 1962).

————. *The Essential Tension: Selected Studies in Scientific Tradition and Change* (Chicago: The University of Chicago Press, 1977).

Kwok, D. W. Y., *Scientism in Chinese Thought (1900-1950)* (New York: Biblo and Tannen, 1971).

Lee, Hong Yung, *From Revolutionary Cadres to Party Technocrats in Socialist China* (Berkeley, CA: University of California Press, 1991).

Li, Cheng and Lynn White, "The Thirteenth Central Committee of the Chinese Communist Party: From Mobilizers to Managers," *Asian Survey*, Vol. XXVIII, No. 4, April 1988.

Li, Jinquan, "On the Historical Status of Confucianist Humanistic Thought," *Chinese Studies in Philosophy*, Fall 1991.

Li, Zehou, *Kang Youwei, Tan Sitong sixiang yanjiu* (*On the Thought of Kang Youwei and Tan Sitong*) (Shanghai: Renmin chubanshe, 1958).

————. *Zhongguo gudai sixiang shilun* (*Ancient Chinese Intellectual History*) (Beijing: Renmin chubanshe, 1985).

————. *Zou wo ziji de lu* (*To Be True To Myself*) (Beijing: Sanlianshudian chubanshe, 1986).

————. *Zhongguo xiandai sixiang shilun* (*Contemporary Chinese Intellectual History*) (Beijing: Dongfang chubanshe, 1987).

————. *Huaxia meixue* (*Chinese Aesthetics*) (Beijing: Zhongwai chubangongsi, 1989).

————. *Zhongguo jindai sixiang shilun* (*Modern Chinese Intellectual History*) (Taibei: Fengyun shidai chubangongsi, 1991).

————. "Guanyu minzuzhuyi" ("On Nationalism"), *Mingpao yuekan* (Hong Kong), February 1993.

Lilienfeld, Robert, "Systems Theory as an Ideology," *Social Research*, Winter, 1975.

Lin, Min, "The Search for Modernity: Chinese Intellectual Discourse and Society, 1978–88—the Case of Li Zehou," *The China Quarterly*, December 1992.

Lin, Yu-sheng, "Guanyu zhongguo yishi de weiji—da Sun longji" ("On The Crisis of Chinese Consciousness—In Response to Sun Longji"), *Ershiyi shiji* (Hong Kong), 3rd edition., February, 1991.

Link, Perry, *Evening Chats in Beijing: Probing China's Predicament* (New York, London: W. W. Norton & Company, 1992).

Liu, Binyan et al., *Ziyou minzhu xiandaihua de husheng* (*Call for Freedom, Democracy and Modernization*) (Taibei: Xinmei chubanshe, 1988).

Liu, Qingfeng, *Rang kexue de guangmang zhaoliang ziji* (*Let the Light of Science Shine Over Ourselves*) (Chengdu: Sichuan renmin chubanshe, 1984).

———. "Ershishiji zhongguo kexuezhuyi de liangci xingqi," ("The Two Surges of Chinese Scientism in the Twentieth Century"), *Ershiyi shiji* (Hong Kong), 4th ed. April, 1991.

———. "Da Huan Xuewen" ("In response to Huan Xuewen"), *Ershiyi shiji* (Hong Kong), October, 1991, 7th ed.

Liu, Xiangyang, "Wenping re" ("Obsession with College Diplomas"), in Xiao Qinfu, *Wuci langchao* (*Five Waves*) (Beijing, Renmindaxue chubanshe, 1989).

Locke, John, *Second Treatise on Civil Government* (New York: New American Library, 1965).

Lu, Keng, "Beijing Hui Wang Ruoshui," ("Meet Wang Ruoshui in Beijing"), *Bai Xing*, (Hong Kong) September 1, 1985.

Macpherson, C. B., *The Real World of Democracy* (Oxford: Oxford University Press, 1976).

Machiavelli, Niccolo, *The Prince*, trans. and ed. by Robert M. Adams (New York: W.W.Norton and Company Inc. 1965).

Magstadt, Thomas M. and Peter M. Schotten, *Understanding Politics—Ideas, Institutions, and Issues* (New York: St. Martin's Press, 1988).

"Makesi maigupiao," ("Marx Buys Stocks"), *Shenzhou Xueren* (*China's Scholars Abroad*), February 1993, p. 47. (No author)

Mandelbaum, Maurice, *History, Man, & Reason: A Study in Nineteenth-Century Thought* (Baltimore and London: The Johns Hopkins Press, 1971).

Manicas, Peter, *A History and Philosophy of Social Sciences* (Oxford: Basil Blackwell, 1987).

———. *War and Democracy* (Oxford: Basil Blackwell, 1989).

Mao, Zedong, *Selected Works of Mao Tse-Tung* (New York: International Publishers, 1964).

Marx, Karl, *The Economic & Philosophic Manuscripts of 1844* (New York: International Publishers, 1964).

———. *The Economic and Philosophic Manuscripts of 1844* (Moscow: Progress Publishers, 1974).

———. *A Contribution to the Critique of Political Economy (1859)*. Cited in "Responses to Hua Shiping's 'All Roads Lead to Democracy.'" *Bulletin of Concerned Asian Scholars*, Vol. 24, No. 1, January–March, 1992.

Meisner, Maurice, "The Chinese Rediscovery of Karl Marx," *Bulletin of Concerned Asian Scholars*, Vol. 17, No. 3, July–September, 1985.

Mencius, *Sacred Books of Confucius* eds. and trans. by Chin Chai and Winberg Chai (New York: University Books, 1965).

Misra, Kalpana, "Rethinking Marxism in Post-Mao China: The Erosion of Official Ideology, 1978-1984," doctoral dissertation in political science, The University of Michigan, 1992.

Moody, Peter, Jr., *Opposition and Dissent in Contemporary China* (Stanford, CA: Hoover Institution Press, 1977).

Moore, John A. Jr. and Myron Roberts, *The Pursuit of Happiness: Government and Politics in America* (New York: Macmillan Publishing Company, 1989).

Nathan, Andrew J., *China's Crisis: Dilemmas of Reform and Prospects for Democracy* (New York: Columbia University Press, 1990).

———. "Is Chinese Culture Distinctive?—A Review Article," *The Journal of Asian Studies*, Vol. 52, No. 4, November 1993.

———. (with Tianjian Shi), "Cultural Requisites for Democracy in China: Some Findings from a Survey," *Daedalus*, Vol. 122, No. 2, Spring 1993.

Neubauer, Deane, "Convergence Theory Revisited," *Occasional Papers in Political Science*, University of Hawaii, January 1990, Vol. 3, No. 3.

Ogden, Suzanne, *China's Unresolved Issues* (Englewood Cliffs, New Jersey: Prentice Hall, 1989).

Owen, R.G., *Scientism, Man, and Religion* (Philadelphia: The Westminster Press, 1952).

Palmer, R. R. and Joel Colton, *A History of the Modern World* (New York: Alfred A. Knopf, 1971).

Pickles, Dorothy, *Democracy* (London: B.T. Batsford Ltd, 1970).

Plato, *The Republic* (New York: Basic Books, 1968).

Pye, Lucian, *Mao Tse-tung—The Man in the Leader* (New York: Basic Books, Inc. Publishers, 1976).

———. "On Chinese Pragmatism in the 1980s," *The China Quarterly*, No. 106, June, 1986.

———. *The Spirit of Chinese Politics* (Cambridge, MA: Harvard University Press, 1992).

Qi, Fang, *Heping yanbian zhanlue de chansheng jiqi fazhan* (*The Origin and Development of the Strategy of Peaceful Restoration of Capitalism*) (Beijing: Dongfang chubanshe, 1990).

Quan, Yanchi, *Zouxia shentan de Mao Zedong* (*Mao Zedong, Who Steps Down From the Shrine of God*) (Beijing: Zhongwai wenhua chubangongsi, 1989).

———. *Lingxiu lei* (*The Tears of the Leader*) (Beijing: Zhonggongzhongyang dangxiao chubanshe, 1990).

Rosenbaum, Walter A., *Political Culture* (New York, Praeger Publishers, Inc., 1975).

Rousseau, Jean-Jacques, *The Social Contract and Discourse on Inequality* (New York: Washington Square Press, 1967).

Sayer, Derek, *Marx's Method* (New Jersey: Humanities Press, 1979).

———. *The Violence of Abstraction: The Analytic Foundations of Historical Materialism* (Oxford and New York: Basil Blackwell, 1987).

Schwartz, Benjamin, Introduction to Yu-sheng Lin's, *The Crisis of Chinese Consciousness* (Madison: The University of Wisconsin Press, 1979).

Selden, Mark, *The Political Economy of Chinese Socialism* (Armonk, New York: M. E. Sharpe, 1988).

Shaw, Yu-ming, *Chinese Modernization* (San Francisco: Chinese Materials Center Publications, 1985).

Snow, C.P., *The Two Cultures and the Scientific Revolution* (New York: Cambridge University Press, 1961).

Sorell, Tom, *Scientism: Philosophy and the Infatuation with Science* (London: Routledge, 1991).

Su, Guoxun, "Lixinghua jiqi xianzhi," ("Rationality and its Limitations"), in Gan Yang ed., *Zhongguo dangdai wenhua yishi* (*Contemporary Chinese Consciousness*) (Hong Kong: Joint Publishing, 1989).

Su, Shaozhi, *Woguo shehuizhuyi jingjiyanjiu zhongde ruoganwenti* (*Certain Issues in the Study of China's Socialist Economy* (Shanghai: Shanghai renmin chubanshe, 1980).

———. *Democratization and Reform* (Nottingham: Spokesman, 1988).

———. *Marxism in China* (Nottingham: Spokesman, 1988).

———. "A Symposium on Marxism in China Today," in *Bulletin of Concerned Asian Scholars*, Vol. 20, No. 1, 1988.

———. "Rethinking Socialism in the Light of China's Reforms," *China Information*, Vol. VI. No. 1, Summer 1991.

———. "A Decade of Crises at the Institute of Marxism-Leninism-Mao Zedong Thought, 1979-89," *The China Quarterly*, No. 134, June 1993.

———. "Su Questions Chinese Marxism," *Messenger*, published by China Times Center for Media and Social Studies, November 15, 1993.

Su, Wei, "Bashiniandai Beijing zhishijie de wenhua quanzi" ("Cultural Circles Among Beijing Intellectuals in the 1980s"), *Zhongguo zhichun*, January, 1992.

Thomas, Paul, *Karl Marx and the Anarchists* (London: Routledge & Kegan Paul Ltd, 1980).

Tianjinshi Geming Weiyuanhui, *Wuchanjieji wenhuadageming zhongyao wenxian xuanbian* (*A Selection of Important Works of the Cultural Revolution*) (Tianjin: Tianjin renmin chubanshe, 1969).

Townsend, James R., "Politics in China," in Gabriel A. Almond and G. Bingham Powell, Jr., *Comparative Politics Today: A World View* (Boston: Little, Brown and Company, 1984).

Tu, Wei-ming, "Ruxue chuantong jiazhi yu minzhu" ("The Confucian Traditional Values and Democracy"), *Dushu*, (Beijing) April, 1989.

———. "Jicheng wu-si, fazhan ruxue" ("Developing Confucianism in the May Fourth Tradition"), *Dushu*, (Beijing) June, 1989.

———. *Rujia ziwo yishi de fansi* (*Self Reflection on the Sense of Self Awareness of Confucianism*) (Taibei: Lianjing chubanshiye gongsi, 1990).

———. "Cultural China: The Periphery as the Center," *Daedalus*, Vol. 120, No. 2, Spring 1991.

Uhalley, Stephen Jr., *A History of the Chinese Communist Party*, (Stanford: Hoover Institution Press, 1988).

von Mises, Ludwig, *Human Action, A Treatise on Economics* (New Haven: Yale University Press, 1963).

Wakeman, Frederick, "The Price of Autonomy: Intellectuals in Ming and Ching Politics," *Daedalus*, 1972, Spring.

Wang, Jin, "Shisida: xin de lichengbei" ("The 14th Party Congress: a New Mile-Stone"), *Renmin ribao*, October 19, 1992.

Wang, Ruoshui, *Zai zhexue zhanxianshang* (*On the Frontier of Philosophy*) (Beijing: Renmin chubanshe, 1980).

———. "Wenhuadageming de jiaoxun shi gerenchongbai" ("The Lesson We Learned from the Cultural Revolution Was Personality Cult"), *Mingbao yuekan* (Hong Kong), February 1980.

———. "On Estrangement," *Selected Writings on Studies of Marxism*, published by the Institute of Marxism-Leninism-Mao Zedong Thought, Chinese Academy of Social Sciences, Beijing, May 1981, No.12.

———. *Wei rendao zhuyi bianhu* (*In Defense of Humanism*) Beijing: Sanlianshudian, 1986.

———. "Makesizhuyi he xuepai wenti" ("Marxism and Schools of Thought), *Dushu*, (Beijing), September, 1986.

———. "Lun rende benzhi he shehui guanxi" ("On the nature of man and social relations"), *Xin Qimeng*, (Beijing) December 1988.

———. "Ren, rende benzhi, rende jiefang" ("Man, Man's Nature and Man's Emancipation"), *Shixue lilun*, (Beijing), February, 1989.

———. "Cong pizuo daoxiang fanyou" ("From Criticizing Leftism to Attacking Rightism"), *Mingbao yuekan* (Hong Kong), March 1989.

———. "Shehuizhuyi meiyou yihuama?" ("Is There No Alienation in a Socialist Society?"), *Xin qimeng, (Beijing), April 1989.*

———. *"Wo de shenbian" ("My Self Defense"), Mingbao yuekan* (Hong Kong), September 1989.

———. "Comments by Wang Ruoshui" [in Shiping Hua's article "All Roads Lead to Democracy"], *Bulletin of Concerned Asian Scholars*, Vol. 24, No. 1, January–March, 1992.

Wang, Shubai, "Mao Zedong de zhongxi wenhua guan" ("Mao Zedong's Ideas on the Cultures of the West and the East"), *Xinhua wenzhai*, (Beijing) May 1987.

Weber, Max, *The Religion of China* (New York: the Free Press, 1951).

———. *The Theory of Social and Economic Organization* (New York: Oxford University Press, 1974).

Wei, Zhengdong, "Wenhua zhongguo de xiang zheng" ("Symbol of Cultural China"), in Lu Keng and Liang Qindong eds., *Zhongguo de jiliang* (China's Backbone) (Hong Kong: Baixing wenhuashiye youxiangongsi).

Wellmuth, Hohn, S.J., *The Nature and Origins of Scientism* (Milwaukee: Marquette University Press, 1944).

White, Lynn and Li Cheng in Chang King-Yuh ed., *Mainland China After the Thirteenth Party Congress*, (Boulder, CO: Westview Press, 1990).

White, Stephen, "Continuity and Change in Soviet Political Culture," *Comparative Political Studies*, Vol. 11, No. 3, October 1978.

Wiarda, Howard J. ed., *New Directions in Comparative Politics* (Boulder, CO: Westview, 1985).

Williams, James, J., "Fang Lizhi's Expanding Universe," *The China Quarterly*, September, 1990.

Wittfogel, Karl A., *Oriental Despotism: A Comparative Study of Total Power* (New York: Vintage Books, 1981).

Xing, Bisi et al. eds., *Makesizhuyi sixiang baoku* (*Treasure-House of Marxist Thought*) (Haikou: Nanhai chubangongsi, 1990).

Xu, Chongwen, *Xifang makesizhuyi luncong* (*A Collection of Articles on Western Marxism*) (Chongqing: Chongqing chubanshe, 1989).

———. *Yong makesizhuyi pingxi xifang sichao* (*To Analyze Western Intellectual Thought with Marxism*) (Chongqing: Chongqing chubanshe, 1990).

Xu, Liangying, *Science and Socialist Construction In China* (New York: M.E. Sharpe, Inc., 1982).

Xu, Xing, *Chinese Politics in Reform* (Hong Kong: Pioneer Publishers, 1986), pp. 185–186.

Xun, Kuang, *Fajia zhuzuo xuan* (*Selections of the Legalists*) (Shanghai: Remin chubanshe, 1975), Vol. 1.

Yan, Jiaqi, *Wo de sixiang zizhuan* (*My Intellectual Autobiography*) (Hong Kong: Sanlian shudian, 1988).

————. "Ducaizhe de zhixu he shangdi de zhixu," ("The Order of the Autocrat and the Order of God"), *Xinwen ziyou daobao* July, 20, 1990.

Yang, Guorong, "Wang Guowei de neizai jinzhang: kexuezhuyi yu renben-zhuyi de duizhi" ("The Tension Within Wang Guowei: the Confrontation Between Scientism and Humanism"), *Ershiyi shiji* (Hong Kong), 11th edition, June 1992.

Yao, Peng et al. eds., *Zhongguo sixiang baoku* (*Treasure-house of Chinese Thought*) (Beijing: Zhongguo guangbo chubanshe, 1990).

Yao, Xianguo, *Liangji fenhua: fuyin haishi zainan* (*Polarization of Wealth: Fortune or Disaster*) (Beijing: Xueyuan chubanshe, 1989).

Yu, Ying-shih, "Zhongguo zhishifenzi de bianyuan hua" ("The Marginalization of Chinese Intellectuals"), *Ershiyi shiji* (Hong Kong), 6th issue, August, 1991.

Zhao, Yuesheng, "Chaoyue-fouding-lixing: lun makusi pipan de shehuizhexue" ("Transcendence-Negation-Rationality: On Marcuse's Critical Social Theory") in Gan ed., *Zhongguo dangdai wenhua yishi*.

Zhongguo zhexueshi bianxiezu, *Zhongguo Zhexueshi* (*A History of Chinese Philosophy*) (Shijiazhuang: Hebei renmin chubanshe, 1980).

Zhu, Jianhua, Xinshu Zhao, and Hairong Li, "Public Political Consciousness in China," *Asian Survey*, Vol. XXX, No. 10, October 1990.

Zou, Yizhi, "Jin Guantao fufu yinxiang" ("Impression of Jin Guantao and his wife Liu Qingfeng"), *Mingbao yuekan* (Hong Kong), September, 1987.

Zhou, Zezong, "Preface" to *Zhongguo de jiliang* (*China's Backbone*) in Lu Keng and Liang Qindong eds., (Hong Kong: Baixing wenhuashiye youxiangongsi, 1990).

Index